Course Booklet

CCNA Exploration

Routing Protocols and Concepts

Version 4.0

ı" ı" ı"
CISCO

Cisco | Networking Academy
Mind Wide Open

CCNA Exploration Course Booklet
Routing Protocols and Concepts, Version 4.0

Cisco Networking Academy

Copyright© 2010 Cisco Systems, Inc.

Published by:
Cisco Press
800 East 96th Street
Indianapolis, IN 46240 USA

Printed in the United States of America

First Printing   September 2009

Library of Congress Cataloging-in-Publication Data is available upon request

ISBN-13: 978-1-58713-251-3

ISBN-10: 1-58713-251-6

Publisher
Paul Boger

Associate Publisher
Dave Dusthimer

Cisco Representative
Erik Ullanderson

Cisco Press Program Manager
Anand Sundaram

Executive Editor
Mary Beth Ray

Managing Editor
Patrick Kanouse

Project Editor
Bethany Wall

Editorial Assistant
Vanessa Evans

Cover Designer
Louisa Adair

Composition
Mark Shirar

This book is part of the Cisco Networking Academy® series from Cisco Press. The products in this series support and complement the Cisco Networking Academy curriculum. If you are using this book outside the Networking Academy, then you are not preparing with a Cisco trained and authorized Networking Academy provider.

For more information on the Cisco Networking Academy or to locate a Networking Academy, Please visit www.cisco.com/edu.

CISCO.

Warning and Disclaimer

This book is designed to provide information about the protocols and concepts of routing. Every effort has been made to make this book as complete and as accurate as possible, but no warranty or fitness is implied.

The information is provided on an "as is" basis. The authors, Cisco Press, and Cisco Systems, Inc. shall have neither liability nor responsibility to any person or entity with respect to any loss or damages arising from the information contained in this book or from the use of the discs or programs that may accompany it.

The opinions expressed in this book belong to the author and are not necessarily those of Cisco Systems, Inc.

Trademark Acknowledgments

All terms mentioned in this book that are known to be trademarks or service marks have been appropriately capitalized. Cisco Press or Cisco Systems, Inc., cannot attest to the accuracy of this information. Use of a term in this book should not be regarded as affecting the validity of any trademark or service mark.

Feedback Information

At Cisco Press, our goal is to create in-depth technical books of the highest quality and value. Each book is crafted with care and precision, undergoing rigorous development that involves the unique expertise of members from the professional technical community.

Readers' feedback is a natural continuation of this process. If you have any comments regarding how we could improve the quality of this book, or otherwise alter it to better suit your needs, you can contact us through email at feedback@ciscopress.com. Please make sure to include the book title and ISBN in your message.

We greatly appreciate your assistance.

Americas Headquarters	Asia Pacific Headquarters	Europe Headquarters
Cisco Systems, Inc.	Cisco Systems (USA) Pte. Ltd.	Cisco Systems International BV
San Jose, CA	Singapore	Amsterdam, The Netherlands

Cisco has more than 200 offices worldwide. Addresses, phone numbers, and fax numbers are listed on the Cisco Website at **www.cisco.com/go/offices.**

CCDE, CCENT, Cisco Eos, Cisco HealthPresence, the Cisco logo, Cisco Lumin, Cisco Nexus, Cisco StadiumVision, Cisco TelePresence, Cisco WebEx, DCE, and Welcome to the Human Network are trademarks; Changing the Way We Work, Live, Play, and Learn and Cisco Store are service marks; and Access Registrar, Aironet, AsyncOS, Bringing the Meeting To You, Catalyst, CCDA, CCDP, CCIE, CCIP, CCNA, CCNP, CCSP, CCVP, Cisco, the Cisco Certified Internetwork Expert logo, Cisco IOS, Cisco Press, Cisco Systems, Cisco Systems Capital, the Cisco Systems logo, Cisco Unity, Collaboration Without Limitation, EtherFast, EtherSwitch, Event Center, Fast Step, Follow Me Browsing, FormShare, GigaDrive, HomeLink, Internet Quotient, IOS, iPhone, iQuick Study, IronPort, the IronPort logo, LightStream, Linksys, MediaTone, MeetingPlace, MeetingPlace Chime Sound, MGX, Networkers, Networking Academy, Network Registrar, PCNow, PIX, PowerPanels, ProConnect, ScriptShare, SenderBase, SMARTnet, Spectrum Expert, StackWise, The Fastest Way to Increase Your Internet Quotient, TransPath, WebEx, and the WebEx logo are registered trademarks of Cisco Systems, Inc. and/or its affiliates in the United States and certain other countries.

All other trademarks mentioned in this document or website are the property of their respective owners. The use of the word partner does not imply a partnership relationship between Cisco and any other company. (0812R)

Contents at a Glance

Contents

Command Syntax Conventions

The conventions used to present command syntax in this book are the same conventions used in the IOS Command Reference. The Command Reference describes these conventions as follows:

- **Boldface** indicates commands and keywords that are entered literally as shown. In actual configuration examples and output (not general command syntax), boldface indicates commands that are manually input by the user (such as a **show** command).

- *Italic* indicates arguments for which you supply actual values.

- Vertical bars (|) separate alternative, mutually exclusive elements.

- Square brackets ([ ]) indicate an optional element.

- Braces ({ }) indicate a required choice.

- Braces within brackets ([{ }]) indicate a required choice within an optional element.

About this Course Booklet

Your Cisco Networking Academy Course Booklet is designed as a study resource you can easily read, highlight, and review on the go, wherever the Internet is not available or practical:

- The text is extracted directly, word-for-word, from the online course so you can highlight important points and take notes in the "Your Chapter Notes" section.

- Headings with the exact page correlations provide a quick reference to the online course for your classroom discussions and exam preparation.

- An icon system directs you to the online curriculum to take full advantage of the images, labs, Packet Tracer activities, and dynamic Flash-based activities embedded within the Networking Academy online course interface.

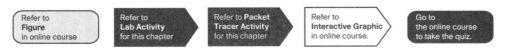

The Course Booklet is a basic, economical paper-based resource to help you succeed with the Cisco Networking Academy online course.

Welcome

Welcome to the CCNA Exploration Routing Protocols and Concepts course. The goal is to develop an understanding of how a router learns about remote networks and determines the best path to those networks. This course includes both static routing and dynamic routing protocols. The specific skills covered in each chapter are described at the start of each chapter.

More than just information

This computer-based learning environment is an important part of the overall course experience for students and instructors in the Networking Academy. These online course materials are designed to be used along with several other instructional tools and activities. These include:

- Class presentation, discussion, and practice with your instructor

- Hands-on labs that use networking equipment within the Networking Academy classroom

- Online scored assessments and gradebook

- Packet Tracer 4.1 simulation tool

- Additional software for classroom activities.

A global community

When you participate in the Networking Academy, you are joining a global community linked by common goals and technologies. Schools, colleges, universities and other entities in over 160 countries participate in the program. You can see an interactive network map of the global Networking Academy community at http://www.academynetspace.com.

The material in this course encompasses a broad range of technologies that facilitate how people work, live, play, and learn by communicating with voice, video, and other data. Networking and the Internet affect people differently in different parts of the world. Although we have worked with instructors from around the world to create these materials, it is important that you work with your instructor and fellow students to make the material in this course applicable to your local situation.

Keep in Touch

These online instructional materials, as well as the rest of the course tools, are part of the larger Networking Academy. The portal for the program is located at http://cisco.netacad.net. There you will obtain access to the other tools in the program such as the assessment server and student grade book), as well as informational updates and other relevant links.

Mind Wide Open®

An important goal in education is to enrich you, the student, by expanding what you know and can do. It is important to realize, however, that the instructional materials and the instructor can only facilitate the process. You must make the commitment yourself to learn new skills. Below are a few suggestions to help you learn and grow.

1. Take notes. Professionals in the networking field often keep Engineering Journals in which they write down the things they observe and learn. Taking notes is an important way to help your understanding grow over time.

2. Think about it. The course provides information both to change what you know and what you can do. As you go through the course, ask yourself what makes sense and what doesn't. Stop and ask questions when you are confused. Try to find out more about topics that interest you. If you are not sure why something is being taught, consider asking your instructor or a friend. Think about how the different parts of the course fit together.

3. Practice. Learning new skills requires practice. We believe this is so important to e-learning that we have a special name for it. We call it e-doing. It is very important that you complete the activities in the online instructional materials and that you also complete the hands-on labs and Packet Tracer® activities.

4. Practice again. Have you ever thought that you knew how to do something and then, when it was time to show it on a test or at work, you discovered that you really hadn't mastered it? Just like learning any new skill like a sport, game, or language, learning a professional skill requires patience and repeated practice before you can say you have truly learned it. The online instructional materials in this course provide opportunities for repeated practice for many skills. Take full advantage of them. You can also work with your instructor to extend Packet Tracer, and other tools, for additional practice as needed.

5. Teach it. Teaching a friend or colleague is often a good way to reinforce your own learning. To teach well, you will have to work through details that you may have overlooked on your first reading. Conversations about the course material with fellow students, colleagues, and the instructor can help solidify your understanding of networking concepts.

6. Make changes as you go. The course is designed to provide feedback through interactive activities and quizzes, the online assessment system, and through interactions with your instructor. You can use this feedback to better understand where your strengths and weaknesses are. If there is an area that you are having trouble with, focus on studying or practicing more in that area. Seek additional feedback from your instructor and other students.

Explore the world of networking

This version of the course includes a special tool called Packet Tracer 4.1®. Packet Tracer is a networking learning tool that supports a wide range of physical and logical simulations. It also provides visualization tools to help you to understand the internal workings of a network.

The Packet Tracer activities included in the course consist of network simulations, games, activities, and challenges that provide a broad range of learning experiences.

Create your own worlds

You can also use Packet Tracer to create your own experiments and networking scenarios. We hope that, over time, you consider using Packet Tracer – not only for experiencing the activities included in the course, but also to become an author, explorer, and experimenter.

The online course materials have embedded Packet Tracer activities that will launch on computers running Windows® operating systems, if Packet Tracer is installed. This integration may also work on other operating systems using Windows emulation.

Course Overview

The primary focus of this course is on routing and routing protocols. The goal is to develop an understanding of how a router learns about remote networks and determines the best path to those networks. This course includes both static routing and dynamic routing protocols. By examining multiple routing protocols, you will gain a better understanding of each of the individual routing protocols and a better perspective of routing in general. Learning the configuration of routing protocols is fairly simple. Developing an understanding of the routing concepts themselves is more difficult, yet is critical for implementing, verifying, and troubleshooting routing operations.

Each static routing and dynamic routing protocol chapter uses a single topology throughout that chapter. You will be using that topology to configure, verify, and troubleshoot the routing operations discussed in the chapter.

The labs and Packet Tracer activities used in this course are designed to help you develop an understanding of how to configure routing operations while reinforcing the concepts learned in each chapter.

Chapter 1 Introduction to Routing and Packet Forwarding - In Chapter 1, you will be introduced to the router, its role in the networks, its main hardware and software components, and the packet forwarding process. You will also be given an overview of directly connected networks, static routing, and dynamic routing protocols, along with a brief introduction to the routing table. Each of these topics is discussed in more detail in later chapters. Chapter1 also includes a review of basic Cisco IOS commands.

Chapter 2 Static Routing - Chapter 2 focuses on the role and configuration of static routes. The routing table process is introduced, and you will be shown how to verify route entries as they are added and deleted from the routing table. This chapter also discusses Cisco Discovery Protocol, which is a tool that you can use to help verify network operations.

Chapter 3 Introduction to Dynamic Routing Protocols – Chapter 3 provides an overview of routing protocol concepts and the various dynamic routing protocols available for routing in IP networks. In this chapter, you will examine the role of routing protocols. There is an overview of the classification of dynamic routing protocols. This overview is useful for comparing and contrasting the different protocols. Most of the information in this chapter is examined in more detail in later chapters.

Chapter 4 Distance Vector Routing Protocols – Chapter 4 presents two different types of routing protocols: distance vector and link-state. You will examine distance vector concepts and operations, including network discovery, routing table maintenance, and the issue of routing loops. In this chapter, you will also be introduced to the concepts used in RIPv1, RIPv2, and EIGRP routing protocols. These routing protocols are discussed in more detail in later chapters.

Chapter 5 RIP version 1 – Chapter 5 is the first chapter that focuses on a specific dynamic routing protocol. In this chapter, you will learn about RIP (Routing Information Protocol) version 1. RIPv1, a classful, distance vector routing protocol, was one of the first IP routing protocols. You will examine the characteristics, operations, and limitations of RIPv1. You will also learn about RIPv1 configuration, verification, and troubleshooting techniques.

Chapter 6 VLSM and CIDR - Chapter 6 reviews VLSM (Variable Length Subnet Masking) and CIDR (Classless Inter-Domain Routing) concepts that were presented in the Network Fundamentals course. You will explore the benefits of VLSM along with the role and benefits of CIDR in today's networks. Next, you will be introduced to the role of classless routing protocols. Classless routing protocols RIPv2, EIGRP, and OSPF are examined in later chapters.

Chapter 7 RIPv2 - Chapter 7 examines the next routing protocol presented in this course, RIPv2. RIPv2 is a classless, distance vector routing protocol. You will see how RIPv2 demonstrates the advantages and operations of a classless routing protocol. The chapter begins with a discussion of the limitations of the classful routing protocol, RIPv1. Then RIPv2 is introduced, to show how a classless routing protocol can be used to overcome these limitations. In this chapter, you will also learn the commands necessary to configure and verify RIPv2.

Chapter 8 The Routing Table: A Closer Look – Chapter 8 examines Cisco's IPv4 routing table in detail. The chapter begins with a discussion of the structure of the routing table. While examining the routing table, you will learn about the lookup process, how the routing table process determines the best match with a packet's destination IP address, and how to enter a route in the routing table. The chapter concludes with a discussion about the differences between classful and classless routing behaviors.

Chapter 9 EIGRP – Chapter 9 focuses on Cisco EIGRP (Enhanced Interior Gateway Routing Protocol). EIGRP is a classless, enhanced distance vector routing protocol. You will examine the advantages and operations of EIGRP's DUAL (Diffusing Update Algorithm). Then you will learn about the configuration of EIGRP, including verification and troubleshooting commands.

Chapter 10 Link-State Routing Protocols – Chapter 10 examines link-state routing protocol concepts. You will be introduced to link-state terminology and the link-state routing process. The chapter discusses the benefits and advantages of a link-state routing protocol compared to a distance vector routing protocol. You will then examine the Shortest Path First (SPF) algorithm and how it is used to build a topology map of the network. The link-state routing protocol OSPF is discussed in the following chapter.

Chapter 11 OSPF – The final chapter in this course is an examination of the classless, link-state routing protocol OSPF (Open Shortest Path First). In this chapter, you will examine OSPF operations and configuration, including verification and troubleshooting commands. By the end of this course, you should feel confident in your knowledge of routing and routing protocols. With continued study and practice, you will be able to put your new skills to work.

CHAPTER 1

Introduction to Routing and Packet Forwarding

Chapter Introduction

Today's networks have a significant impact on our lives - changing the way we live, work, and play. Computer networks - and in a larger context the Internet - allow people to communicate, collaborate, and interact in ways they never did before. We use the network in a variety of ways, including web applications, *IP* telephony, video conferencing, interactive gaming, electronic commerce, education, and more.

At the center of the network is the router. Stated simply, a router connects one network to another network. Therefore, the router is responsible for the delivery of packets across different networks. The destination of the IP packet might be a web server in another country or an e-mail server on the local area network. It is the responsibility of the routers to deliver those packets in a timely manner. The effectiveness of internetwork communications depends, to a large degree, on the ability of routers to forward packets in the most efficient way possible.

Routers are now being added to satellites in space. These routers will have the ability to route IP traffic between satellites in space in much the same way that packets are moved on Earth, thereby reducing delays and offering greater networking flexibility.

In addition to packet forwarding, a router provides other services as well. To meet the demands on today's networks, routers are also used to:

- Ensure 24x7 (24 hours a day, 7 days a week) availability. To help guarantee network reachability, routers use alternate paths in case the primary path fails.

- Provide integrated services of data, video, and voice over wired and wireless networks. Routers use Quality of service (QoS) prioritization of IP packets to ensure that real-time traffic, such as voice, video and critical data are not dropped or delayed.

- Mitigate the impact of worms, viruses, and other attacks on the network by permitting or denying the forwarding of packets.

All of these services are built around the router and its primary responsibility of forwarding packets from one network to the next. It is only because of the router's ability to route packets between networks that devices on different networks can communicate. This chapter will introduce you to the router, its role in the networks, its main hardware and software components, and the routing process itself.

1.1 Inside the Router

1.1.1 Routers are Computers

Routers are Computers

Refer to
Figure
in online course

A router is a computer, just like any other computer including a PC. The very first router, used for the Advanced Research Projects Agency Network (ARPANET), was the Interface Message Processor (IMP). The IMP was a Honeywell 316 minicomputer; this computer brought the ARPANET to life on August 30, 1969.

Note: The ARPANET was developed by Advanced Research Projects Agency (ARPA) of the United States Department of Defense. The ARPANET was the world's first operational *packet* switching network and the predecessor of today's Internet.

Routers have many of the same hardware and software components that are found in other computers including:

- CPU

- RAM

- ROM

- *Operating System*

Click Play to see the animation.

Refer to
Figure
in online course

Routers are at the network center

Typical users may be unaware of the presence of numerous routers in their own network or in the Internet. Users expect to be able to access web pages, send e-mails, and download music - whether the server they are accessing is on their own network or on another network half-way around the world. However, networking professionals know it is the router that is responsible for forwarding packets from network-to-network, from the original source to the final destination.

A router connects multiple networks. This means that it has multiple interfaces that each belong to a different IP network. When a router receives an IP packet on one interface, it determines which interface to use to forward the packet onto its destination. The interface that the router uses to forward the packet may be the network of the final destination of the packet (the network with the destination IP address of this packet), or it may be a network connected to another router that is used to reach the destination network.

Each network that a router connects to typically requires a separate interface. These interfaces are used to connect a combination of both *Local Area Networks (LANs)* and *Wide Area Networks (WANs)*. LANs are commonly *Ethernet* networks that contain devices such as PCs, printers, and servers. WANs are used to connect networks over a large geographical area. For example, a WAN connection is commonly used to connect a LAN to the *Internet Service Provider (ISP)* network.

In the figure, we see that routers R1 and R2 are responsible for receiving the packet on one network and forwarding the packet out another network toward the destination network.

Refer to
Figure
in online course

Routers determine the *best path*

The primary responsibility of a router is to direct packets destined for local and remote networks by:

- Determining the best path to send packets

- Forwarding packets toward their destination

The router uses its *routing table* to determine the best path to forward the packet. When the router receives a packet, it examines its destination IP address and searches for the best match with a network address in the router's routing table. The routing table also includes the interface to be used to forward the packet. Once a match is found, the router encapsulates the IP packet into the data link frame of the outgoing or exit interface, and the packet is then forwarded toward its destination.

It is very likely that a router will receive a packet that is encapsulated in one type of data link frame, such as an Ethernet frame and when forwarding the packet, the router will encapsulate it in a different type of data link frame, such as Point-to-Point Protocol (*PPP*). The data link encapsulation depends on the type of interface on the router and the type of medium it connects to. The different data link technologies that a router connects to can include LAN technologies, such as Ethernet, and WAN *serial* connections, such as T1 connection using PPP, *Frame Relay*, and *Asynchronous Transfer Mode (ATM)*.

In the figure, we can follow a packet from the source PC to the destination PC. Notice that it is the responsibility of the router to find the destination network in its routing table and forward the packet on toward its destination. In this example, router R1 receives the packet encapsulated in an Ethernet frame. After decapsulating the packet, R1 uses the destination IP address of the packet to search its routing table for a matching network address. After a destination network address is found in the routing table, R1 encapsulates the packet inside a PPP frame and forwards the packet to R2. A similar process is performed by R2.

Static routes and *dynamic routing* protocols are used by routers to learn about remote networks and build their routing tables. These routes and protocols are the primary focus of the course and will be discussed in detail in later chapters along with the process that routers use in searching their routing tables and forwarding the packets.

Links

Refer to Figure in online course

"How Routers Work" http://computer.howstuffworks.com/router.htm

Refer to Packet Tracer Activity for this chapter

This Packet Tracer Activity shows a complex network of routers with many different technologies. Be sure to view the activity in Simulation Mode so that you can see the traffic traveling from multiple sources to multiple destinations over various types of *media*. Please be patient as this complex topology may take some time to load.

1.1.2 Router CPU and Memory

Refer to Figure in online course

Although there are several different types and models of routers, every router has the same general hardware components. Depending on the model, those components are located in different places inside the router. The figure shows the inside of an 1841 router. To see the internal router components, you must unscrew the metal cover and take it off the router. **Usually you do not need to open the router unless you are upgrading memory.**

Refer to Figure in online course

Router Components and their Functions

Like a PC, a router also includes:

- Central Processing Unit (CPU)

- Random-Access Memory (RAM)

- *Read-Only Memory (ROM)*

Roll over components in the figure to see a brief description of each.

CPU

The CPU executes operating system instructions, such as system initialization, routing functions, and switching functions.

RAM

RAM stores the instructions and data needed to be executed by the CPU. RAM is used to store these components:

- *Operating System:* The Cisco IOS (Internetwork Operating System) is copied into RAM during bootup.

- *Running Configuration File:* This is the configuration file that stores the configuration commands that the router IOS is currently using. With few exceptions, all commands configured on the router are stored in the running configuration file, known as running-config.

- *IP Routing Table:* This file stores information about directly connected and remote networks. It is used to determine the best path to forward the packet.

- *ARP* Cache: This cache contains the IPv4 address to *MAC address* mappings, similar to the ARP cache on a PC. The ARP cache is used on routers that have LAN interfaces such as Ethernet interfaces.

- *Packet Buffer:* Packets are temporarily stored in a buffer when received on an interface or before they exit an interface.

RAM is volatile memory and loses its content when the router is powered down or restarted. However, the router also contains permanent storage areas, such as ROM, *flash* and NVRAM.

ROM

ROM is a form of permanent storage. Cisco devices use ROM to store:

- The bootstrap instructions

- Basic diagnostic software

- Scaled-down version of IOS

ROM uses firmware, which is software that is embedded inside the integrated circuit. Firmware includes the software that does not normally need to be modified or upgraded, such as the bootup instructions. Many of these features, including ROM monitor software, will be discussed in a later course. ROM does not lose its contents when the router loses power or is restarted.

Flash Memory

Flash memory is nonvolatile computer memory that can be electrically stored and erased. Flash is used as permanent storage for the operating system, Cisco IOS. In most models of Cisco routers, the IOS is permanently stored in flash memory and copied into RAM during the bootup process, where it is then executed by the CPU. Some older models of Cisco routers run the IOS directly from flash. Flash consists of SIMMs or PCMCIA cards, which can be upgraded to increase the amount of flash memory.

Flash memory does not lose its contents when the router loses power or is restarted.

NVRAM

NVRAM (Nonvolatile RAM) does not lose its information when power is turned off. This is in contrast to the most common forms of RAM, such as DRAM, that requires continual power to maintain its information. NVRAM is used by the Cisco IOS as permanent storage for the startup configuration file (startup-config). All configuration changes are stored in the running-config file in RAM, and with few exceptions, are implemented immediately by the IOS. To save those changes in case the router is restarted or loses power, the running-config must be copied to NVRAM, where it is stored as the startup-config file. NVRAM retains its contents even when the router reloads or is powered off.

ROM, RAM, NVRAM, and flash are discussed in the following section which introduces the IOS and the bootup process. They are also discussed in more detail in a later course relative to managing the IOS.

It is more important for a networking professional to understand the function of the main internal components of a router than the exact location of those components inside a specific router. The internal physical architecture will differ from model to model.

Links

View the "Cisco 1800 Series Portfolio Multimedia Demo," http://www.cisco.com/cdc_content_elements/flash/isr_demo/demo.htm

1.1.3 Internetwork Operating System

Refer to **Figure** in online course

Internetwork Operating System

The operating system software used in Cisco routers is known as Cisco Internetwork Operating System (IOS). Like any operating system on any computer, Cisco IOS manages the hardware and software resources of the router, including memory allocation, processes, security, and file systems. Cisco IOS is a multitasking operating system that is integrated with routing, switching, internetworking, and telecommunications functions.

Although the Cisco IOS may appear to be the same on many routers, there are many different IOS images. An IOS image is a file that contains the entire IOS for that router. Cisco creates many different types of IOS images, depending upon the model of the router and the features within the IOS. Typically the more features in the IOS, the larger the IOS image, and therefore, the more flash and RAM that is required to store and load the IOS. For example, some features include the ability to run *IPv6* or the ability for the router to perform NAT (Network Address Translation).

As with other operating systems Cisco IOS has its own user interface. Although some routers provide a graphical user interface (GUI), the command line interface (CLI) is a much more common method of configuring Cisco routers. The CLI is used throughout this curriculum.

Upon bootup, the startup-config file in NVRAM is copied into RAM and stored as the running-config file. IOS executes the configuration commands in the running-config. Any changes entered by the network administrator are stored in the running-config and are immediately implemented by the IOS. In this chapter, we will review some of the basic IOS commands used to configure a Cisco router. In later chapters, we will learn the commands used to configure, verify, and troubleshoot *static routing* and various routing protocols such as RIP, EIGRP, and OSPF.

Note: Cisco IOS and the bootup process is discussed in more detail in a later course.

1.1.4 Router Boot-up Process

Refer to **Figure** in online course

Bootup Process

There are four major phases to the bootup process:

1. Performing the POST

2. Loading the bootstrap program

3. Locating and loading the Cisco IOS software

4. Locating and loading the startup configuration file or entering setup mode

1. Performing the POST

The *Power-On Self Test (POST)* is a common process that occurs on almost every computer during bootup. The POST process is used to test the router hardware. When the router is powered on, software on the ROM chip conducts the POST. During this self-test, the router executes diagnostics from ROM on several hardware components including the CPU, RAM, and NVRAM. After the POST has been completed, the router executes the bootstrap program.

2. Loading the Bootstrap Program

After the POST, the bootstrap program is copied from ROM into RAM. Once in RAM, the CPU executes the instructions in the bootstrap program. The main task of the bootstrap program is to locate the Cisco IOS and load it into RAM.

Note: At this point, if you have a console connection to the router, you will begin to see output on the screen.

3. Locating and Loading Cisco IOS

Locating the Cisco IOS software. The IOS is typically stored in flash memory, but can also be stored in other places such as a TFTP (Trivial File Transfer Protocol) server.

If a full IOS image can not be located, a scaled-down version of the IOS is copied from ROM into RAM. This version of IOS is used to help diagnose any problems and can be used to load a complete version of the IOS into RAM.

Note: A TFTP server is usually used as a backup server for IOS but it can also be used as a central point for storing and loading the IOS. IOS management and using the TFTP server is discussed in a later course.

Loading the IOS. Some of the older Cisco routers ran the IOS directly from flash, but current models copy the IOS into RAM for execution by the CPU.

Note: Once the IOS begins to load, you may see a string of pounds signs (#), as shown in the figure, while the image decompresses.

4. Locating and Loading the Configuration File

Locating the Startup Configuration File. After the IOS is loaded, the bootstrap program searches for the startup configuration file, known as startup-config, in NVRAM. This file has the previously saved configuration commands and parameters including:

- interface addresses
- routing information
- passwords
- any other configurations saved by the network administrator

If the startup configuration file, startup-config, is located in NVRAM, it is copied into RAM as the running configuration file, running-config.

Note: If the startup configuration file does not exist in NVRAM, the router may search for a TFTP server. If the router detects that it has an active link to another configured router, it sends a broadcast searching for a configuration file across the active link. This condition will cause the router to pause, but you will eventually see a console message like the following one:

<router pauses here while it broadcasts for a configuration file across an active link>
```
%Error opening tftp://255.255.255.255/network-confg (Timed out)
%Error opening tftp://255.255.255.255/cisconet.cfg (Timed out)
```

Executing the Configuration File. If a startup configuration file is found in NVRAM, the IOS loads it into RAM as the running-config and executes the commands in the file, one line at a time. The running-config file contains interface addresses, starts routing processes, configures router passwords and defines other characteristics of the router.

Enter Setup Mode (Optional). If the startup configuration file can not be located, the router prompts the user to enter setup mode. *Setup mode* is a series of questions prompting the user for basic configuration information. Setup mode is not intended to be used to enter complex router configurations, and it is not commonly used by network administrators.

When booting a router that does not contain a startup configuration file, you will see the following question after the IOS has been loaded:

```
Would you like to enter the initial configuration dialog? [yes/no]: no
```
Setup mode will not be used in this course to configure the router. When prompted to enter setup mode, always answer **no**. If you answer **yes** and enter setup mode, you can press **Ctrl-C** at any time to terminate the setup process.

When setup mode is not used, the IOS creates a default running-config. The default running-config is a basic configuration file that includes the router interfaces, management interfaces, and certain default information. The default running-config does not contain any interface addresses, routing information, passwords, or other specific configuration information.

Command Line Interface

Depending on the platform and IOS, the router may ask the following question before displaying the prompt:

```
Would you like to terminate autoinstall? [yes]: <Enter>
 Press the Enter key to accept the default answer.
Router>
```

Note: If a startup configuration file was found, the running-config may contain a hostname and the prompt will display the hostname of the router.

Once the prompt displays, the router is now running the IOS with the current running configuration file. The network administrator can now begin using IOS commands on this router.

Note: The bootup process is discussed in more detail in a later course.

Verifying Router Bootup Process

Refer to
Figure
in online course

The **show version** command can be used to help verify and troubleshoot some of the basic hardware and software components of the router. The **show version** command displays information about the version of the Cisco IOS software currently running on the router, the version of the bootstrap program, and information about the hardware configuration, including the amount of system memory.

The output from the **show version** command includes:

IOS version

```
Cisco Internetwork Operating System Software
IOS (tm) C2600 Software (C2600-I-M), Version 12.2(28), RELEASE SOFTWARE (fc5)
```

This is the version of the Cisco IOS software in RAM and that is being used by the router.

ROM Bootstrap Program

```
ROM: System Bootstrap, Version 12.1(3r)T2, RELEASE SOFTWARE (fc1)
```

This shows the version of the system bootstrap software, stored in ROM memory, that was initially used to boot up the router.

Location of IOS

`System image file is "`**`flash:c2600-i-mz.122-28.bin`**`"`

This shows where the bootstrap program is located and loaded the Cisco IOS, and the complete filename of the IOS image.

CPU and Amount of RAM

`cisco 2621 (`**`MPC860`**`) processor (revision 0x200) with` **`60416K/5120K bytes of memory`**

The first part of this line displays the type of CPU on this router. The last part of this line displays the amount of DRAM. Some series of routers, like the 2600, use a fraction of DRAM as packet memory. Packet memory is used for buffering packets.

To determine the total amount of DRAM on the router, add both numbers. In this example, the Cisco 2621 router has 60,416 KB (kilobytes) of free DRAM used for temporarily storing the Cisco IOS and other system processes. The other 5,120 KB is dedicated for packet memory. The sum of these numbers is 65,536K, or 64 megabytes (MB) of total DRAM.

Note: It may be necessary to upgrade the amount of RAM when upgrading the IOS.

Interfaces

`2 FastEthernet/IEEE 802.3 interface(s)`
`2 Low-speed serial(sync/async) network interface(s)`

This section of the output displays the physical interfaces on the router. In this example, the Cisco 2621 router has two FastEthernet interfaces and two low-speed serial interfaces.

Amount of NVRAM

`32K bytes of non-volatile configuration memory.`

This is the amount of NVRAM on the router. NVRAM is used to store the startup-config file.

Amount of Flash

`16384K bytes of processor board System flash (Read/Write)`

This is the amount of flash memory on the router. Flash is used to permanently store the Cisco IOS.

Note: It may be necessary to upgrade the amount of flash when upgrading the IOS.

Configuration Register

`Configuration register is 0x2102`

The last line of the **show version** command displays the current configured value of the software configuration register in hexadecimal. If there is a second value displayed in parentheses, it denotes the configuration register value that will be used during the next reload.

The configuration register has several uses, including password recovery. The factory default setting for the configuration register is 0x2102. This value indicates that the router will attempt to load a Cisco IOS software image from flash memory and load the startup configuration file from NVRAM.

Note: The configuration register is discussed in more detail in a later course.

Refer to **Packet Tracer Activity** for this chapter

Use this Packet Tracer Activity to experience setup mode and investigate the **show running-configuration** command.

1.1.5 Router Interfaces

Refer to **Figure** in online course

Management Ports

Routers have physical connectors that are used to manage the router. These connectors are known as management ports. Unlike Ethernet and serial interfaces, management ports are not used for packet forwarding. The most common management port is the *console port*. The console port is used to connect a terminal, or most often a PC running terminal emulator software, to configure the router without the need for network access to that router. The console port must be used during initial configuration of the router.

Another management port is the auxiliary port. Not all routers have auxiliary ports. At times the auxiliary port can be used in ways similar to a console port. It can also be used to attach a modem. Auxiliary ports will not be used in this curriculum.

The figure shows the console and AUX ports on the router.

Router Interfaces

The term *interface* on Cisco routers refers to a physical connector on the router whose main purpose is to receive and forward packets. Routers have multiple interfaces that are used to connect to multiple networks. Typically, the interfaces connect to various types of networks, which means that different types of media and connectors are required. Often a router will need to have different types of interfaces. For example, a router usually has FastEthernet interfaces for connections to different LANs and various types of WAN interfaces to connect a variety of serial links including T1, *DSL* and *ISDN*. The figure shows the FastEthernet and serial interfaces on the router.

Like interfaces on a PC, the ports and interfaces on a router are located on the outside of the router. Their external location allows for convenient attachment to the appropriate network cables and connectors.

Note: A single interface on a router can be used to connect to multiple networks; however, this is beyond the scope of this course and is discussed in a later course.

Like most networking devices, Cisco routers use *LED* indicators to provide status information. An interface LED indicates the activity of the corresponding interface. If an LED is off when the interface is active and the interface is correctly connected, this may be an indication of a problem with that interface. If an interface is extremely busy, its LED will always be on. Depending on the type of router, there may be other LEDs as well. For more information on LED displays on the 1841, see the link below.

Links

"Troubleshooting Cisco 1800 Series Routers (Modular)," http://www.cisco.com/en/US/docs/routers/access/1800/1841/hardware/installation/guide/18troub.html

Refer to
Figure
in online course

Interfaces Belong to Different Networks

As shown in the figure, every interface on the router is a member or host on a different IP network. Each interface must be configured with an IP address and subnet mask of a different network. Cisco IOS will not allow two active interfaces on the same router to belong to the same network.

Router interfaces can be divided into two major groups:

- *LAN interfaces -* such as Ethernet and FastEthernet
- *WAN interfaces -* such as serial, ISDN, and Frame Relay

LAN Interfaces

As the name indicates, LAN interfaces are used to connect the router to the LAN, similar to how a PC Ethernet NIC is used to connect the PC to the Ethernet LAN. Like a PC Ethernet NIC, a router Ethernet interface also has a Layer 2 MAC address and participates in the Ethernet LAN in the same way as any other *hosts* on that LAN. For example, a router Ethernet interface participates in the ARP process for that LAN. The router maintains an ARP cache for that interface, sends ARP requests when needed, and responds with ARP replies when required.

A router Ethernet interface usually uses an RJ-45 jack that supports unshielded twisted-pair (UTP) cabling. When a router is connected to a switch, a straight-through *cable* is used. When two routers are connected directly through the Ethernet interfaces, or when a PC NIC is connected directly to a router Ethernet interface, a crossover cable is used.

Use the Packet Tracer Activity later in this section to test your cabling skills.

WAN Interfaces

WAN interfaces are used to connect routers to external networks, usually over a larger geographical distance. The Layer 2 encapsulation can be of different types, such as PPP, Frame Relay, and HDLC (High-Level Data Link Control). Similar to LAN interfaces, each WAN interface has its own IP address and subnet mask, which identifies it as a member of a specific network.

Note: MAC addresses are used on LAN interfaces, such as Ethernet, and are not used on WAN interfaces. However, WAN interfaces use their own Layer 2 addresses depending on the technology. Layer 2 WAN encapsulation types and addresses are covered in a later course.

Router Interfaces

The router in the figure has four interfaces. Each interface has a Layer 3 IP address and subnet mask that configures it for a different network. The Ethernet interfaces also have Layer 2 Ethernet MAC addresses.

The WAN interfaces are using different Layer 2 encapsulations. Serial 0/0/0 is using HDLC and Serial 0/0/1 is using PPP. Both of these serial point-to-point protocols use a broadcast address for the Layer 2 destination address when encapsulating the IP packet into a data link frame.

In the lab environment, you are restricted as to how many LAN and WAN interfaces you can use to configure hands-on labs. With Packet Tracer, however, you have the flexibility to create more complex network designs.

Refer to **Packet Tracer Activity** for this chapter

Use the Packet Tracer Activity to practice selecting the correct cable to connect devices.

Refer to **Packet Tracer Activity** for this chapter

Use the Packet Tracer Activity to explore using the **Physical**, **Config**, and **CLI** tabs for a router.

1.1.6 Routers and the Network Layer

Refer to **Figure** in online course

Routers and the Network Layer

The main purpose of a router is to connect multiple networks and forward packets destined either for its own networks or other networks. A router is considered a Layer 3 device because its primary forwarding decision is based on the information in the Layer 3 IP packet, specifically the destination IP address. This process is known as routing.

When a router receives a packet, it examines its destination IP address. If the destination IP address does not belong to any of the router's directly connected networks, the router must forward this packet to another router. In the figure, R1 examines the destination IP address of the packet. After searching the routing table, R1 forwards the packet onto R2. When R2 receives the packet, it also examines the packet's destination IP address. After searching its routing table, R2 forwards the packet out its directly connected Ethernet network to PC2.

When each router receives a packet, it searches its routing table to find the best match between the destination IP address of the packet and one of the network addresses in the routing table. Once a match is found, the packet is encapsulated in the layer 2 data link frame for that outgoing interface. The type of data link encapsulation depends on the type of interface, such as Ethernet or HDLC.

Eventually the packet reaches a router that is part of a network that matches the destination IP address of the packet. In this example, router R2 receives the packet from R1. R2 forwards the packet out its Ethernet interface, which belongs to the same network as the destination device, PC2.

This sequence of events is explained in more detail later in this chapter.

Refer to
Figure
in online course

Routers Operate at Layers 1, 2, and 3

A router makes its primary forwarding decision at Layer 3, but as we saw earlier, it participates in Layer 1 and Layer 2 processes as well. After a router has examined the destination IP address of a packet and consulted its routing table to make its forwarding decision, it can forward that packet out the appropriate interface toward its destination. The router encapsulates the Layer 3 IP packet into the data portion of a Layer 2 data link frame appropriate for the exit interface. The type of frame can be an Ethernet, HDLC, or some other Layer 2 encapsulation - whatever encapsulation is used on that particular interface. The Layer 2 frame is encoded into the Layer 1 physical signals that are used to represent bits over the physical link.

To understand this process better, refer to the figure. Notice that PC1 operates at all seven layers, encapsulating the data and sending the frame out as a stream of encoded bits to R1, its default gateway.

R1 receives the stream of encoded bits on its interface. The bits are decoded and passed up to Layer 2, where R1 decapsulates the frame. The router examines the destination address of the data link frame to determine if it matches the receiving interface, including a broadcast or multicast address. If there is a match with the data portion of the frame, the IP packet is passed up to Layer 3, where R1 makes its routing decision. R1 then re-encapsulates the packet into a new Layer 2 data link frame and forwards it out the outbound interface as a stream of encoded bits.

R2 receives the stream of bits, and the process repeats itself. R2 decapsulates the frame and passes the data portion of the frame, the IP packet, to Layer 3 where R2 makes its routing decision. R2 then re-encapsulates the packet into a new Layer 2 data link frame and forwards it out the outbound interface as a stream of encoded bits.

This process is repeated once again by router R3, which forwards the IP packet, encapsulated inside a data link frame and encoded as bits, to PC2.

Each router in the path from source to destination performs this same process of decapsulation, searching the routing table, and then re-encapsulation. This process is important to your understanding of how routers participate in networks. Therefore, we will revisit this discussion in more depth in a later section.

1.2 CLI Configuration and Addressing

1.2.1 Implementing Basic Addressing Schemes

Refer to
Figure
in online course

When designing a new network or mapping an existing network, document the network. At a minimum, the documentation should include a topology diagram that indicates the physical connectivity and an addressing table that lists all of the following information:

- Device names

- Interfaces used in the design

- IP addresses and subnet masks

■ Default gateway addresses for end devices, such as PCs

Populating an Address Table

The figure shows a network topology with the devices interconnected and configured with IP addresses. Under the topology is a table used to document the network. The table is partially populated with the data documenting the network (devices, IP addresses, subnet masks, and interfaces).

Router R1 and host PC1 are already documented. Finish populating the table and the blank spaces on the diagram dragging the pool of IP addresses shown below the table to the correct locations.

Refer to **Packet Tracer Activity** for this chapter

Use the Packet Tracer Activity to connect the devices. Configure the device names to match the figure and use the **Place Note** feature to add network address labels.

1.2.2 Basic Router Configuration

Refer to **Figure** in online course

Basic Router Configuration

When configuring a router, certain basic tasks are performed including:

■ Naming the router

■ Setting passwords

■ Configuring interfaces

■ Configuring a banner

■ Saving changes on a router

■ Verifying basic configuration and router operations

You should already be familiar with these configuration commands; however, we will do a brief review. We begin our review with the assumption that the router does not have a current startup-config file.

The first prompt appears at user mode. User mode allows you to view the state of the router, but does not allow you to modify its configuration. Do not confuse the term "user" as used in user mode with users of the network. User mode is intended for the network technicians, operators, and engineers who have the responsibility to configure network devices.

```
Router>
```

The **enable** command is used to enter the *privileged EXEC mode*. This mode allows the user to make configuration changes on the router. The router prompt will change from a ">" to a "#" in this mode.

```
Router>enable
Router#
```

Hostnames and Passwords

The figure shows the basic router configuration command syntax used to configure R1 in the following example. You can open Packet Tracer Activity 1.2.2 and follow along or wait until the end of this section to open it.

First, enter the global configuration mode.

```
Router#config t
```

Next, apply a unique hostname to the router.

```
Router(config)#hostname R1
R1(config)#
```

Now, configure a password that is to be used to enter privileged EXEC mode. In our lab environment, we will use the password *class*. However, in production environments, routers should have strong passwords. See the links at the end of this section for more information on creating and using strong passwords.

```
Router(config)#enable secret class
```

Next, configure the console and *Telnet* lines with the password *cisco*. Once again, the password *cisco* is used only in our lab environment. The command login enables password checking on the line. If you do not enter the command login on the console line, the user will be granted access to the line without entering a password.

```
R1(config)#line console 0
 R1(config-line)#password cisco
 R1(config-line)#login
 R1(config-line)#exit
 R1(config)#line vty 0 4
 R1(config-line)#password cisco
 R1(config-line)#login
R1(config-line)#exit
```

Configuring a Banner

From the global configuration mode, configure the message-of-the-day (motd) banner. A delimiting character, such as a "#" is used at the beginning and at the end of the message. The delimiter allows you to configure a multiline banner, as shown here.

```
R1(config)#banner motd #
 Enter TEXT message. End with the character '#'.
 ********************************************
 WARNING!! Unauthorized Access Prohibited!!
 ********************************************
#
```

Configuring an appropriate banner is part of a good security plan. At a very minimum, a banner should warn against unauthorized access. Never configure a banner that "welcomes" an unauthorized user.

Links

For discussions about using strong passwords, see:

"Cisco Response to Dictionary Attacks on Cisco LEAP," at http://www.cisco.com/en/US/products/hw/wireless/ps430/prod_bulletin09186a00801cc901.html#wp1002291

"Strong passwords: How to create and use them," at http://www.microsoft.com/athome/security/privacy/password.mspx

Refer to
Figure
in online course

Router Interface Configuration

You will now configure the individual router interfaces with IP addresses and other information. First, enter the interface configuration mode by specifying the interface type and number. Next, configure the IP address and subnet mask:

```
R1(config)#interface Serial0/0/0
R1(config-if)#ip address 192.168.2.1 255.255.255.0
```

It is good practice to configure a description on each interface to help document the network information. The description text is limited to 240 characters. On production networks a description can be helpful in troubleshooting by providing information about the type of network that the interface is connected to and if there are any other routers on that network. If the interface connects to an ISP or service carrier, it is helpful to enter the third party connection and contact information; for example:

```
Router(config-if)#description Ciruit#VBN32696-123 (help desk:1-800-555-1234)
```

In lab environments, enter a simple description that will help in troubleshooting situations; for example:

`R1(config-if)#description Link to R2`

After configuring the IP address and description, the interface must be activated with the **no shut-down** command. This is similar to powering on the interface. The interface must also be connected to another device (a hub, a switch, another router, etc.) for the Physical layer to be active.

`Router(config-if)#no shutdown`

Note: When cabling a point-to-point serial link in our lab environment, one end of the cable is marked DTE and the other end is marked DCE. The router that has the DCE end of the cable connected to its serial interface will need the additional **clock rate** command configured on that serial interface. This step is only necessary in a lab environment and will be explained in more detail in Chapter 2, "Static Routing".

`R1(config-if)#clock rate 64000`

Repeat the interface configuration commands on all other interfaces that need to be configured. In our topology example, the FastEthernet interface needs to be configured.

```
R1(config)#interface FastEthernet0/0
 R1(config-if)#ip address 192.168.1.1 255.255.255.0
 R1(config-if)#description R1 LAN
R1(config-if)#no shutdown
```

Each Interface Belongs to a Different Network

At this point, note that each interface must belong to a different network. Although the IOS allows you to configure an IP address from the same network on two different interfaces, the router will not activate the second interface.

For example, what if you attempt to configure the FastEthernet 0/1 interface on R1 with an IP address on the 192.168.1.0/24 network? FastEthernet 0/0 has already been assigned an address on that same network. If you attempt to configure another interface, FastEthernet 0/1, with an IP address that belongs to the same network, you will get the following message:

```
R1(config)#interface FastEthernet0/1
 R1(config-if)#ip address 192.168.1.2 255.255.255.0

192.168.1.0 overlaps with FastEthernet0/0
```

If there is an attempt to enable the interface with the **no shutdown** command, the following message will appear:

```
R1(config-if)#no shutdown

192.168.1.0 overlaps with FastEthernet0/0

FastEthernet0/1: incorrect IP address assignment
```

Notice that the output from the **show ip interface brief** command shows that the second interface configured for the 192.168.1.0/24 network, FastEthernet 0/1, is still down.

```
R1#show ip interface brief
 <output omitted>
FastEthernet0/1 192.168.1.2 YES manual administratively down down
```

Refer to
Figure
in online course

Verifying Basic Router Configuration

Currently in the example, all of the previous basic router configuration commands have been entered and were immediately stored in the running configuration file of R1. The running-config file is stored in RAM and is the configuration file used by IOS. The next step is to verify the commands entered by displaying the running configuration with the following command:

`R1#show running-config`

Now that the basic configuration commands have been entered, it is important to save the running-config to the nonvolatile memory, the NVRAM of the router. That way, in case of a power outage or an accidental reload, the router will be able to boot with the current configuration. After the router's configuration has been completed and tested, it is important to save the running-config to the startup-config as the permanent configuration file.

R1#`copy running-config startup-config`

After applying and saving the basic configuration, you can use several commands to verify that you have correctly configured the router. Click the appropriate button in the figure to see a listing of each command's output. All of these commands are discussed in detail in later chapters. For now, begin to become familiar with the output.

R1#`show running-config`

This command displays the current running configuration that is stored in RAM. With a few exceptions, all configuration commands that were used will be entered into the running-config and implemented immediately by the IOS.

R1#`show startup-config`

This command displays the startup configuration file stored in NVRAM. This is the configuration that the router will use on the next reboot. This configuration does not change unless the current running configuration is saved to NVRAM with the **copy running-config startup-config** command. Notice in the figure that the startup configuration and the running configuration are identical. They are identical because the running configuration has not changed since the last time it was saved. Also notice that the **show startup-config** command also displays how many bytes of NVRAM the saved configuration is using.

R1#`show ip route`

This command displays the routing table that the IOS is currently using to choose the best path to its destination networks. At this point, R1 only has routes for its directly connected networks via its own interfaces.

R1#`show interfaces`

This command displays all of the interface configuration parameters and statistics. Some of this information is discussed later in the curriculum and in CCNP.

R1#`show ip interface brief`

This command displays abbreviated interface configuration information, including IP address and interface status. This command is a useful tool for troubleshooting and a quick way to determine the status of all router interfaces.

Refer to **Packet Tracer Activity** for this chapter

Use the Packet Tracer Activity to practice basic router configuration and verification commands.

1.3 Building the Routing Table

1.3.1 Introducing the Routing Table

Refer to **Figure** in online course

Introducing the Routing Table

The primary function of a router is to forward a packet toward its destination network, which is the destination IP address of the packet. To do this, a router needs to search the routing information stored in its routing table.

A routing table is a data file in RAM that is used to store route information about directly connected and remote networks. The routing table contains network/next hop associations. These associations tell a router that a particular destination can be optimally reached by sending the packet to a specific router that represents the "next hop" on the way to the final destination. The next hop association can also be the outgoing or exit interface to the final destination.

The network/exit-interface association can also represent the destination network address of the IP packet. This association occurs on the router's directly connected networks.

A directly connected network is a network that is directly attached to one of the router interfaces. When a router interface is configured with an IP address and subnet mask, the interface becomes a host on that attached network. The network address and subnet mask of the interface, along with the interface type and number, are entered into the routing table as a directly connected network. When a router forwards a packet to a host, such as a web server, that host is on the same network as a router's directly connected network.

A remote network is a network that is not directly connected to the router. In other words, a remote network is a network that can only be reached by sending the packet to another router. Remote networks are added to the routing table using either a dynamic routing protocol or by configuring static routes. Dynamic routes are routes to remote networks that were learned automatically by the router, using a dynamic routing protocol. Static routes are routes to networks that a network administrator manually configured.

Note: The routing table-with its directly-connected networks, static routes, and dynamic routes-will be introduced in the following sections and discussed in even greater detail throughout this course.

The following analogies may help clarify the concept of connected, static, and dynamic routes:

- *Directly Connected Routes* - To visit a *neighbor*, you only have to go down the street on which you already live. This path is similar to a directly-connected route because the "destination" is available directly through your "connected interface," the street.

- *Static Routes* - A train uses the same railroad tracks every time for a specified route. This path is similar to a static route because the path to the destination is always the same.

- *Dynamic Routes* - When driving a car, you can "dynamically" choose a different path based on traffic, weather, or other conditions. This path is similar to a dynamic route because you can choose a new path at many different points on your way to the destination.

The show ip route command

As shown in the figure the routing table is displayed with the **show ip route** command. At this point, there have not been any static routes configured nor any dynamic routing protocol enabled. Therefore, the routing table for R1 only shows the router's directly connected networks. For each network listed in the routing table, the following information is included:

- **C** - The information in this column denotes the source of the route information, directly connected network, static route or a dynamic routing protocol. The **C** represents a directly connected route.

- **192.168.1.0/24** - This is the network address and subnet mask of the directly connected or remote network. In this example, both entries in the routing table, 192.168.1./24 and 192.168.2.0/24, are directly connected networks.

- **FastEthernet 0/0** - The information at the end of the route entry represents the exit interface and/or the IP address of the *next-hop* router. In this example, both FastEthernet 0/0 and Serial0/0/0 are the exit interfaces used to reach these networks.

When the routing table includes a route entry for a remote network, additional information is included, such as the routing metric and the *administrative distance*. Routing *metrics*, administrative distance, and the **show ip route** command are explained in more detail in later chapters.

PCs also have a routing table. In the figure, you can see the **route print** command output. The command reveals the configured or acquired default gateway, connected, *loopback*, multicast, and broadcast networks. The output from **route print** command will not be analyzed during this course. It is shown here to emphasize the point that all IP configured devices should have a routing table.

1.3.2 Directly-Connected Networks

Refer to
Figure
in online course

Adding a Connected Network to the Routing Table

As stated in the previous section, when a router's interface is configured with an IP address and subnet mask, that interface becomes a host on that network. For example, when the FastEthernet 0/0 interface on R1 in the figure is configured with the IP address 192.168.1.1 and the subnet mask 255.255.255.0, the FastEthernet 0/0 interface becomes a member of the 192.168.1.0/24 network. Hosts that are attached to the same LAN, like PC1, are also configured with an IP address that belongs to the 192.168.1.0/24 network.

When a PC is configured with a host IP address and subnet mask, the PC uses the subnet mask to determine what network it now belongs to. This is done by the operating system ANDing the host IP address and subnet mask. A router uses the same logic when an interface is configured.

A PC is normally configured with a single host IP address because it only has a single network interface, usually an Ethernet NIC. Routers have multiple interfaces; therefore, each interface must be a member of a different network. In the figure, R1 is a member of two different networks: 192.168.1.0/24 and 192.168.2.0/24. Router R2 is also a member of two networks: 192.168.2.0/24 and 192.168.3.0/24.

After the router's interface is configured and the interface is activated with the **no shutdown** command, the interface must receive a carrier signal from another device (router, switch, hub, etc.) before the interface state is considered "up." Once the interface is "up," the network of that interface is added to the routing table as a directly connected network.

Before any static or dynamic routing is configured on a router, the router only knows about its own directly connected networks. These are the only networks that are displayed in the routing table until static or dynamic routing is configured. Directly connected networks are of prime importance for routing decisions. Static and dynamic routes cannot exist in the routing table without a router's own directly connected networks. The router cannot send packets out an interface if that interface is not enabled with an IP address and subnet mask, just as a PC cannot send IP packets out its Ethernet interface if that interface is not configured with an IP address and subnet mask.

Note: The process of configuring router interfaces and adding network address to the routing table are discussed in the following chapter.

Refer to **Packet
Tracer Activity**
for this chapter

Use the Packet Tracer Activity to learn how the IOS installs and removes directly connected routes.

1.3.3 Static Routing

Refer to
Figure
in online course

Static Routing

Remote networks are added to the routing table either by configuring static routes or enabling a dynamic routing protocol. When the IOS learns about a remote network and the interface that it will use to reach that network, it adds that route to the routing table as long as the exit interface is enabled.

A static route includes the network address and subnet mask of the remote network, along with the IP address of the next-hop router or exit interface. Static routes are denoted with the code **S** in the routing table as shown in the figure. Static routes are examined in detail in the next chapter.

When to Use Static Routes

Static routes should be used in the following cases:

- *A network consists of only a few routers.* Using a dynamic routing protocol in such a case does not present any substantial benefit. On the contrary, dynamic routing may add more administrative overhead.

- *A network is connected to the Internet only through a single ISP.* There is no need to use a dynamic routing protocol across this link because the ISP represents the only exit point to the Internet.

- *A large network is configured in a hub-and-spoke* topology. A hub-and-spoke topology consists of a central location (the hub) and multiple branch locations (spokes), with each spoke having only one connection to the hub. Using dynamic routing would be unnecessary because each branch has only one path to a given destination-through the central location.

Typically, most routing tables contain a combination of static routes and dynamic routes. But, as stated earlier, the routing table must first contain the directly connected networks used to access these remote networks before any static or dynamic routing can be used.

Refer to **Packet Tracer Activity** for this chapter

Use the Packet Tracer Activity to learn how the IOS installs and removes static routes.

1.3.4 Dynamic Routing

Refer to **Figure** in online course

Dynamic Routing

Remote networks can also be added to the routing table by using a dynamic routing protocol. In the figure, R1 has automatically learned about the 192.168.4.0/24 network from R2 through the dynamic routing protocol, RIP (Routing Information Protocol). RIP was one of the first IP routing protocols and will be fully discussed in later chapters.

Note: R1's routing table in the figure shows that R1 has learned about two remote networks: one route that dynamically used RIP and a static route that was configured manually. This is an example of how routing tables can contain routes learned dynamically and configured statically and is not necessarily representative of the best configuration for this network.

Dynamic routing protocols are used by routers to share information about the reachability and status of remote networks. Dynamic routing protocols perform several activities, including:

- Network discovery
- Updating and maintaining routing tables

Automatic Network Discovery

Network discovery is the ability of a routing protocol to share information about the networks that it knows about with other routers that are also using the same routing protocol. Instead of configuring static routes to remote networks on every router, a dynamic routing protocol allows the routers to automatically learn about these networks from other routers. These networks - and the best path to each network - are added to the router's routing table and denoted as a network learned by a specific dynamic routing protocol.

Maintaining Routing Tables

After the initial network discovery, *dynamic routing protocols* update and maintain the networks in their routing tables. Dynamic routing protocols not only make a best path determination to various networks, they will also determine a new best path if the initial path becomes unusable (or if the topology changes). For these reasons, dynamic routing protocols have an advantage over static routes. Routers that use dynamic routing protocols automatically share routing information with other routers and compensate for any topology changes without involving the network administrator.

IP Routing Protocols

There are several dynamic routing protocols for IP. Here are some of the more common dynamic routing protocols for routing IP packets:

- RIP (Routing Information Protocol)
- *IGRP* (Interior Gateway Routing Protocol)
- EIGRP (Enhanced Interior Gateway Routing Protocol)
- OSPF (Open Shortest Path First)
- IS-IS (Intermediate System-to-Intermediate System)
- BGP (Border Gateway Protocol)

Note: RIP (versions 1 and 2), EIGRP, and OSPF are discussed in this course. EIGRP and OSPF are also explained in more detail in CCNP, along with IS-IS and BGP. IGRP is a legacy routing protocol and has been replaced by EIGRP. Both IGRP and EIGRP are Cisco proprietary routing protocols, whereas all other routing protocols listed are standard, non-proprietary protocols.

Once again, remember that in most cases, routers contain a combination of static routes and dynamic routes in the routing tables. Dynamic routing protocols will be discussed in more detail in Chapter 3, "Introduction to Dynamic Routing Protocols."

Use the Packet Tracer Activity to learn how the IOS installs and removes dynamic routes.

Refer to **Packet Tracer Activity** for this chapter

Refer to **Figure** in online course

1.3.5 Routing Table Principles

Routing Table Principles

At times in this course we will refer to three principles regarding routing tables that will help you understand, configure, and troubleshoot routing issues. These principles are from Alex Zinin's book, *Cisco IP Routing*.

1. Every router makes its decision alone, based on the information it has in its own routing table.

2. The fact that one router has certain information in its routing table does not mean that other routers have the same information.

3. Routing information about a path from one network to another does not provide routing information about the reverse, or return, path.

What is the effect of these principles? Let's look at the example in the figure.

1. After making its routing decision, router R1 forwards the packet destined for PC2 to router R2. R1 only knows about the information in its own routing table, which indicates that router R2 is the next-hop router. R1 does not know whether or not R2 actually has a route to the destination network.

2. It is the responsibility of the network administrator to make sure that all routers within their control have complete and accurate routing information so that packets can be forwarded between any two networks. This can be done using static routes, a dynamic routing protocol, or a combination of both.

3. Router R2 was able to forward the packet toward PC2's destination network. However, the packet from PC2 to PC1 was dropped by R2. Although R2 has information in its routing table

about the destination network of PC2, we do not know if it has the information for the return path back to PC1's network.

Asymmetric Routing

Because routers do not necessarily have the same information in their routing tables, packets can traverse the network in one direction, using one path, and return via another path. This is called *asymmetric routing*. Asymmetric routing is more common in the Internet, which uses the BGP routing protocol than it is in most internal networks.

This example implies that when designing and troubleshooting a network, the network administrator should check the following routing information:

- Is there a path from source to destination available in both directions?

- Is the path taken in both directions the same path? (Asymmetrical routing is not uncommon, but sometimes can pose additional issues.)

Refer to **Packet Tracer Activity** for this chapter

Use the Packet Tracer Activity to investigate a fully-converged network with connected, static, and dynamic routing.

1.4   Path Determination and Switching Functions

1.4.1   Packet Fields and Frame Fields

Refer to **Figure** in online course

Packet Fields and Frame Fields

As we discussed previously, routers make their primary forwarding decision by examining the destination IP address of a packet. Before sending a packet out the proper exit interface, the IP packet needs to be encapsulated into a Layer 2 data link frame. Later in this section we will follow an IP packet from source to destination, examining the encapsulation and decapsulation process at each router. But first, we will review the format of a Layer 3 IP packet and a Layer 2 Ethernet frame.

Internet Protocol (IP) Packet Format

The Internet Protocol specified in RFC 791 defines the IP packet format. The IP packet header has specific fields that contain information about the packet and about the sending and receiving hosts. Below is a list of the fields in the IP header and a brief description for each one. You should already be familiar with destination IP address, source IP address, version, and Time To Live (*TTL*) fields. The other fields are important but are outside the scope of this course.

- *Version -* Version number (4 bits); predominant version is IP version 4 (IPv4)

- *IP header length -* Header length in 32-bit words (4 bits)

- *Precedence and type of service -* How the datagram should be handled (8 bits); the first 3 bits are precedence bits (this use has been superseded by Differentiated Services Code Point [DSCP], which uses the first 6 bits [last 2 reserved])

- *Packet length -* Total length (header + data) (16 bits)

- *Identification -* Unique IP datagram value (16 bits)

- *Flags -* Controls fragmenting (3 bits)

- *Fragment offset -* Supports fragmentation of *datagrams* to allow differing maximum transmission units (MTUs) in the Internet (13 bits)

- *Time to Live (TTL) -* Identifies how many routers can be traversed by the datagram before being dropped (8 bits)

- *Protocol -* Upper-layer protocol sending the datagram (8 bits)

- *Header checksum -* Integrity check on the header (16 bits)

- *Source IP address -* 32-bit source IP address (32 bits)

- *Destination IP address -* 32-bit destination IP address (32 bits)

- *IP options -* Network testing, debugging, security, and others (0 or 32 bits, if any)

Refer to **Figure** in online course

MAC Layer Frame Format

The Layer 2 data link frame usually contains header information with a data link source and destination address, trailer information, and the actual transmitted data. The data link source address is the Layer 2 address of the interface that sent the data link frame. The data link destination address is the Layer 2 address of the interface of the destination device. Both the source and destination data link interfaces are on the same network. As a packet is forwarded from router to router, the Layer 3 source and destination IP addresses will not change; however, the Layer 2 source and destination data link addresses will change. This process will be examined more closely later in this section.

Note: When NAT (Network Address Translation) is used, the destination IP address does change, but this process is of no concern to IP and is a process performed within a company's network. Routing with NAT is discussed in a later course.

The Layer 3 IP packet is encapsulated in the Layer 2 data link frame associated with that interface. In this example, we will show the Layer 2 Ethernet frame. The figure shows the two compatible versions of Ethernet. Below is a list of the fields in an Ethernet frame and a brief description of each one.

- *Preamble -* Seven bytes of alternating 1s and 0s, used to synchronize signals

- *Start-of-frame (SOF) delimiter -* 1 byte signaling the beginning of the frame

- *Destination address -* 6 byte MAC address of the sending device on the local segment

- *Source address -* 6 byte MAC address of the receiving device on the local segment

- *Type/length -* 2 bytes specifying either the type of upper layer protocol (Ethernet II frame format) or the length of the data field (IEEE 802.3 frame format)

- *Data and pad -* 46 to 1500 bytes of data; zeros used to pad any data packet less than 46 bytes

- *Frame check sequence (FCS) -* 4 bytes used for a cyclical redundancy check to make sure the frame is not corrupted

1.4.2 Best Path and Metric

Refer to **Figure** in online course

Best Path

Determining a router's best path involves the evaluation of multiple paths to the same destination network and selecting the optimum or "shortest" path to reach that network. Whenever multiple paths to reach the same network exist, each path uses a different exit interface on the router to reach that network. The best path is selected by a routing protocol based on the value or metric it uses to determine the distance to reach a network. Some routing protocols, such as RIP, use simple hop-count, which the number of routers between a router and the destination network. Other routing protocols, such as OSPF, determine the shortest path by examining the bandwidth of the links, and using the links with the fastest bandwidth from a router to the destination network.

Dynamic routing protocols typically use their own rules and metrics to build and update routing tables. A metric is the quantitative value used to measure the distance to a given route. The best path to a network is the path with the lowest metric. For example, a router will prefer a path that is 5 hops away over a path that is 10 hops away.

The primary objective of the routing protocol is to determine the best paths for each route to include in the routing table. The routing algorithm generates a value, or a metric, for each path through the network. Metrics can be based on either a single characteristic or several characteristics of a path. Some routing protocols can base route selection on multiple metrics, combining them into a single metric. The smaller the value of the metric, the better the path.

Comparing Hop Count and Bandwidth Metrics

Two metrics that are used by some dynamic routing protocols are:

- *Hop count-* Hop count is the number of routers that a packet must travel through before reaching its destination. Each router is equal to one hop. A hop count of four indicates that a packet must pass through four routers to reach its destination. If multiple paths are available to a destination, the routing protocol, such as RIP, picks the path with the least number of hops.

- *Bandwidth-* Bandwidth is the data capacity of a link, sometimes referred to as the speed of the link. For example, Cisco's implementation of the OSPF routing protocol uses bandwidth as its metric. The best path to a network is determined by the path with an accumulation of links that have the highest bandwidth values, or the fastest links. The use of bandwidth in OSPF will be explained in Chapter 11.

Note: *Speed* is technically not an accurate description of bandwidth because all bits travel at the same speed over the same physical medium. Bandwidth is more accurately defined as the number of bits that can be transmitted over a link per second.

When hop count is used as the metric, the resulting path may sometimes be suboptimal. For example, consider the network shown in the figure. If RIP is the routing protocol used by the three routers, then R1 will choose the suboptimal route through R3 to reach PC2 because this path has fewer hops. Bandwidth is not considered. However, if OSPF is used as the routing protocol, then R1 will choose the route based on bandwidth. Packets will be able to reach their destination sooner using the two, faster T1 links as compared to the single, slower 56 Kbps link.

Refer to **Packet Tracer Activity** for this chapter

Use the Packet Tracer Activity to determine the best path using routing tables.

1.4.3 Equal Cost Load Balancing

Refer to **Figure** in online course

Equal Cost Load Balancing

You may be wondering what happens if a routing table has two or more paths with the same metric to the same destination network. When a router has multiple paths to a destination network and the value of that metric (hop count, bandwidth, etc.) is the same, this is known as an *equal cost metric*, and the router will perform *equal cost load balancing*. The routing table will contain the single destination network but will have multiple exit interfaces, one for each equal cost path. The router will forward packets using the multiple exit interfaces listed in the routing table.

If configured correctly, load balancing can increase the effectiveness and performance of the network. Equal cost load balancing can be configured to use both dynamic routing protocols and static routes. Equal cost load balancing is discussed in more detail in Chapter 8, "The Routing Table: A Closer Look".

Equal Cost Paths and Unequal Cost Paths

Just in case you are wondering, a router can send packets over multiple networks even when the metric is not the same if it is using a routing protocol that has this capability. This is known as *unequal cost load balancing*. EIGRP (as well as IGRP) are the only routing protocols that can be configured for unequal cost load balancing. Unequal cost load balancing in EIGRP is not discussed in this course but is covered in CCNP.

Refer to **Packet Tracer Activity** for this chapter

Use the Packet Tracer Activity to explore a routing table that is using equal *cost load balancing*.

1.4.4 Path Determination

Refer to **Figure** in online course

Path Determination

Packet forwarding involves two functions:

- Path determination function

- Switching function

The path determination function is the process of how the router determines which path to use when forwarding a packet. To determine the best path, the router searches its routing table for a network address that matches the packet's destination IP address.

One of three path determinations results from this search:

Directly Connected Network - If the destination IP address of the packet belongs to a device on a network that is directly connected to one of the router's interfaces, that packet is forwarded directly to that device. This means that the destination IP address of the packet is a host address on the same network as this router's interface.

Remote Network - If the destination IP address of the packet belongs to a remote network, then the packet is forwarded to another router. Remote networks can only be reached by forwarding packets to another router.

No Route Determined - If the destination IP address of the packet does not belong to either a connected or remote network, and if the router does not have a default route, then the packet is discarded. The router sends an *ICMP* unreachable message to the source IP address of the packet.

In the first two results, the router re-encapsulates the IP packet into the Layer 2 data link frame format of the exit interface. The type of Layer 2 encapsulation is determined by the type of interface. For example, if the exit interface is FastEthernet, the packet is encapsulated in an Ethernet frame. If the exit interface is a serial interface configured for PPP, the IP packet is encapsulated in a PPP frame.

The following section demonstrates this process.

1.4.5 Switching Function

Refer to **Figure** in online course

Switching Function

After the router has determined the exit interface using the path determination function, the router needs to encapsulate the packet into the data link frame of the outgoing interface.

The switching function is the process used by a router to accept a packet on one interface and forward it out another interface. A key responsibility of the switching function is to encapsulate packets in the appropriate data link frame type for the outgoing data link.

What does a router do with a packet received from one network and destined for another network? The router performs the following three major steps:

1. Decapsulates the Layer 3 packet by removing the Layer 2 frame header and trailer.

2. Examines the destination IP address of the IP packet to find the best path in the routing table.

3. Encapsulates Layer 3 packet into a new Layer 2 frame and forwards the frame out the exit interface.

Click Play to view the animation.

As the Layer 3 IP packet is forwarded from one router to the next, the IP packet remains unchanged, with the exception of the Time To Live (TTL) field. When a router receives an IP packet, it decrements the TTL by one. If the resulting TTL value is zero, the router discards the packet. The TTL is used to prevent IP packets from traveling endlessly over networks due to a routing loop or other misfunction in the network. Routing loops are discussed in a later a chapter.

As the IP packet is decapsulated from one Layer 2 frame and encapsulated into a new Layer 2 frame, the data link destination address and source address will change as the packet is forwarded from one router to the next. The Layer 2 data link source address represents the Layer 2 address of the outbound interface. The Layer 2 destination address represents the Layer 2 address of the next-hop router. If the next hop is the final destination device, it will be the Layer 2 address of that device.

It is very likely that the packet will be encapsulated in a different type of Layer 2 frame than the one in which it was received. For example, the packet might be received by the router on a FastEthernet interface, encapsulated in an Ethernet frame, and forwarded out a serial interface encapsulated in a PPP frame.

Remember, as a packet travels from the source device to the final destination device, the Layer 3 IP addresses do not change. However, the Layer 2 data link addresses change at every hop as the packet is decapsulated and re-encapsulated in a new frame by each router.

Refer to
Figure
in online course

Path Determination and Switching Function Details

Can you describe the exact details of what happens to a packet at Layer 2 and Layer 3 as it travels from source to destination? If not, study the animation and follow along with the discussion until you can describe the process on your own.

Click Play to view the animation.

Step 1: PC1 has a packet to be sent to PC2

PC1 encapsulates the IP packet into an Ethernet frame with the destination MAC address of R1's FastEthernet 0/0 interface.

How does PC1 know to forward to packet to R1 and not directly to PC2? PC1 has determined that the IP source and IP destination addresses are on different networks.

PC1 knows the network it belongs to by doing an **AND** operation on its own IP address and subnet mask, which results in its network address. PC1 does this same **AND** operation using the packet destination IP address and the PC1 subnet mask. If the result is the same as its own network, PC1 knows that the destination IP address is on its own network and it does not need to forward the packet to the default gateway, the router. If the **AND** operation results in a different network address, PC1 knows that the destination IP address is not on its own network and that it must forward this packet to the default gateway, the router.

Note: If an **AND** operation with the destination IP address of the packet and the subnet mask of PC1 results in a different network address than what PC1 has determined to be its own network address, this address does not necessarily reflect the actual remote network address. PC1 only knows that if the destination IP address is on its own network, the masks will be the same and the network addresses would be the same. The mask of the remote network might be a different mask. If the destination IP address results in a different network address, PC1 will not know the actual remote network address - it only knows that it is not on its own network.

How does PC1 determine the MAC address of the default gateway, router R1? PC1 checks its ARP table for the IP address of the default gateway and its associated MAC address.

What if this entry does not exist in the ARP table? PC1 sends an ARP request and router R1 sends back an ARP reply.

Step 2: Router R1 receives the Ethernet frame

1. Router R1 examines the destination MAC address, which matches the MAC address of the receiving interface, FastEthernet 0/0. R1 will therefore copy the frame into its buffer.

2. R1 sees that the Ethernet Type field is 0x800, which means that the Ethernet frame contains an IP packet in the data portion of the frame.

3. R1 decapsulates the Ethernet frame.

4. Because the destination IP address of the packet does not match any of R1's directly connected networks, the router consults its routing table to route this packet. R1 searches the routing table for a network address and subnet mask that would include this packet's destination IP address as a host address on that network. In this example, the routing table has a route for the 192.168.4.0/24 network. The destination IP address of the packet is 192.168.4.10, which is a host IP address on that network.

R1's route to the 192.168.4.0/24 network has a next-hop IP address of 192.168.2.2 and an exit interface of FastEthernet 0/1. This means that the IP packet will be encapsulated in a new Ethernet frame with the destination MAC address of the next-hop router's IP address. Because the exit interface is on an Ethernet network, R1 must resolve the next-hop IP address with a destination MAC address.

5. R1 looks up the next-hop IP address of 192.168.2.2 in its ARP cache for its FastEthernet 0/1 interface. If the entry is not in the ARP cache, R1 sends an ARP request out its FastEthernet 0/1 interface. R2 sends back an ARP reply. R1 then updates its ARP cache with an entry for 192.168.2.2 and the associated MAC address.

6. The IP packet is now encapsulated into a new Ethernet frame and forwarded out R1's FastEthernet 0/1 interface.

Refer to **Figure** in online course

Step 3: Packet arrives at router R2

Click Play to view the animation.

1. Router R2 examines the destination MAC address, which matches the MAC address of the receiving interface, FastEthernet 0/0. R1 will therefore copy the frame into its buffer.

2. R2 sees that the Ethernet Type field is 0x800, which means that the Ethernet frame contains an IP packet in the data portion of the frame.

3. R2 decapsulates the Ethernet frame.

4. Because the destination IP address of the packet does not match any of R2's interface addresses, the router consults its routing table to route this packet. R2 searches the routing table for the packet's destination IP address using the same process R1 used.

R2's routing table has a route to the 192.168.4.0/24 route, with a next-hop IP address of 192.168.3.2 and an exit interface of Serial 0/0/0. Because the exit interface is not an Ethernet network, R2 does not have to resolve the next-hop-IP address with a destination MAC address.

When the interface is a point-to-point serial connection, R2 encapsulates the IP packet into the proper data link frame format used by the exit interface (HDLC, PPP, etc.). In this case, the Layer 2 encapsulation is PPP; therefore, the data link destination address is set to a broadcast. Remember, there are no MAC addresses on serial interfaces.

5. The IP packet is now encapsulated into a new data link frame, PPP, and sent out the serial 0/0/0 exit interface.

Refer to
Figure
in online course

Step 4: The packet arrives at R3

1. R3 receives and copies the data link PPP frame into its buffer.

2. R3 decapsulates the data link PPP frame.

3. R3 searches the routing table for the destination IP address of the packet. The search of the routing table results in a network that is one of R3's directly connected networks. This means that the packet can be sent directly to the destination device and does not need to be sent to another router.

Because the exit interface is a directly connected Ethernet network, R3 needs to resolve the destination IP address of the packet with a destination MAC address.

4. R3 searches for the packet's destination IP address of 192.168.4.10 in its ARP cache. If the entry is not in the ARP cache, R3 sends an ARP request out its FastEthernet 0/0 interface. PC2 sends back an ARP reply with its MAC address. R3 updates its ARP cache with an entry for 192.168.4.10 and the MAC address that was returned in the ARP reply.

5. The IP packet is encapsulated into a new data link, Ethernet frame and sent out R3's FastEthernet 0/0 interface.

Step 5: The Ethernet Frame with encapsulated IP packet arrives at PC2

1. PC2 examines the destination MAC address, which matches the MAC address of the receiving interface, its Ethernet NIC. PC2 will therefore copy the rest of the frame into its buffer.

2. PC2 sees that the Ethernet Type field is 0x800, which means that the Ethernet frame contains an IP packet in the data portion of the frame.

3. PC2 decapsulates the Ethernet frame and passes the IP packet to the IP process of its operating system.

Summary

We have just examined the encapsulation and decapsulation process of a packet as it is forwarded from router to router, from the originating source device the final destination device. We have also been introduced to the routing table lookup process, which will be discussed more thoroughly in a later chapter. We have seen that routers are not involved only in Layer 3 routing decisions, but that they also participate in Layer 2 processes, including encapsulation, and on Ethernet networks, ARP. Routers also participate in Layer 1, which is used to transmit and receive the data bits over the physical medium.

Routing tables contain both directly connected networks and remote networks. It is because routers contain addresses for remote networks in their routing tables that routers know where to send packets destined other networks, including the Internet. In the following chapters will learn how the routers build and maintain these routing tables - either by the use of manually entered static routes or through the use of dynamic routing protocols.

1.5 Router Configuration Labs

1.5.1 Cabling a Network and Basic Router Configuration

Refer to
Lab Activity
for this chapter

Complete this lab if you need a solid review of device cabling, establishing a console connection, and command-line interface (CLI) basics. If you are comfortable with these skills, you can substitute **Lab 1.5.2 Basic Router Configuration** for this lab.

Refer to **Packet Tracer Activity** for this chapter

Use Packet Tracer Activity 1.5.1 to repeat a simulation of Lab 1.5.1. Remember, however, that Packet Tracer is not a substitute for a hands-on lab experience with real equipment.

A summary of the instructions is provided within the activity. Use the Lab PDF for more details.

1.5.2 Basic Router Configuration

Refer to **Lab Activity** for this chapter

Complete this lab if you have solid skills in device cabling, establishing a console connection, and command-line interface (CLI) basics. If you need a review of these skills, you can substitute **Lab 1.5.1 Cabling a Network and Basic Router Configuration** for this lab.

Refer to **Packet Tracer Activity** for this chapter

Use Packet Tracer Activity 1.5.2 to repeat a simulation of Lab 1.5.2. Remember, however, that Packet Tracer is not a substitute for a hands-on lab experience with real equipment.

A summary of the instructions is provided within the activity. Use the Lab PDF for more details.

1.5.3 Challenge Router Configuration

Refer to **Lab Activity** for this chapter

This lab challenges your subnetting and configuration skills. Given an address space and network requirements, you are expected to design and implement an addressing scheme in a two-router topology.

Refer to **Packet Tracer Activity** for this chapter

Use Packet Tracer Activity 1.5.3 to repeat a simulation of Lab 1.5.3. Remember, however, that Packet Tracer is not a substitute for a hands-on lab experience with real equipment.

A summary of the instructions is provided within the activity. Use the Lab PDF for more details.

Summary and Review

Summary

Refer to **Figure** in online course

This chapter introduced the router. Routers are computers and include many of the same hardware and software components found in a typical PC, such as CPU, RAM, ROM, and an operating system.

The main purpose of a router is to connect multiple networks and forward packets from one network to the next. This means that a router typically has multiple interfaces. Each interface is a member or host on a different IP network.

The router has a routing table, which is a list of networks known by the router. The routing table includes network addresses for its own interfaces, which are the directly connected networks, as well as network addresses for remote networks. A remote network is a network that can only be reached by forwarding the packet to another router.

Remote networks are added to the routing table in two ways: either by the network administrator manually configuring static routes or by implementing a dynamic routing protocol. Static routes do not have as much overhead as dynamic routing protocols; however, static routes can require more maintenance if the topology is constantly changing or is unstable.

Dynamic routing protocols automatically adjust to changes without any intervention from the network administrator. Dynamic routing protocols require more CPU processing and also use a certain amount of link capacity for routing updates and messages. In many cases, a routing table will contain both static and dynamic routes.

Routers make their primary forwarding decision at Layer 3, the Network layer. However, router interfaces participate in Layers 1, 2, and 3. Layer 3 IP packets are encapsulated into a Layer 2 data link frame and encoded into bits at Layer 1. Router interfaces participate in Layer 2 processes associated with their encapsulation. For example, an Ethernet interface on a router participates in the ARP process like other hosts on that LAN.

In the next chapter, we will examine the configuration of static routes and introduce the IP routing table.

Refer to **Figure** in online course

Refer to **Packet Tracer Activity** for this chapter

The Packet Tracer Skills Integration Challenge Activity for this chapter integrates all the knowledge and skills you acquired in previous courses and the first chapter of this course. In this activity, you build a network from the ground up. Starting with an addressing space and network requirements, you must implement a network design that satisfies the specifications.

Packet Tracer Skills Integration Instructions (PDF)

To Learn More

Refer to **Figure** in online course

Create a topology similar to that in 1.4.5.2, with several routers, and a LAN at each end. On one LAN add a client host, and on the other end add a web server. On each LAN include a switch between the computer and the router. Assume that each router has a route to each of the LANs, similar to that in 1.4.5.2.

What happens when the host requests a web page from the web server? Look at all of the processes and protocols involved starting with the user entering a URL such as www.cisco.com. This includes protocols learned in Exploration 1 as well as information learned in this chapter.

See if you can determine each of the processes that happen starting with the client needing to resolve www.cisco.com to an IP address which results in the client having to do an ARP Request for the DNS server. What are all of the protocols and processes involved starting with the DNS request to getting the first packet with http information from the web server.

- How is DNS involved?

- How is ARP involved?

- What affect does TCP have between the client and the server? Is the first packet the web server receives from the client the request for the web page?

- What do the switches do when they receive an Ethernet frame? How do they update their MAC address tables and how do they determine how to forward the frame?

- What do the routers do when they receive an IP packet?

- What is the decapsulation and encapsulation process of each frame received and forwarded by the router?

- Is any ARP processes required by the web server and its default gateway (its router)?

Go to the online course to take the quiz.

Chapter Quiz

Take the chapter quiz to test your knowledge.

Your Chapter Notes

CHAPTER 2

Static Routing

Chapter Introduction

Chapter Introduction

Routing is at the core of every data network, moving information across an internetwork from source to destination. Routers are the devices responsible for the transfer of packets from one network to the next.

As we learned in the previous chapter, routers learn about remote networks either dynamically using routing protocols or manually using static routes. In many cases routers use a combination of both dynamic routing protocols and static routes. This chapter focuses on static routing.

Static routes are very common and do not require the same amount of processing and overhead as we will see with dynamic routing protocols.

In this chapter, we will follow a sample topology as we configure static routes and learn troubleshooting techniques. In the process, we will examine several key IOS commands and the results they display. We will also introduce the routing table using both directly connected networks and static routes.

As you work through the Packet Tracer activities associated with these commands, take the time to experiment with the commands and examine the results. Reading the routing tables will soon become second nature.

2.1 Routers and Network

2.1.1 Role of the Router

Role of the Router

The router is a special-purpose computer that plays a key role in the operation of any data network. Routers are primarily responsible for interconnecting networks by:

- Determining the best path to send packets
- Forwarding packets toward their destination

Routers perform packet forwarding by learning about remote networks and maintaining routing information. The router is the junction or intersection that connects multiple IP networks. The routers primary forwarding decision is based on Layer 3 information, the destination IP address.

The router's routing table is used to find the best match between the destination IP of a packet and a network address in the routing table. The routing table will ultimately determine the exit interface to forward the packet and the router will encapsulate that packet in the appropriated data link frame for that outgoing interface.

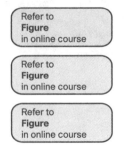

2.1.2 Introducing the Topology

Introducing the Topology

The figure shows the topology used in this chapter. The topology consists of three routers, labeled R1, R2, and R3. Routers R1 and R2 are connected through one WAN link, and routers R2 and R3 are connected through another WAN link. Each router is connected to a different Ethernet LAN, represented by a switch and a PC.

Each router in this example is a Cisco 1841. A Cisco 1841 router has the following interfaces:

- Two FastEthernet interfaces: FastEthernet 0/0 and FastEthernet 0/1

- Two serial interfaces: Serial 0/0/0 and Serial0/0/1

The interfaces on your routers may vary from those on the 1841, but you should be able to follow the commands in this chapter-with some slight modifications-and complete the hands-on labs. In addition, Packet Tracer activities are available throughout the discussion of static routing so that you can practice skills as they are presented. Lab 2.8.1, "Basic Static Route Configuration," mirrors the topology, configurations, and commands discussed in this chapter.

2.1.3 Examining the Connections of the Router

Router Connections

Connecting a router to a network requires a router interface connector to be coupled with a cable connector. As you can see in the figure, Cisco routers support many different connector types.

Serial Connectors

Click 1 in the figure.

For WAN connections, Cisco routers support the EIA/TIA-232, EIA/TIA-449, V.35, X.21, and EIA/TIA-530 standards for serial connections, as shown. Memorizing these connection types is not important. Just know that a router has a DB-60 port that can support five different cabling standards. Because five different cable types are supported with this port, the port is sometimes called a five-in-one serial port. The other end of the serial cable is fitted with a connector that is appropriate to one of the five possible standards.

Note: The documentation for the device to which you want to connect should indicate the standard for that device.

Click 2 and 3 in the figure.

Newer routers support the smart serial interface that allows for more data to be forwarded across fewer cable pins. The serial end of the smart serial cable is a 26-pin connector. It is much smaller than the DB-60 connector used to connect to a five-in-one serial port. These transition cables support the same five serial standards and are available in either DTE or DCE configurations.

Note: For a thorough explanation of DTE and DCE, see Lab 1.5.1, "Cabling a Network and Basic Router Configuration."

These cable designations are only important to you when configuring your lab equipment to simulate a "real-world" environment. In a production setting, the cable type is determined for you by the WAN service you are using.

Ethernet Connectors

Click 4 in the figure.

A different connector is used in an Ethernet-based LAN environment. An RJ-45 connector for the unshielded twisted-pair (UTP) cable is the most common connector used to connect LAN interfaces. At each end of an RJ-45 cable, you should be able to see eight colored strips, or pins. An Ethernet cable uses pins 1, 2, 3, and 6 for transmitting and receiving data.

Two types of cables can be used with Ethernet LAN interfaces:

- A straight-through, or patch cable, with the order of the colored pins the same on each end of the cable

- A crossover cable, with pin 1 connected to pin 3, and pin 2 connected to pin 6

Straight-through cables are used for:

- Switch-to-router

- Switch-to-PC

- Hub-to-PC

- Hub-to-server

Crossover cables are used for:

- Switch-to-switch

- PC-to-PC

- Switch-to-hub

- Hub-to-hub

- Router-to-router

- Router-to-server

Note: Wireless connectivity is discussed in another course.

Refer to **Packet Tracer Activity** for this chapter

Use the Packet Tracer Activity to build the topology that you will use for the rest of this chapter. You will add all the necessary devices and connect them with the correct cabling.

2.2 Router Configuration Review

2.2.1 Examining Router Interfaces

Refer to **Figure** in online course

Examining Router Interfaces

As we learned in Chapter 1, the `show ip route` command is used to display the routing table. Initially, the routing table is empty if no interfaces have been configured.

As you can see in the routing table for R1, no interfaces have been configured with an IP address and subnet mask.

Note: Static routes and dynamic routes will not be added to the routing table until the appropriate local interfaces, also known as the exit interfaces, have been configured on the router. This procedure will be examined more closely in later chapters.

Interfaces and their Status

The status of each interface can be examined by using several commands.

Click show interfaces in the figure.

The **show interfaces** command shows the status and gives a detailed description for all interfaces on the router. As you can see, the output from the command can be rather lengthy. To view the same information, but for a specific interface, such as FastEthernet 0/0, use the **show interfaces** command with a parameter that specifies the interface. For example:

```
R1#show interfaces fastethernet 0/0
FastEthernet0/0 is
administratively down, line protocol is down
```

Notice that the interface is **administratively down** and the **line protocol is down**. Administratively down means that the interface is currently in the shutdown mode, or turned off. Line protocol is down means, in this case, that the interface is not receiving a carrier signal from a switch or the hub. This condition may also be due to the fact that the interface is in shutdown mode.

You will notice that the **show interfaces** command does not show any IP addresses on R1's interfaces. The reason for this is because we have not yet configured IP addresses on any of the interfaces.

Additional Commands for Examining Interface Status

Click show ip interface brief in the figure.

The **show ip interface brief** command can be used to see a portion of the interface information in a condensed format.

Click show running-config in the figure.

The **show running-config** command displays the current configuration file that the router is using. Configuration commands are temporarily stored in the running configuration file and implemented immediately by the router. Using this command is another way to verify the status of an interface such as FastEthernet 0/0.

```
R1#show running-config
<some output omitted>
interface FastEthernet0/0

no ip address

shutdown
<some output omitted>
```

However, using **show running-config** is not necessarily the best way to verify interface configurations. Use the **show ip interface brief** command to quickly verify that interfaces are **up** and **up** (administratively **up** and line protocol is **up**).

2.2.2 Configuring an Ethernet Interface

Refer to
Figure
in online course

Configuring an Ethernet Interface

As shown, R1 does not yet have any routes. Let's add a route by configuring an interface and explore exactly what happens when that interface is activated. By default, all router interfaces are **shutdown**, or turned off. To enable this interface, use the **no shutdown** command, which changes the interface from **administratively down** to **up**.

```
R1(config)#interface fastethernet 0/0
R1(config-if)#ip address 172.16.3.1 255.255.255.0
R1(config-if)#no shutdown
```

The following message is returned from the IOS:

```
*Mar 1 01:16:08.212: %LINK-3-UPDOWN: Interface FastEthernet0/0,
changed state to up
*Mar 1 01:16:09.214: %LINEPROTO-5-UPDOWN: Line protocol on Interface
FastEthernet0/0,
```

```
changed state to up
```
Both of these messages are important. The first **changed state to up** message indicates that, physically, the connection is good. If you do not get this first message, be sure that the interface is properly connected to a switch or a hub.

Note: Although enabled with **no shutdown**, an Ethernet interface will not be active, or **up**, unless it is receiving a carrier signal from another device (switch, hub, PC, or another router).

The second changed state to **up** message indicates that the Data Link layer is operational. On LAN interfaces, we do not normally change the Data Link layer parameters. However, WAN interfaces in a lab environment require clocking on one side of the link as discussed in Lab 1.5.1, "Cabling a Network and Basic Router Configuration," as well as later in the section, "Configuring a Serial Interface." If you do not correctly set the clock rate, then line protocol (the Data Link layer) **will not change to up**.

Unsolicited Messages from IOS

Click Unsolicited Messages from IOS in the figure.

The IOS often sends unsolicited messages similar to the **changed state to up** messages just discussed. As you can see in the figure, sometimes these messages will occur when you are in the middle of typing a command, such as configuring a description for the interface. The IOS message does not affect the command, but it can cause you to lose your place when typing.

Click Logging Synchronous in the figure.

In order to keep the unsolicited output separate from your input, enter line configuration mode for the consoled port and add the **logging synchronous** command, as shown. You will see that messages returned by IOS no longer interfere with your typing.

Refer to
Figure
in online course

Reading the Routing Table

Now look at routing table shown in the figure. Notice R1 now has a "directly connected" FastEthernet 0/0 interface a new network. The interface was configured with the 172.16.3.1/24 IP address which makes it a member of the 172.16.3.0/24 network.

Examine the following line of output from the table:

```
C 172.16.3.0 is directly connected, FastEthernet0/0
```
The **C** at the beginning of the route indicates that this is a directly connected network. In other words, R1 has an interface that belongs to this network. The meaning of **C** is defined in the list of codes at the top of the routing table.

The **/24** subnet mask for this route is displayed in the line above the actual route.

```
172.16.0.0/24 is subnetted, 1 subnets
C 172.16.3.0 is directly connected, FastEthernet0/0
```

Routers Usually Store Network Addresses

With very few exceptions, routing tables have routes for network addresses rather than individual host addresses. The 172.16.3.0/24 route in the routing table means that this route matches all packets with a destination address belonging to this network. Having a single route represent an entire network of host IP addresses makes the routing table smaller, with fewer routes, which results in faster routing table lookups. The routing table could contain all 254 individual host IP addresses for the 172.16.3.0/24 network, but that is an inefficient way of storing addresses.

A phone book is a good analogy for a routing table structure. A phone book is a list of names and phone numbers, sorted in alphabetical order by last name. When looking for a number, we can assume that the fewer names there are in the book, the faster it will be to find a particular name. A phone book of 20 pages and perhaps 2,000 entries will be much easier to search than a book of 200 pages and 20,000 entries.

The phone book only contains one listing for each phone number. For example, the Stanford family might be listed as:

Stanford, Harold, 742 Evergreen Terrace, 555-1234

This is the single entry for everyone who lives at this address and has the same phone number. The phone book could contain a listing for every individual, but this would increase the size of the phone book. For example, there could be a separate listing for Harold Stanford, Margaret Stanford, Brad Stanford, Leslie Stanford, and Maggie Stanford - all with the same address and phone number. If this were done for every family, the phone book would be larger and take longer to search.

Routing tables work the same way: one entry in the table represents a "family" of devices that all share the same network or address space (the difference between a network and an address space will become clearer as you move through the course). The fewer the entries in the routing table, the faster the lookup process. To keep routing tables smaller, network addresses with subnet masks are listed instead of individual host IP addresses.

Note: Occasionally, a "host route" is entered in the routing table, which represents an individual host IP address. It is listed with the device's host IP address and a /32 (255.255.255.255) subnet mask. The topic of host routes is discussed in another course.

2.2.3 Verifying Ethernet interface

Commands to Verify Interface Configuration

Refer to
Figure
in online course

The `show interfaces fastethernet 0/0` command in the figure now shows that the interface is **up**, and the line protocol is **up**. The `no shutdown` command changed the interface from **administratively down** to **up**. Notice that the IP address is now displayed.

Click `show ip interface brief` in the figure.

The `show ip interface brief` command also shows verifies this same information. Under the status and protocol, you should see "up".

The `show running-config` command shows the current configuration of this interface. When the interface is disabled, the `running-config` command displays `shutdown`; however, when the interface is enabled, `no shutdown` is not displayed.

```
R1#show running-config
<output omitted>
interface FastEthernet0/0
ip address 172.16.3.1 255.255.255.0
<output omitted>
```

As explained in Chapter 1, a router cannot have multiple interfaces that belong to the same IP subnet. Each interface must belong to a separate subnet. For example, a router cannot have both its FastEthernet 0/0 interface configured as 172.16.3.1/24 address and mask and its FastEthernet 0/1 interface configured as 172.16.3.2/24.

The IOS will return the following error message if you attempt to configure the second interface with the same IP subnet as the first interface:

```
R1(config-if)#int fa0/1
R1(config-if)#ip address 172.16.3.2 255.255.255.0

172.16.3.0 overlaps with FastEthernet0/0
R1(config-if)#
```

Typically, the router's Ethernet or FastEthernet interface will be the default gateway IP address for any devices on that LAN. For example, PC1 would be configured with a host IP address belonging to the 172.16.3.0/24 network, with the default gateway IP address 172.16.3.1. 172.16.3.1 is router R1's FastEthernet IP address. Remember, a router's Ethernet or FastEthernet interface will also participate in the ARP process as a member of that Ethernet network.

Refer to
Figure
in online course

Ethernet Interfaces Participate in ARP

A router's Ethernet interface participates in a LAN network just like any other device on that network. This means that these interfaces have a Layer 2 MAC address, as shown in the figure. The **show interfaces** command displays the MAC address for the Ethernet interfaces.

`R1#`**`show interfaces fastethernet 0/0`**

As demonstrated in Chapter 1, an Ethernet interface participates in ARP requests and replies and maintains an ARP table. If a router has a packet destined for a device on a directly connected Ethernet network, it checks the ARP table for an entry with that destination IP address in order to map it to the MAC address. If the ARP table does not contain this IP address, the Ethernet interface sends out an ARP request. The device with the destination IP address sends back an ARP reply that lists its MAC address. The IP address and MAC address information is then added to the ARP table for that Ethernet interface. The router is now able to encapsulate the IP packet into an Ethernet frame with the destination MAC address from its ARP table. The Ethernet frame, with the encapsulated packet, is then sent via that Ethernet interface.

Refer to **Packet Tracer Activity** for this chapter

Use the Packet Tracer Activity to practice configuring Ethernet interfaces. Follow the additional instructions provided in the activity to examine the ARP process in simulation mode.

2.2.4 Configuring A Serial Interface

Refer to
Figure
in online course

Configuring a Serial Interface

Next, let's configure the Serial 0/0/0 interface on router R1. This interface is on the 172.16.2.0/24 network and is assigned the IP address and subnet mask of 172.16.2.1/24. The process we use for the configuration of the serial interface 0/0/0 is similar to the process we used to configure the FastEthernet 0/0 interface.

`R1(config)#`**`interface serial 0/0/0`**
`R1(config-if)#`**`ip address 172.16.2.1 255.255.255.0`**
`R1(config-if)#`**`no shutdown`**

After entering the commands above, the state of the serial interface may vary depending upon the type of WAN connection. This will be discussed in more detail in a later course. In this course, we will be using dedicated, serial point-to-point connections between two routers. The serial interface will be in the **up** state only after the other end of the serial link has also been properly configured. We can display the current state of serial 0/0/0 using the **show interfaces serial 0/0/0** command, as shown in the figure.

As you can see, the link is still down. The link is down because we have not yet configured and enabled the other end of the serial link.

`R1#`**`show interfaces serial 0/0/0`**
```
Serial0/0/0 is administratively
down, line protocol is
down
```
We will now configure the other end of this link, Serial 0/0/0 link for router R2.

Note: There is no requirement that both ends of the serial link use the same interface, in this case, Serial 0/0/0. However, because both interfaces are members of the same network, they both must have IP addresses that belong to the 172.16.2.0/24 network. (The terms *network* and *subnet* can be used interchangeably in this case.) R2's interface Serial 0/0/0 is configured with the IP address and subnet mask 172.16.2.2/24.

```
R2(config)#interface serial 0/0/0
R2(config-if)#ip address 172.16.2.2 255.255.255.0
R2(config-if)#no shutdown
```

If we now issue the **show interfaces serial 0/0/0** command on either router, we still see that the link is **up/down**.

```
R2#show interfaces serial 0/0/0
Serial0/0/0 is
up, line protocol is
down
<output omitted>
```

The physical link between R1 and R2 is **up** because both ends of the serial link have been configured correctly with an IP address/mask and enabled with the **no shutdown** command. However, the line protocol is still **down**. This is because the interface is not receiving a clock signal. There is still one more command that we need to enter, the **clock rate** command, on the router with the DCE cable. The **clock rate** command will set the clock signal for the link. Configuring the clock signal will be discussed in the next section.

2.2.5 Examining Router Interfaces

Refer to
Figure
in online course

Physically Connecting a WAN Interface

The WAN Physical layer describes the interface between the data terminal equipment (DTE) and the data circuit-terminating equipment (DCE). Generally, the DCE is the service provider and the DTE is the attached device. In this model, the services offered to the DTE are made available either through a modem or a CSU/DSU.

Typically, the router is the DTE device and is connected to a CSU/DSU, which is the DCE device. The CSU/DSU (DCE device) is used to convert the data from the router (DTE device) into a form acceptable to the WAN service provider. The CSU/DSU (DCE device) is also responsible for converting the data from the WAN service provider into a form acceptable by the router (DTE device). The router is usually connected to the CSU/DSU using a serial DTE cable, as shown.

Serial interfaces require a clock signal to control the timing of the communications. In most environments, the service provider (a DCE device such as a CSU/DSU) will provide the clock. By default, Cisco routers are DTE devices. However, in a lab environment, we are not using any CSU/DSUs and, of course, we do not have a WAN service provider.

Roll over the cables and devices in the figure to see what they are.

Refer to
Figure
in online course

Configuring Serial Links in a Lab Environment

For serial links that are directly interconnected, as in a lab environment, one side of a connection must be considered a DCE and provide a clocking signal. Although Cisco serial interfaces are DTE devices by default, they can be configured as DCE devices.

To configure a router to be the DCE device:

1. Connect the DCE end of the cable to the serial interface.

2. Configure the clock signal on the serial interface using the **clock rate** command.

The serial cables used in the lab are typically one of two types.

- A DTE/DCE crossover cable on which one end is DTE and the other end is DCE

■ A DTE cable connected to a DCE cable

In our lab topology, the Serial 0/0/0 interface on R1 is connected with the DCE end of the cable, and the serial 0/0/0 interface on R2 is connected to the DTE end of the cable. The cable should be labeled either DTE or DCE.

You can also distinguish DTE from DCE by looking at the connector between the two cables. The DTE cable has a male connector, whereas the DCE cable has a female connector.

If a cable is connected between the two routers, you can use the **show controllers** command to determine which end of the cable is attached to that interface. In the command output, notice that R1 has the DCE cable attached to its serial 0/0 interface and that no clock rate is set.

```
R1#show controllers serial 0/0/0
Interface Serial0/0/0
Hardware is PowerQUICC
MPC860

DCE V.35, no clock
<output omitted>
```

Once the cable is attached, the clock can now be set with the **clock rate** command. The available clock rates, in bits per second, are 1200, 2400, 9600, 19200, 38400, 56000, 64000, 72000, 125000, 148000, 500000, 800000, 1000000, 1300000, 2000000, and 4000000. Some bit rates might not be available on certain serial interfaces. Because Serial 0/0/0 interface on R1 has the DCE cable attached, we will configure that interface with a clock rate.

```
R1(config)#interface serial 0/0/0
R1(config-if)#clock rate 64000
01:10:28: %LINEPROTO-5-UPDOWN: Line protocol on Interface Serial0/0/0, changed
state to up
```

Note: If a router's interface with a DTE cable is configured with the clock rate command, the IOS will disregard the command and there will be no ill effects.

Refer to
Figure
in online course

Verifying the Serial Interface Configuration

As you can see from the figure, we can determine that the line protocol is now up and verify this on both ends of the serial link by using the **show interfaces** and **show ip interface brief** commands. Remember, the serial interface will be up only if both ends of the link are configured correctly. In our lab environment, we have configured the clock rate on the end with the DCE cable.

We can further verify that the link is up/up by pinging the remote interface.

```
R1#ping 172.16.2.2
```

Finally, we can see the 172.16.2.0/24 serial network in the routing tables of both routers. If we issue the **show ip route** command on R1, we will see the directly connected route for the 172.16.2.0/24 network.

```
R1#show ip route
```

Now take a look at router R1's running configuration by using the **show running-config** command.

```
R1#show running-config
```

Note: Although the **clock rate** command is two words, the IOS spells **clockrate** as a single word in the running configuration and startup configuration files.

2.3 Exploring Directly Connected Networks

2.3.1 Verifying Changes to the Routing Table

Refer to
Figure
in online course

Routing Table Concepts

As you can see in the figure, the **show ip route** command reveals the content of the routing table. Let's review the purpose of a routing table. A routing table is a data structure used to store routing information acquired from different sources. The main purpose of a routing table is to provide the router with paths to different destination networks.

The routing table consists of a list of "known" network addresses - that is, those addresses that are directly connected, configured statically, and learned dynamically. R1 and R2 only have routes for directly connected networks.

Refer to
Figure
in online course

Observing Routes as They are Added to the Routing Table

We will now take a closer look at how directly connected routes are added to, and deleted from, the routing table. In contrast to **show** commands, **debug** commands can be used to monitor router operations in real time. The **debug ip routing** command will let us see any changes that the router performs when adding or removing routes. We will configure the interfaces on the R2 router and examine this process.

First, we will enable debugging with the **debug ip routing** command so that we can see the directly connected networks as they are added to the routing table.

```
R2#debug ip routing
IP routing debugging is on
```

Configuring the IP address and Subnet Mask

Next, we will configure the IP address and subnet mask for the FastEthernet 0/0 interface on R2 and use the **no shutdown** command. Because the FastEthernet interface connects to the 172.16.1.0/24 network, it must be configured with a host IP address for that network.

```
R2(config)#interface fastethernet 0/0
R2(config-if)#ip address 172.16.1.1 255.255.255.0
R2(config-if)#no shutdown
```

The following message will be returned from the IOS:

```
02:35:30: %LINK-3-UPDOWN: Interface FastEthernet0/0, changed state to
up
02:35:31: %LINEPROTO-5-UPDOWN: Line protocol on Interface FastEthernet0/0, changed
state to
up
```

After the **no shutdown** command is entered and the router determines that the interface and line protocol are in the **up** and **up** state, the debug output shows R2 adding this directly connected network to the routing table.

```
02:35:30: RT: add 172.16.1.0/24 via 0.0.0.0, connected metric [0/0]
02:35:30: RT:
interface FastEthernet0/0 added to routing table
```

Click Routing Table 1 in the figure.

The routing table now shows the route for the directly connected network 172.16.1.0/24, as seen in the figure.

The **debug ip routing** command displays routing table processes for any route, whether that route is a directly connected network, a static route, or a dynamic route.

Click Disable Debug in the figure.

Disable **debug ip routing** by using either the **undebug ip routing** command or the **undebug all** command.

Changing an IP Address

To change an IP address or subnet mask for an interface, reconfigure the IP address and subnet mask for that interface. This change will overwrite the previous entry. There are ways to configure a single interface with multiple IP addresses, as long as each address is on a different subnet. This topic will be discussed in a later course.

To remove a directly connected network from a router, use these two commands: **shutdown** and **no ip address**.

The **shutdown** command is used to disable interfaces. This command can be used by itself if you want to retain the IP address/mask configuration on the interface but want to shut it down temporarily. In our example, this command will disable R2's FastEtherent interface. The IP address, however, will still be in the configuration file, **running-config**.

After the **shutdown** command is used, you can remove the IP address and subnet mask from the interface. The order in which you perform these two commands does not matter.

Click Debug 2 in the figure.

Using **debug ip routing** we can see the routing table process, we will delete the configuration for R2's FastEthernet 0/0 interface.

```
R2(config)#interface fastethernet 0/0
R2(config-if)#shutdown
```

We can see the routing table process removing the directly connected route.

```
02:53:58: RT:
interface FastEthernet0/0 removed from routing table
02:53:58: RT: del 172.16.1.0/24 via 0.0.0.0, connected metric [0/0]
02:53:58: RT:
delete subnet route to 172.16.1.0/24
```

The IOS also indicates that the interface and line protocol are now **down**:

```
02:54:00: %LINK-5-CHANGED: Interface FastEthernet0/0, changed state to adminis-
tratively
down
02:54:01: %LINEPROTO-5-UPDOWN: Line protocol on Interface FastEthernet0/0, changed
state to
down
```

We will now remove the IP address on the interface.

```
R2(config-if)#no ip address
```

Disable debugging:

```
R2#undebug all
All possible debugging has been turned off
```

Click Routing Table 2 in the figure.

To verify that the route was removed from the routing table, we use the command **show ip route**. Notice that the route to 172.16.1.0/24 has been removed.

Reconfiguring the interface to continue with the chapter.

For the purposes of the rest of this chapter, we will assume that the addressing for FastEthernet 0/0 was not removed. To reconfigure the interface, simply enter the commands again:

```
R2(config)#interface fastethernet 0/0
R2(config-if)#ip address 172.16.1.1 255.255.255.0
R2(config-if)#no shutdown
```

WARNING: Debug commands, especially the **debug all** command, should be used sparingly. These commands can disrupt router operations. Debug commands are useful when configuring or troubleshooting a network; however, they can make intensive use of CPU and memory resources.

It is recommended that you run as few debug processes as necessary and disable them immediately when they are no longer needed. Debug commands should be used with caution on production networks because they can affect the performance of the device.

Refer to **Packet Tracer Activity** for this chapter

Use the Packet Tracer Activity to practice configuring Serial interfaces. You will also use **debug ip routing** to observe the routing table processes.

2.3.2 Devices on Directly Connected Networks

Refer to **Figure** in online course

Accessing Devices on Directly Connected Networks

To return to our configuration in the sample topology, we will now assume that all directly connected networks are configured for all three routers. The figure shows the rest of the configurations for routers R2 and R3.

Click show ip interface brief in the figure.

The output in this figure verifies that all configured interfaces are "**up**" and "**up**".

Click show ip route in the figure.

By reviewing the routing tables in the figure, we can verify that all directly connected networks are installed for routing.

The crucial step in configuring your network is to verify that all the interfaces are "up" and "up" and that the routing tables are complete. Regardless of what routing scheme you ultimately configure - static, dynamic, or a combination of both - verify your initial network configurations with the **show ip interface brief** command and the **show ip route** command before proceeding with more complex configurations.

When a router only has its interfaces configured, and the routing table contains the directly connected networks but no other routes, only devices on those directly connected networks are reachable.

- R1 can communicate with any device on the 172.16.3.0/24 and 172.16.2.0/24 networks.

- R2 can communicate with any device on the 172.16.1.0/24, 172.16.2.0/24, and 192.168.1.0/24 networks.

- R3 can communicate with any device on the 192.168.1.0/24 and 192.168.2.0/24 networks.

Because these routers only know about their directly connected networks, the routers can only communicate with those devices on their own directly connected LANs and serial networks.

For example, PC1 in the topology has been configured with the IP address 172.16.3.10 and the subnet mask 255.255.255.0. PC1 has also been configured with the default gateway IP address 172.16.3.1, which is the router's FastEtherent 0/0 interface IP address. Because R1 only knows about directly connected networks, it can forward packets from PC1 to devices on the 172.16.2.0/24 network, such as 172.16.2.1 and 172.16.2.2. Packets from PC1 with any other destination IP address, such as PC2 at 172.16.1.10, would be dropped by R1.

Let's take a look at the routing table for R2 in the figure. R2 only knows about its three directly connected networks. Try to predict what will happen if we ping one of the FastEthernet interfaces on one of the other routers.

Click ping in the figure.

Notice that the pings failed, as indicated by the series of five periods. It failed because R2 does not have a route in its routing table that matches either 172.16.3.1 or 192.168.2.1, which is the ping packet's destination IP address. To have a match between the packet's destination IP address of 172.16.3.1 and a route in the routing table, the address must match the number of left-most bits of the network address as indicated by the prefix of the route. For R2, all the routes have a /24 prefix, therefore, the left-most 24 bits are checked for each route.

Checking Each Route in Turn

The first route in the table for R1 is 172.16.1.0/24.

```
172.16.0.0/24 is subnetted, 2 subnets
C 172.16.1.0 is directly connected, FastEthernet0/0
```

The IOS routing table process checks to see if the 24 left-most bits of the packet's destination IP address, 172.16.3.1, match the 172.16.1.0/24 network.

Play the first animation in the figure.

If you convert these addresses to binary and compare them, as shown in the animation, you will see that the first 24 bits of this route do not match because the 23rd bit does not match. Therefore, this route is rejected.

```
 172.16.0.0/
24 is subnetted, 2 subnets
C 172.16.2.0 is directly connected, Serial0/0/0
```

In the animation, we see that the first 24 bits of the second route do not match because the 24th bit does not match. Therefore, this route is also rejected, and the process moves on to the next route in the routing table.

```
C 192.168.1.0/
24 is directly connected, Serial0/0/1
```

The third route is also not a match. As shown, 10 of the first 24 bits do not match. Therefore, this route is rejected. Because there are no more routes in the routing table, the pings are discarded. The router makes its forwarding decision at Layer 3, a "best effort" to forward the packet, but it makes no guarantees.

Click Pings are sent to R3 on the figure and play the animation.

Let's look at the second animation to see what happens if the router R2 pings the 192.168.1.1 interface on router R3.

This time the ping succeeds! It is successful because R2 has a route in its routing table that matches 192.168.1.1, which is the ping packet's destination IP address. The first two routes, 172.16.1.0/24 and 172.16.2.0/24, are rejected. But the last route, 192.168.1.0/24, matches the first 24 bits of the destination IP address. The ping packet is encapsulated in the Layer 2 HDLC protocol of Serial0/0/1, the exit interface, and forwarded via the Serial0/0/1 interface. R2 is now done making the forwarding decisions for this packet; the decisions made by other routers regarding this packet are not its concern.

Note: The routing table lookup process will be discussed in further detail in Chapter 8, "The Routing Table: A Closer Look."

Use the Packet Tracer Activity to test connectivity between directly connected devices.

2.3.3 Cisco Discovery Protocol (CDP)

Network discovery with CDP

Cisco Discovery Protocol (CDP) is a powerful network monitoring and troubleshooting tool. CDP is an information-gathering tool used by network administrators to get information about directly connected Cisco devices. CDP is a proprietary tool that enables you to access a summary of protocol and address information about Cisco devices that are directly connected. By default, each Cisco device sends periodic messages, which are known as CDP advertisements, to directly connected Cisco devices. These advertisements contain information such as the types of devices that are connected, the router interfaces they are connected to, the interfaces used to make the connections, and the model numbers of the devices.

Most network devices, by definition, do not work in isolation. A Cisco device frequently has other Cisco devices as neighbors on the network. Information gathered from other devices can assist you in making network design decisions, troubleshooting, and making changes to equipment. CDP can be used as a network discovery tool, helping you to build a logical topology of a network when such documentation is missing or lacking in detail.

Familiarity with the general concept of *neighbors* is important for understanding CDP as well as for future discussions about dynamic routing protocols.

Layer 3 Neighbors

At this point in our topology configuration, we only have directly connected neighbors. At Layer 3, routing protocols consider *neighbors* to be devices that share the same network address space.

For example, R1 and R2 are neighbors. Both are members of the 172.16.2.0/24 network. R2 and R3 are also neighbors because they both share the 192.168.1.0/24 network. But R1 and R3 are *not* neighbors because they do not share any network address space. If we connected R1 and R3 with a cable and configured each with an IP address from the same network, then they would be neighbors.

Layer 2 Neighbors

CDP operates at Layer 2 only. Therefore, CDP neighbors are Cisco devices that are directly connected physically and share the same data link. In the CDP Protocol figure, the network administrator is logged in to S3. S3 will receive CDP advertisements from S1, S2, and R2 only.

Assuming that all routers and switches in the figure are Cisco devices running CDP, what neighbors would R1 have? Can you determine the CDP neighbors for each device?

Click the Topology button in the figure.

In our chapter topology, we can see the following CDP neighbor relationships:

- R1 and S1 are CDP neighbors.
- R1 and R2 are CDP neighbors.
- R2 and S2 are CDP neighbors.
- R2 and R3 are CDP neighbors.
- R3 and S3 are CDP neighbors.

Notice the difference between Layer 2 and Layer 3 neighbors. The switches are not neighbors to the routers at Layer 3, because the switches are operating at Layer 2 only. However, the switches are Layer 2 neighbors to their directly connected routers.

Let's see how CDP can be helpful to a network administrator.

Refer to
Figure
in online course

CDP Operation

Examine the output from the **show cdp neighbors** and **show cdp neighbors detail** commands in the figure. Notice that R3 has gathered some detailed information about R2 and the switch connected to the Fast Ethernet interface on R3.

CDP runs at the Data Link layer connecting the physical media to the upper-layer protocols (ULPs). Because CDP operates at the Data Link layer, two or more Cisco network devices, such as routers that support different Network layer protocols (for example, IP and Novell *IPX*), can learn about each other.

When a Cisco device boots up, CDP starts up by default. CDP automatically discovers neighboring Cisco devices running CDP, regardless of which protocol or suites are running. CDP exchanges hardware and software device information with its directly connected CDP neighbors.

CDP provides the following information about each CDP neighbor device:

- *Device identifiers -* For example, the configured host name of a switch

- *Address list -* Up to one Network layer address for each protocol supported

- *Port identifier -* The name of the local and remote port-in the form of an ASCII character string such as ethernet0

- *Capabilities list -* For example, whether this device is a router or a switch

- *Platform -* The hardware platform of the device; for example, a Cisco 7200 series router

Refer to **Packet Tracer Activity** for this chapter

Use the Packet Tracer Activity to explore the features of the Cisco Discovery Protocol (CDP). Practice enabling and disabling CDP - globally and on a per-interface basis. Investigate the power of using CDP to discover the topology of a network.

2.3.4 Using CDP for Network Discovery

Refer to **Figure** in online course

CDP show commands

The information gathered by the CDP protocol can be examined with the **show cdp neighbors** command. For each CDP neighbor, the following information is displayed:

- Neighbor device ID

- Local interface

- Holdtime value, in seconds

- Neighbor device capability code

- Neighbor hardware platform

- Neighbor remote port ID

Click show cdp neighbors detail in the figure.

The **show cdp neighbors detail** command also reveals the IP address of a neighboring device. CDP will reveal the neighbor's IP address regardless of whether or not you can ping the neighbor. This command is very helpful when two Cisco routers cannot route across their shared data link. The **show cdp neighbors detail** command will help determine if one of the CDP neighbors has an IP configuration error.

For network discovery situations, knowing the IP address of the CDP neighbor is often all the information needed to telnet into that device. With an established Telnet session, information can be gathered about a neighbor's directly connected Cisco devices. In this fashion, you can telnet around a network and build a logical topology. In the next Packet Tracer Activity, you will do just that.

Disabling CDP

Could CDP be a security risk? Yes, it could be. You may already have seen CDP packets in your packet capturing labs from a previous course. Because some IOS versions send out CDP advertisements by default, it is important to know how to disable CDP.

Click Disabling CDP in the figure.

If you need to disable CDP globally, for the entire device, use this command:

Router(config)#**no cdp run**

If you want to use CDP but need to stop CDP advertisements on a particular interface, use this command:

Router(config-if)#**no cdp enable**

Refer to **Packet Tracer Activity** for this chapter

CDP **show** commands can be used to discover information about unknown devices in a network. CDP **show** commands display information about directly connected Cisco devices, including an IP address that can be used to reach the device. You can then telnet to the device and repeat the process until the entire network is mapped.

Use the Packet Tracer Activity to discover and map an unknown network using CDP and Telnet.

2.4 Static Routes with "Next Hop" Addresses

2.4.1 Purpose and Command Syntax of ip route

Refer to **Figure** in online course

Purpose and Command Syntax of ip route

As we have discussed previously, a router can learn about remote networks in one of two ways:

- Manually, from configured static routes

- Automatically, from a dynamic routing protocol

The rest of this chapter focuses on configuring static routes. Dynamic routing protocols are introduced in the next chapter.

Static routes

Static routes are commonly used when routing from a network to a stub network. **A stub network is a network accessed by a single route.** For an example, see the figure. Here we see that any network attached to R1 would only have one way to reach other destinations, whether to networks attached to R2 or to destinations beyond R2. Therefore, network 172.16.3.0 is a stub network and R1 is a stub router.

Running a routing protocol between R1 and R2 is a waste of resources because R1 has only one way out for sending non-local traffic. Therefore, static routes are configured for connectivity to remote networks that are not directly connected to a router. Again, referring to the figure, we would configure a static route on R2 to the LAN attached to R1. We will also see how to configure a default static route from R1 to R2 later in the chapter so that R1 can send traffic to any destination beyond R2.

Refer to **Figure** in online course

The ip route command

The command for configuring a static route is **ip route**. The complete syntax for configuring a static route is:

Router(config)#**ip route prefix mask** {*ip-address* ¦ *interface-type interface-number* [*ip-address*]} [*distance*] [*name*] [**permanent**] [**tag** tag]

Most of these parameters are not relevant for this chapter or for your CCNA studies. As shown in the figure, we will use a simpler version of the syntax:

Router(config)#**ip route** *network-address subnet-mask* {*ip-address* ¦ *exit-interface* }

The following parameters are used:

- **network-address -** Destination network address of the remote network to be added to the routing table

- **subnet-mask** - Subnet mask of the remote network to be added to the routing table. The subnet mask can be modified to summarize a group of networks.

One or both of the following parameters must also be used:

- **ip-address** - Commonly referred to as the next-hop router's IP address
- **exit-interface** - Outgoing interface that would be used in forwarding packets to the destination network

Note: The *ip-address* parameter is commonly referred to as the "next-hop" router's IP address. The actual next-hop router's IP address is commonly used for this parameter. However, the *ip-address* parameter could be any IP address, as long as it is resolvable in the routing table. This is beyond the scope of this course, but we've added this point to maintain technical accuracy.

2.4.2 Configuring Static Routes

Refer to **Figure** in online course

Installing a Static Route in the Routing Table

Remember R1 knows about its directly connected networks. These are the routes currently in its routing table. The remote networks that R1 does **not** know about are:

- 172.16.1.0/124 - The LAN on R2
- 192.168.1.0/24 - The serial network between R2 and R3
- 192.168.2.0/24 - The LAN on R3

Click Static Route in the figure.

First, enable **debug ip routing** to have the IOS display a message when the new route is added to the routing table. Then, use the **ip route** command to configure static routes on R1 for each of these networks. The figure shows the first route configured.

```
R1#debug ip routing
R1#conf t
R1(config)#ip route 172.16.1.0 255.255.255.0 172.16.2.2
```

Let's examine each element in this output:

- **ip route** - Static route command
- **172.16.1.0** - Network address of remote network
- **255.255.255.0** - Subnet mask of remote network
- **172.16.2.2** - Serial 0/0/0 interface IP address on R2, which is the "next-hop" to this network

When the IP address is the actual next-hop router's IP address, this IP address is reachable from one of this router's directly connected networks. In other words, the next-hop IP address **172.16.2.2** is on router R1's directly connected Serial 0/0/0 network **172.16.2.0/24**.

Verifying the Static Route

The output from **debug ip routing** shows that this route has been added to the routing table.

```
00:20:15: RT:
add 172.16.1.0/24 via 172.16.2.2, static metric [1/0]
```

Notice in the figure that entering **show ip route** on R1 shows the new routing table. The static route entry is highlighted.

Let's examine this output:

- **S** - Routing table code for static route

- **172.16.1.0** - Network address for the route

- **/24** - Subnet mask for this route; this is displayed in the line above, known as the parent route, and discussed in Chapter 8

- **[1/0]** - Administrative distance and metric for the static route (explained in a later chapter)

- **via 172.16.2.2** - IP address of the next-hop router, the IP address of R2's Serial 0/0/0 interface

Any packets with a destination IP address that have the 24 left-most bits matching **172.16.1.0** will use this route.

> Refer to
> **Figure**
> in online course

Configuring Routes to Two More Remote Networks

The commands to configure the routes for the other two remote networks are shown in the figure. Notice that all three static routes configured on R1 have the same next-hop IP address: 172.16.2.2. Using the topology diagram as a reference, we can see that this is true because packets for all of the remote networks must be forwarded to router R2, the next-hop router.

Use the **show ip route** command again to examine the new static routes in the routing table, as shown.

```
S 192.168.1.0/
24 [1/0] via 172.16.2.2
S 192.168.2.0/
24 [1/0] via 172.16.2.2
```

The /24 subnet masks are located on the same line as the network address. For now, this difference is not important. It will be explained in detail in Chapter 8, "The Routing Table: A Closer Look."

Click Verify Static Route Configuration in the figure.

The static routes that have been configured can also be verified by examining the running configuration with the **show running-config** command.

Now is a good time to save the configuration to NVRAM:

```
R1#copy running-config startup-config
```

2.4.3 Routing Table Principles and Static Routes

> Refer to
> **Figure**
> in online course

Routing Table Principles

Now that three static routes are configured, can you predict whether packets destined for these networks will reach their destination? Will packets from all these networks destined for network 172.16.3.0/24 reach their destination?

Let's introduce three routing table principles, as described by Alex Zinin in his book, *Cisco IP Routing*.

Principle 1: "Every router makes its decision alone, based on the information it has in its own routing table."

R1 has three static routes in its routing table and makes forwarding decisions based solely upon the information in the routing table. R1 does not consult the routing tables in any other routers. Nor does it know whether or not those routers have routes to other networks. Making each router aware of remote networks is the responsibility of the network administrator.

Principle 2: "The fact that one router has certain information in its routing table does not mean that other routers have the same information."

R1 does not know what information other routers have in their routing table. For example, R1 has a route to the 192.168.2.0/24 network through router R2. Any packets that match this route belong to the 192.168.2.0/24 network and will be forwarded to router R2. R1 does not know whether or not R2 has a route to the 192.168.2.0/24 network. Again, the network administrator would be responsible for ensuring that the next-hop router also has a route to this network.

Using Principle 2, we still need to configure the proper routing on the other routers (R2 and R3) to make sure that they have routes to these three networks.

Principle 3: "Routing information about a path from one network to another does not provide routing information about the reverse, or return path."

Most of the communication over networks is bidirectional. This means that packets must travel in both directions between the end devices involved. A packet from PC1 may reach PC3 because all the routers involved have routes to the destination network 192.168.2.0/24. However, the success of any returning packets going from PC3 to PC1 depends upon whether or not the routers involved have a route to the return path, PC1's 172.16.3.0/24 network.

Using Principle 3 as guidance, we will configure proper static routes on the other routers to make sure they have routes back to the 172.16.3.0/24 network.

Refer to
Figure
in online course

Applying the Principles

With these principles in mind, how would you answer the questions we posed regarding packets that originate from PC1?

1. Would packets from PC1 reach their destination?

In this case, packets destined for 172.16.1.0/24 and 192.168.1.0/24 networks would reach their destination. This is because router R1 has a route to these networks through R2. When packets reach router R2, these networks are directly connected on R2 and are routed using its routing table.

Packets destined for 192.168.2.0/24 network would not reach their destination. R1 has a static route to this network through R2. However, when R2 receives a packet, it will drop it because R2 does not yet contain a route for this network in its routing table.

2. Does this mean that any packets from these networks destined for 172.16.3.0/24 network will reach their destination?

If R2 or R3 receives a packet destined for 172.16.3.0/24, the packet will not reach its destination, because neither router has a route to the 172.16.3.0/24 network.

Click R2 and R3 Static Routes in the figure.

With the commands shown in the figure, all routers now have routes to all remote networks.

Click show ip route in the figure.

Examine the routing tables in the figure to verify that all routers now have routes to all remote networks.

Click ping in the figure.

Connectivity can be further verified by pinging remote router interfaces from router R1, as shown in the figure.

Full connectivity is now achieved for the devices in our topology. Any PC, on any LAN, can now access PCs on all other LANs.

2.4.4 Resolving to an Exit Interface

Refer to
Figure
in online course

Recursive Route Lookup

Before any packet is forwarded by a router, the routing table process must determine the exit interface to use to forward the packet. This is known as route resolvability. Let's examine this process by looking at the routing table for R1 in the figure. R1 has a static route for the remote network 192.168.2.0/24, which forwards all packets to the next-hop IP address 172.16.2.2.

```
S 192.168.2.0/24 [1/0] via 172.16.2.2
```

Finding a route is only the first step in the lookup process. R1 must determine how to reach the next-hop IP address 172.16.2.2. It will do a second search looking for a match for 172.16.2.2. In this case, the IP address 172.16.2.2 matches the route for the directly connected network 17216.2.0/24.

```
C 172.16.2.0 is directly connected, Serial0/0/0
```

The 172.16.2.0 route is a directly connected network with the exit interface Serial 0/0/0. This lookup tells the routing table process that this packet will be forwarded out that interface. Therefore, it actually takes two routing table lookup processes to forward any packet to the 192.168.2.0/24 network. When the router has to perform multiple lookups in the routing table before forwarding a packet, it is performing a process known as a *recursive lookup*. In this example:

1. The packet's destination IP address is matched to the static route 192.168.2.0/24 with the next-hop IP address 172.16.2.2.

2. The next-hop IP address of the static route, 172.16.2.2, is matched to the directly connected network 172.16.2.0/24 with the exit interface of Serial 0/0/0.

Every route that references only a next-hop IP address, and does not reference an exit-interface, must have the next-hop IP address resolved using another route in the routing table that has an exit interface.

Typically, these routes are resolved to routes in the routing table that are directly connected networks, because these entries will always contain an exit interface. We will see in the next section that static routes can be configured with an exit interface. This means that they do not need to be resolve using another route entry.

Refer to
Figure
in online course

Exit Interface is Down

Let's consider what would happen if an exit interface goes down. For example, what would happen to R1's static route to 192.16.2.0/24 if its Serial 0/0/0 interface went down? If the static route cannot be resolved to an exit interface, in this case Serial 0/0/0, the static route is removed from the routing table.

Examine this process with **debug ip routing** on R1 and then configure the Serial 0/0/0 to **shutdown**, as shown.

Notice from the debug output that all three static routes were deleted when the Serial 0/0/0 interface was shut down. They were deleted because all three static routes were resolved to Serial 0/0/0. However, the static routes are still in the R1's running configuration. If the interface comes back up (is enabled again with **no shutdown**), the IOS routing table process will reinstall these static routes back into the routing table.

2.5 Static Routes with Exit Interfaces

Refer to
Figure
in online course

2.5.1 Configuring a Static Route with an Exit Interface

Configuring a Static Route with an Exit Interface

Let's investigate another way to configure the same static routes. Currently, R1's static route for the 192.168.2.0/24 network is configured with the next-hop IP address of 172.16.2.2. In the running configuration, note the following line:

```
ip route 192.168.2.0 255.255.255.0 172.16.2.2
```

Refer to
Figure
in online course

As you will recall from the previous section, this static route requires a second routing table lookup to resolve the 172.16.2.2 next-hop IP address to an exit interface. However, most static routes can be configured with an exit interface, which allows the routing table to resolve the exit interface in a single search instead of two searches.

Static Route and an Exit Interface

Let's reconfigure this static route to use an exit interface instead of a next-hop IP address. The first thing to do is to delete the current static route. This is done using the **no ip route** command as shown in the figure.

Next, configure R1's static route to **192.168.2.0/24** using the exit interface Serial 0/0/0

Then use the **show ip route** command to examine the change in the routing table. Notice that the entry in the routing table no longer refers to the next-hop IP address but refers directly to the exit interface. This exit interface is the same one that the static route was resolved to when it used the next-hop IP address.

```
S 192.168.2.0/24
is directly connected, Serial0/0/0
```

Now, when the routing table process has a match for a packet and this static route, it will be able to resolve the route to an exit interface in a single lookup. As you can see in the figure, the other two static routes still must be processed in two steps, resolving to the same Serial 0/0/0 interface.

Note: The static route displays the route as **directly connected**. It is important to understand that this does not mean that this route is a directly connected network or directly connected route. This route is still a static route. We will examine the importance of this fact when we discuss Administrative Distances in the next chapter. We will learn that this type of static route still has an Administrative Distance of "1". For now, just note that this route is still a static route with an administrative distance of "1" and is not a directly connected network.

Static routes and point-to-point networks

Static routes that are configured with exit interfaces instead of next-hop IP addresses are ideal for most serial point-to-point networks. Point-to-point networks that use protocols such as HDLC and PPP do not use the next-hop IP address in the packet forwarding process. The routed IP packet is encapsulated in an HDLC Layer 2 frame with a broadcast Layer 2 destination address.

These types of point-to-point serial links are like pipes. A pipe has only two ends. What enters one end can only have a single destination - the other end of the pipe. Any packets that are sent via R1's Serial 0/0/0 interface can only have one destination: R2's Serial 0/0/0 interface. R2's serial interface happens to be the IP address 172.16.2.2.

Note: Under certain conditions, the network administrator will not want to configure the static route with an exit interface but with the next-hop IP address. This type of situation is beyond the scope of this course but is important to note.

2.5.2 Modifying Static Routes

Refer to
Figure
in online course

Modifying Static Routes

There are times when a previously configured static route needs to be modified:

- The destination network no longer exists, and therefore the static route should be deleted.

- There is a change in the topology, and either the intermediate address or the exit interface has to be changed.

There is no way to modify an existing static route. The static route must be deleted and a new one configured.

To delete a static route, add **no** in front of the **ip route** command, followed by the rest of the static route to be removed.

In the previous section, we had a static route:

`ip route 192.168.2.0 255.255.255.0 172.16.2.2`

We can delete that static route with the **no ip route** command:

`no ip route 192.168.2.0 255.255.255.0 172.16.2.2`

As you will recall, we deleted the static route because we wanted to modify it to use an exit interface instead of a next-hop IP address. We configured a new static route using the exit interface:

`R1(config)#ip route 192.168.2.0 255.255.255.0`
`serial 0/0/0`

It is more efficient for the routing table lookup process to have static routes with exit interfaces - at least for serial point-to-point outbound networks. Let's reconfigure the rest of the static routes on R1, R2, and R3 to use exit interfaces.

As you can see in the figure, as we delete each route, we will configure a new route to the same network using an exit interface.

2.5.3 Verifying the Static Route Configuration

Refer to
Figure
in online course

Verifying the Static Route Configuration

Whenever changes are made to static routes - or to other aspects of the network - verify that the changes took effect and that they produce the desired results.

Verifying Static Route Changes

In the previous section, we deleted and reconfigured the static routes for all three routers. Remember, the running configuration contains the current router configuration - the commands and parameters that the router is currently using. Verify your changes by examining the running configuration. The figure shows the portions of each router's running configuration that show the current static route.

Click show ip route in the figure.

This figure shows the routing table for all three routers. Notice that static routes with exit interfaces have been added to the routing table and that the previous static routes with next-hop addresses have been deleted.

Click ping in the figure.

The ultimate test is to route packets from source to destination. Using the **ping** command, we can test that packets from each router are reaching their destination and that the return path is also working properly. This figure shows successful ping outputs.

Refer to **Packet Tracer Activity** for this chapter

Use the Packet Tracer Activity to practice removing static routes and reconfiguring static routes using the exit interface argument. Then verify the new configuration and test connectivity.

2.5.4 Static Routes with Ethernet Interfaces

Refer to **Figure** in online course

Ethernet Interfaces and ARP

Sometimes the exit interface is an Ethernet network.

Suppose that the network link between R1 and R2 is an Ethernet link and that the FastEthernet 0/1 interface of R1 is connected to that network, as shown in the figure. A static route, using a next-hop IP address for the 192.168.2.0/24 network, can be set using this command:

```
R1(config)#ip route 192.168.2.0 255.255.255.0 172.16.2.2
```

As discussed in the previous section "Configuring an Ethernet interface", the IP packet must be encapsulated into an Ethernet frame with an Ethernet destination MAC address. If the packet should be sent to a next-hop router, the destination MAC address will be the address of the next-hop router's Ethernet interface. In this case, the Ethernet destination MAC address will be matched to the next-hop IP address 172.16.2.2. R1 checks its FastEthernet 0/1 ARP table for an entry with 172.16.2.2 and a corresponding MAC address.

Sending an ARP Request

If this entry is not in the ARP table, R1 sends an ARP request via its FastEthernet 0/1 interface. The Layer 2 broadcast is requesting that if any device has the IP address 172.16.2.2, it should respond with its MAC address. Because R2's FastEthernet 0/1 interface has the IP address 172.16.2.2, it sends back an ARP reply with the MAC address for that interface.

R1 receives the ARP reply and adds the 172.16.2.2 IP address, and the associated MAC address, to its ARP table. The IP packet is now encapsulated into an Ethernet frame with the destination MAC address found in the ARP table. The Ethernet frame with the encapsulated packet is then sent out the FastEthernet 0/1 interface to router R2.

Refer to **Figure** in online course

Static routes and Ethernet exit interfaces

Let's configure a static route with an Ethernet exit interface instead of a next-hop IP address. Change the static route for 192.168.2.0/24 to use an exit interface with this command:

```
R1(config)#ip route 192.168.2.0 255.255.255.0 fastethernet 0/1
```

The difference between an Ethernet network and a point-to-point serial network is that a point-to-point network has only one other device on that network - the router at the other end of the link. With Ethernet networks, there may be many different devices sharing the same multi-access network, including hosts and even multiple routers. By only designating the Ethernet exit interface in the static route, the router will not have sufficient information to determine which device is the next-hop device.

R1 knows that the packet needs to be encapsulated in an Ethernet frame and sent out the FastEthernet 0/1 interface. However, R1 does not know the next-hop IP address and therefore it cannot determine the destination MAC address for the Ethernet frame.

Depending upon the topology and the configurations on other routers, this static route may or may not work. We will not go into the details here, but it is recommended that when the exit interface is an Ethernet network, you do not use only the exit interface in the static route.

One might ask: Is there any way to configure a static route over an Ethernet network so that it does not have to use the recursive lookup of the next-hop IP address? Yes - this can be done by configuring the static route to include both the exit interface and the next-hop IP address.

As you can see in the figure, the exit interface would be FastEthernet 0/1 and the next-hop IP address would be 172.16.2.2.

`R1(config)#ip route 192.168.2.0 255.255.255.0 fastethernet 0/1 172.16.2.2`

The routing table entry for this route would be:

`S 192.168.2.0/24 [1/0] via 172.16.2.2 FastEthernet0/1`

The routing table process will only need to perform a single lookup to get both the exit interface and the next-hop IP address.

Advantages of using an exit interface with static routes

There is an advantage to utilizing exit interfaces in static routes for both serial point-to-point and Ethernet outbound networks. The routing table process only has to perform a single lookup to find the exit interface instead of a second lookup to resolve a next-hop address.

For static routes with outbound point-to-point serial networks, it is best to configure static routes with only the exit interface. For point-to-point serial interfaces, the next-hop address in the routing table is never used by the packet delivery procedure, and so it is not needed.

For static routes with outbound Ethernet networks, it is best to configure the static routes with both the next-hop address and the exit-interface.

Note: For more information about the issues that can occur with static routes that only use an Ethernet or FastEthernet exit interface, see the book *Cisco IP Routing*, by Alex Zinin.

2.6 Summary and Default Static Routes

2.6.1 Summary Static Routes

Refer to
Figure
in online course

Summarizing Routes to Reduce the Size of the Routing Table

Creating smaller routing tables makes the routing table lookup process more efficient, because there are fewer routes to search. If one static route can be used instead of multiple static routes, the size of the routing table will be reduced. In many cases, a single static route can be used to represent dozens, hundreds, or even thousands of routes.

We can use a single network address to represent multiple subnets. For example, the networks 10.0.0.0/16, 10.1.0.0/16, 10.2.0.0/16, 10.3.0.0/16, 10.4.0.0/16, 10.5.0.0/16, all the way through 10.255.0.0/16 can be represented by a single network address: 10.0.0.0/8.

Route Summarization

Multiple static routes can be summarized into a single static route if:

- The destination networks can be summarized into a single network address, and

- The multiple static routes all use the same exit-interface or next-hop IP address

This is called *route summarization* .

In our example, R3 has three static routes. All three routes are forwarding traffic out the same Serial0/0/1 interface. The three static routes on R3 are:

```
ip route 172.16.1.0 255.255.255.0 Serial0/0/1
ip route 172.16.2.0 255.255.255.0 Serial0/0/1
ip route 172.16.3.0 255.255.255.0 Serial0/0/1
```

If possible, we would like to summarize all of these routes into a single static route. 172.16.1.0/24, 172.16.2.0/24 and 172.16.3.0/24 can be summarized to the 172.16.0.0/22 network. Because all three routes use the same exit interface, they can be summarized to the single 172.16.0.0 255.255.252.0 network, and we can create a single summary route.

Calculating a summary route

Here's the process of creating the summary route 172.16.0.0/22, as shown in the figure:

1. Write out the networks that you want to summarize in binary.

2. To find the subnet mask for summarization, start with the left-most bit.

3. Work your way to the right, finding all the bits that match consecutively.

4. When you find a column of bits that do *not* match, stop. You are at the summary boundary.

5. Now, count the number of left-most matching bits, which in our example is 22. This number becomes your subnet mask for the summarized route, /22 or 255.255.252.0

6. To find the network address for summarization, copy the matching 22 bits and add all 0 bits to the end to make 32 bits.

By following these steps, we can discover that the three static routes on R3 can be summarized into a single static route, using the summary network address of 172.16.0.0 255.255.252.0:

```
ip route 172.16.0.0 255.255.252.0 Serial0/0/1
```

Configuring a *Summary Route*

To implement the summary route, we must first delete the three current static routes:

```
R3(config)#no ip route 172.16.1.0 255.255.255.0 serial0/0/1
R3(config)#no ip route 172.16.2.0 255.255.255.0 serial0/0/1
R3(config)#no ip route 172.16.3.0 255.255.255.0 serial0/0/1
```

Next, we will configure the summary static route:

```
R3(config)#ip route 172.16.0.0 255.255.252.0 serial0/0/1
```

Click Effect of Summary Route in the figure.

To verify the new static route, examine R3's routing table with the show ip route command, as shown:

```
172.16.0.0/
22 is subnetted, 1 subnets

S 172.16.0.0 is directly connected, Serial0/0/1
```

With this summary route, the destination IP address of a packet only needs to match the left-most 22 bits of the 172.16.0.0 network address. Any packet with a destination IP address belonging to the 172.16.1.0/24, 172.16.2.0/24, or 172.16.3.0/24 network matches this summarized route.

Click Verify Summary Route in the figure.

As you can see in the figure, we can test the reconfiguration using the **ping** command. We verify that we still have proper connectivity throughout the network.

Note: As of March 2007, there are over 200,000 routes in the Internet core routers. Most of these are summarized routes.

2.6.2 Default Static Route

Most Specific Match

It is possible that the destination IP address of a packet will match multiple routes in the routing table. For example, what if we had the following two static routes in the routing table:

```
172.16.0.0/
```

```
24 is subnetted, 3 subnets
```

```
S 172.16.1.0 is directly connected, Serial0/0/0 and
```

```
S 172.16.0.0/16 is directly connected, Serial0/0/1
```
Consider a packet with the destination IP address 172.16.1.10. This IP address matches both routes. The routing table lookup process will use the most-specific match. Because 24 bits match the 172.16.1.0/24 route, and only 16 bits of the 172.16.0.0/16 route match, the static route with the 24 bit match will be used. This is the longest match. The packet will then be encapsulated in a Layer 2 frame and sent via the Serial 0/0/0 interface. Remember, the subnet mask in the route entry is what determines how many bits must match the packet's destination IP address for this route to be a match.

Note: This process is the same for all routes in the routing table including static routes, routes learned from a routing protocol and directly connected networks. The routing table lookup process will be explained in more detail in a later chapter.

The default static route matches all packets

A default static route is a route that will match all packets. Default static routes are used:

- When no other routes in the routing table match the packet's destination IP address. In other words, when a more specific match does not exist. A common use is when connecting a company's edge router to the ISP network.

- When a router has only one other router to which it is connected. This condition is known as a stub router.

Configuring a Default Static Route

The syntax for a default static route is similar to any other static route, except that the network address is 0.0.0.0 and the subnet mask is 0.0.0.0:

```
Router(config)#ip route 0.0.0.0 0.0.0.0 [exit-interface ¦ ip-address ]
```
The 0.0.0.0 0.0.0.0 network address and mask is called a "quad-zero" route.

R1 is a stub router. It is only connected to R2. Currently R1 has three static routes, which are used to reach all of the remote networks in our topology. All three static routes have the exit interface Serial 0/0/0, forwarding packets to the next-hop router R2.

The three static routes on R1 are:

```
ip route 172.16.1.0 255.255.255.0 serial 0/0/0
ip route 192.168.1.0 255.255.255.0 serial 0/0/0
ip route 192.168.2.0 255.255.255.0 serial 0/0/0
```

R1 is an ideal candidate to have all of its static routes replaced by a single default route. First, delete the three static routes:

```
R1(config)#no ip route 172.16.1.0 255.255.255.0 serial 0/0/0
R1(config)#no ip route 192.168.1.0 255.255.255.0 serial 0/0/0
R1(config)#no ip route 192.168.2.0 255.255.255.0 serial 0/0/0
```

Next, configure the single default static route using the same Serial 0/0/0 exit interface as the three previous static routes:

```
R1(config)#ip route 0.0.0.0 0.0.0.0 serial 0/0/0
```

Refer to
Figure
in online course

Verifying a Default Static Route

Verify the change to the routing table with the show ip route command, as shown in the Figure:

```
S* 0.0.0.0/0 is directly connected, Serial0/0/0
```
Note the * or asterisk next to the **S**. As you can see from the **Codes** table in the figure, the asterisk indicates that this static route is a **candidate default** route. That is why it is called a "default

static" route. We will see in later chapters that a "default" route does not always have to be a "static" route.

The key to this configuration is the /**0** mask. We previously said that it is the subnet mask in the routing table that determines how many bits must match between the destination IP address of the packet and the route in the routing table. A /0 mask indicates that zero or no bits are needed to match. As long as a more specific match doesn't exist, the default static route will match all packets.

Default routes are very common on routers. Instead of routers having to store routes for all of the networks in the Internet, they can store a single default route to represent any network that is not in the routing table. This topic will be discussed in more detail when we discuss dynamic routing protocols.

Refer to **Packet Tracer Activity** for this chapter

Use the Packet Tracer Activity to practice configuring summary routes and default routes. Then verify the new configuration by testing for connectivity.

2.7 Managing and Troubleshooting Static Routes

2.7.1 Static Routes and Packet Forwarding

Refer to **Figure** in online course

Static Routes and Packet Forwarding

The following is an example of the packet forwarding process with static routes. As you can see in the animation, PC1 is sending a packet to PC3:

1. The packet arrives on the FastEthernet 0/0 interface of R1.

2. R1 does not have a specific route to the destination network, 192.168.2.0/24; therefore, R1 uses the default static route.

3. R1 encapsulates the packet in a new frame. Because the link to R2 is a point-to-point link, R1 adds an "all 1s" address for the Layer 2 destination address.

4. The frame is forwarded out the serial 0/0/0 interface. The packet arrives on the Serial 0/0/0 interface on R2.

5. R2 decapsulates the frame and looks for a route to the destination. R2 has a static route to 192.168.2.0/24 out Serial0/0/1.

6. R2 encapsulates the packet in a new frame. Because the link to R3 is a point-to-point link, R2 adds an "all 1s" address for the Layer 2 destination address.

7. The frame is forwarded out the Serial0/0/1 interface. The packet arrives on the Serial0/0/1 interface on R3.

8. R3 decapsulates the frame and looks for a route to the destination. R3 has a connected route to 192.168.2.0/24 out FastEthernet 0/1.

9. R3 looks up the ARP table entry for 192.168.2.10 to find the Layer 2 MAC address for PC3.

     a.   `If no entry exists, R3 sends an ARP request out FastEthernet 0/0.`
     b.   `PC3 responds with an ARP reply which includes the PC3 MAC address.`

10. R3 encapsulates the packet in a new frame with the MAC address of interface FastEthernet 0/0 as the source Layer 2 address and the MAC address of PC3 as the destination MAC address.

11. The frame is forwarded out the FastEthernet 0/0 interface. The packet arrives on the NIC interface of PC3.

This process is no different from the process demonstrated in Chapter 1. As was explained in Chapter 1, you must be able to describe this process in detail. Knowing how a router performs its two basic functions-path determination and packet forwarding - is fundamental to all routing discussions. In Lab 2.8.1, "Basic Static Route Configuration," you have an opportunity to demonstrate your knowledge of the path determination and packet forwarding process.

2.7.2 Troubleshooting a Missing Route

Refer to
Figure
in online course

Troubleshooting a Missing Route

Networks are subject to many different forces that can cause their status to change quite often:

- An interface fails.

- A service provider drops a connection.

- There is an over-saturation of links.

- An administrator enters a wrong configuration.

When there is a change in the network, connectivity may be lost. As a network administrator, you are the one responsible for pinpointing and solving the problem.

What steps can you take?

By now, you should be very familiar with some tools that can help you isolate routing problems. Listed in the figure, they include:

```
ping
traceroute
show ip route
```

Although we have not used traceroute yet in this course, you should be very familiar with its capabilities from previous studies. Recall that traceroute commands will find a break in the path from source to destination.

As we go further into this course, you will discover more tools. For example, **show ip interface brief** gives you a quick summary of interface status. CDP can help you gather information about the IP configuration of a directly connected Cisco device using the **show cdp neighbors detail** command.

2.7.3 Solving the Missing Route

Refer to
Figure
in online course

Solving the Missing Route

Finding a missing (or misconfigured) route is relatively straightforward if you methodically use the correct tools.

Consider this problem: PC1 cannot ping PC3. A traceroute reveals that R2 is responding but that there is no response from R3. Displaying the routing table on R2 reveals that the 172.16.3.0/24 network is configured incorrectly. The exit interface is configured to send packets to R3. Obviously, from the topology, we can see that R1 has the 172.16.3.0/24 network. Therefore, R2 must use Serial 0/0/0 as the exit interface - not Serial0/0/1.

To remedy the situation, remove the incorrect route and add the route for network 172.16.3.0/24 with the Serial 0/0/0 specified as the exit interface.

```
R2(config)#no ip route 172.16.3.0 255.255.255.0 serial0/0/1
R2(config)#ip route 172.16.3.0 255.255.255.0 serial 0/0/0
```

Refer to **Packet Tracer Activity** for this chapter

Use the Packet Tracer Activity to see how the loop explained in this section can occur. In Simulation mode, watch as R2 and R3 loop a packet for 172.16.3.10 until the TTL field reaches zero. Then fix the problem and test for connectivity between PC1 and PC3.

2.8 Static Route Configuration Labs

2.8.1 Basic Static Route Configuration

Refer to
Lab Activity
for this chapter

In this lab activity, you will create a network like the one used in this chapter. You will cable the network and perform the initial router configurations required for connectivity. After completing the basic configuration, you will test connectivity between the devices on the network. You will then configure the static routes that are needed to allow communication between the hosts.

Refer to **Packet Tracer Activity** for this chapter

Use this Packet Tracer Activity to repeat a simulation of Lab 2.8.1. Remember, however, that Packet Tracer is not a substitute for a hands-on lab experience with real equipment.

A summary of the instructions is provided within the activity. Use the Lab PDF for more details.

2.8.2 Challenge Static Route Configuration

Refer to
Lab Activity
for this chapter

In this lab activity, you will be given a network address that must be subnetted to complete the addressing of the network. The addressing for the LAN connected to the ISP router and the link between the HQ and ISP routers has already been completed. Static routes will also need to be configured so that hosts on networks that are not directly connected will be able to communicate with each other.

Refer to **Packet Tracer Activity** for this chapter

Use this Packet Tracer Activity to repeat a simulation of Lab 2.8.2. Remember, however, that Packet Tracer is not a substitute for a hands-on lab experience with real equipment.

A summary of the instructions is provided within the activity. Use the Lab PDF for more details.

2.8.3 Troubleshooting Static Routes

Refer to
Lab Activity
for this chapter

In this lab, you will begin by loading corrupted configuration scripts on each of the routers. These scripts contain errors that will prevent end-to-end communication across the network. You will need to troubleshoot each router to determine the configuration errors, and then use the appropriate commands to correct the configurations. When you have corrected all of the configuration errors, all of the hosts on the network should be able to communicate with each other.

Refer to **Packet Tracer Activity** for this chapter

Use this Packet Tracer Activity to repeat a simulation of Lab 2.8.3. Remember, however, that Packet Tracer is not a substitute for a hands-on lab experience with real equipment.

A summary of the instructions is provided within the activity. Use the Lab PDF for more details.

Summary and Review

Refer to
Figure
in online course

Summary

In this chapter you learned how static routes can be used to reach remote networks. Remote networks are networks that can only be reached by forwarding the packet to another router. Static routes are easily configured. However, in large networks this manual operation can become quite cumbersome. As we will see in later chapters, static routes are still used - even when a dynamic routing protocol is implemented.

Static routes can be configured with a next-hop IP address, which is commonly the IP address of the next-hop router. When a next-hop IP address is used, the routing table process must resolve this address to an exit interface. On point-to-point serial links it is usually more efficient to configure the static route with an exit interface. On multiaccess networks such as Ethernet, both a next-hop IP address and an exit interface can be configured on the static route.

Static routes have a default administrative distance of "1". This administrative distance also applies to static routes configured with a next-hop address as well as an exit-interface.

A static route will only be entered in the routing table if the next-hop IP address can be resolved through an exit interface. Whether the static route is configured with a next-hop IP address or exit interface, if the exit interface that is used to forward that packet is not in the routing table, the static route will not be included in the routing table.

In many cases, several static routes can be configured as a single summary route. This means fewer entries in the routing table and results in a faster routing table lookup process. The ultimate summary route is a default route, configured with a 0.0.0.0 network address and a 0.0.0.0 subnet mask. If there is not a more specific match in the routing table, the routing table will use the default route to forward the packet to another router.

Note: The routing table lookup process is examined more closely in Chapter 8, "The Routing Table: A Closer Look."

Refer to
Figure
in online course

Refer to **Packet
Tracer Activity**
for this chapter

The Packet Tracer Skills Integration Challenge Activity for this chapter integrates all the knowledge and skills you acquired in the first two chapters of this course. In this activity, you will build a network from the ground up. Starting with an addressing space and network requirements, you must implement a network design that satisfies the specifications. Then implement an effective static routing configuration.

Packet Tracer Skills Integration Instructions (PDF)

To Learn More

Floating Static Routes

Refer to
Figure
in online course

A floating static route is a backup route to a route which is either a dynamic route or another static route. The default administrative distance of a static route is "1". See if you can create a static route using a different exit-interface or next-hop IP address which would only be added to the routing table if the primary static route fails.

Hints: Remember, if the router has two routes to the same destination network with two different administrative distance values, it will add the route with the lower administrative distance. A static route will be removed from the routing table if the exit-interface or next-hop IP address is no longer available.

Discard Route

A common configuration in many networks is to have a static default route on the edge router forwarding packets to the ISP. The ISP router then has a static route pointing to the customer's network.

For example, Customer A has the network address of 172.16.0.0/16, which is subnetted into several /24 subnets. The edge router of Customer A has a static default route forwarding all other traffic to the ISP router:

```
ip route 0.0.0.0 0.0.0.0 serial 0/0/0
```

The ISP router has a static default route for forwarding traffic to Customer A's network:

```
ip route 172.16.0.0 255.255.0.0 serial 0/0/1
```

A problem can occur when packets are originated from the Customer A's network for a subnet that does not exist. Customer A's edge router will use its default route to forward those packets onto the ISP, The ISP router will receive those packets and send them back to Customer A's edge router because they are part of the 172.16.0.0/16 network, The edge router will once again send them back to the ISP. The packets are caught in a loop until the TTL of the packet expires.

Configure a static route on the Customer A's edge router to discard those packets instead of forwarding them onto the ISP router.

Further Reading on Static Routing

Although static routes can be easily understood and configured, there are some situations when the IOS processing of static routes can be quite complex. This is especially true when there are various static routes configured that cover the same range of networks.

Alex Zinin's book, *Cisco IP Routing*, covers static routing and IOS's static route processing in detail. This book goes beyond just the configuration and looks at the inner-workings of the Cisco IOS and its routing processes.

Go to
the online course
to take the quiz.

Chapter Quiz

Take the chapter quiz to test your knowledge.

Your Chapter Notes

CHAPTER 3

Introduction to Dynamic Routing Protocols

Chapter Introduction

Refer to **Figure** in online course

The data networks that we use in our everyday lives to learn, play, and work range from small, local networks to large, global internetworks. At home, you may have a router and two or more computers. At work, your organization may have multiple routers and switches servicing the data communication needs of hundreds or even thousands of PCs.

In the previous chapters you discovered how routers are used in packet forwarding and that routers learn about remote networks using both static routes and dynamic routing protocols. You also know how routes to remote networks can be configured manually using static routes.

This chapter introduces dynamic routing protocols, including how different routing protocols are classified, what metrics they use to determine best path, and the benefits of using a dynamic routing protocol.

Dynamic routing protocols are usually used in larger networks to ease the administrative and operational overhead of using only static routes. Typically, a network uses a combination of both a dynamic routing protocol and static routes. In most networks, a single dynamic routing protocol is used, however there are cases where different parts of the network may use different routing protocols.

Since the early 1980's, several different dynamic routing protocols have emerged. In this chapter we will begin to discuss some of the characteristics and differences in these routing protocols, however this will become more evident in later chapters when we discuss several of these routing protocols in detail.

Although many networks will only use a single routing protocol or use only static routes, it is important for a network professional to understand the concepts and operations of all the different routing protocols. A network professional must be able to make an informed decision regarding when to use a dynamic routing protocol and which routing protocol is the best choice for a particular environment.

3.1 Introduction and Advantages

3.1.1 Perspective and Background

The Evolution of Dynamic Routing Protocols

Refer to **Figure** in online course

Dynamic routing protocols have been used in networks since the early 1980s. The first version of RIP was released in 1982, but some of the basic algorithms within the protocol were used on the ARPANET as early as 1969.

As networks have evolved and become more complex, new routing protocols have emerged. The figure shows the classification of routing protocols.

One of the earliest routing protocols was *Routing Information Protocol (RIP)*. RIP has evolved into a newer version RIPv2. However, the newer version of RIP still does not *scale* to larger network implementations. To address the needs of larger networks, two advanced routing protocols were developed: *Open Shortest Path First (OSPF)* and Intermediate System-to-Intermediate System (IS-IS). Cisco developed Interior Gateway Routing Protocol (IGRP) and *Enhanced IGRP (EIGRP)*, which also scales well in larger network implementations.

Additionally, there was the need to interconnect different internetworks and provide routing among them. *Border Gateway Routing (BGP)* protocol is now used between ISPs as well as between ISPs and their larger private clients to exchange routing information.

With the advent of numerous consumer devices using IP, the IPv4 addressing space is nearly exhausted. Thus IPv6 has emerged. To support the communication based on IPv6, newer versions of the IP routing protocols have been developed (see the IPv6 row in the table).

Note: This chapter presents an overview of the different dynamic routing protocols. More details about RIP, EIGRP, and OSPF routing protocols will be discussed in later chapters. The IS-IS and BGP routing protocols are explained in the CCNP curriculum. IGRP is the predecessor to EIGRP and is now obsolete.

> Refer to
> **Figure**
> in online course

The Role of Dynamic Routing Protocol

What exactly are dynamic routing protocols? Routing protocols are used to facilitate the exchange of routing information between routers. Routing protocols allow routers to dynamically share information about remote networks and automatically add this information to their own routing tables. This is shown in the animation.

Routing protocols determine the best path to each network which is then added to the routing table. One of the primary benefits to using a dynamic routing protocol is that routers exchange routing information whenever there is a topology change. This exchange allows routers to automatically learn about new networks and also to find alternate paths when there is a link failure to a current network.

Compared to static routing, dynamic routing protocols require less administrative overhead. However, the expense of using dynamic routing protocols is dedicating part of a router's resources for protocol operation including CPU time and network link bandwidth. Despite the benefits of dynamic routing, static routing still has its place. There are times when static routing is more appropriate and other times when dynamic routing is the better choice. More often than not, you will find a combination of both types of routing in any network that has a moderate level of complexity. We will discuss the advantages and disadvantages of static and dynamic routing later in this chapter.

3.1.2 Network discovery and routing table maintenance

> Refer to
> **Figure**
> in online course

The Purpose of Dynamic Routing Protocols

A routing protocol is a set of processes, algorithms, and messages that are used to exchange routing information and populate the routing table with the routing protocol's choice of best paths. The purpose of a routing protocol includes:

- Discovery of remote networks

- Maintaining up-to-date routing information

- Choosing the best path to destination networks

- Ability to find a new best path if the current path is no longer available

What are the components of a routing protocol?

- *Data structures* - Some routing protocols use tables and/or databases for its operations. This information is kept in RAM.

- *Algorithm* - An algorithm is a finite list of steps used in accomplishing a task. Routing protocols use algorithms for facilitating routing information and for best path determination.

- *Routing protocol messages* - Routing protocols use various types of messages to discover neighboring routers, exchange routing information, and other tasks to learn and maintain accurate information about the network.

Dynamic Routing Protocol Operation

All routing protocols have the same purpose - to learn about remote networks and to quickly adapt whenever there is a change in the topology. The method that a routing protocol uses to accomplish this depends upon the algorithm it uses and the operational characteristics of that protocol. The operations of a dynamic routing protocol vary depending upon the type of routing protocol and the routing protocol itself. In general, the operations of a dynamic routing protocol can be described as follows:

- The router sends and receives routing messages on its interfaces.

- The router shares routing messages and routing information with other routers that are using the same routing protocol.

- Routers exchange routing information to learn about remote networks.

- When a router detects a topology change the routing protocol can advertise this change to other routers.

Play the animation to see dynamic routing protocols in operation.

Note: Understanding dynamic routing protocol operation and concepts and using them in real networks requires a solid knowledge of IP addressing and subnetting. Three subnetting scenarios are available at the end of this chapter for your practice.

3.1.3 Advantages

Refer to
Figure
in online course

Static Routing Usage

Before identifying the benefits of dynamic routing protocols, we need to consider the reasons why we would use static routing. Dynamic routing certainly has several advantages over static routing. However, static routing is still used in networks today. In fact, networks typically use a combination of both static and dynamic routing.

Static routing has several primary uses, including:

- Providing ease of routing table maintenance in smaller networks that are not expected to grow significantly.

- Routing to and from stub networks (see Chapter 2).

- Use of a single default route, used to represent a path to any network that does not have a more specific match with another route in the routing table.

Static Routing Advantages and Disadvantages

In the table dynamic and static routing features are directly compared. From this comparison, we can list the advantages of each routing method. The advantages of one method are the disadvantages of the other.

Static routing advantages:

■ Minimal CPU processing.

■ Easier for administrator to understand.

■ Easy to configure.

Static routing disadvantages:

■ Configuration and maintenance is time-consuming.

■ Configuration is error-prone, especially in large networks.

■ Administrator intervention is required to maintain changing route information.

■ Does not scale well with growing networks; maintenance becomes cumbersome.

■ Requires complete knowledge of the whole network for proper implementation.

Dynamic Routing Advantages and Disadvantages

Dynamic routing advantages:

■ Administrator has less work maintaining the configuration when adding or deleting networks.

■ Protocols automatically react to the topology changes.

■ Configuration is less error-prone.

■ More scalable, growing the network usually does not present a problem.

Dynamic routing disadvantages:

■ Router resources are used (CPU cycles, memory and link bandwidth).

■ More administrator knowledge is required for configuration, verification, and troubleshooting.

3.2 Classifying Dynamic Routing Protocols

3.2.1 Overview

Refer to
Figure
in online course

Dynamic Routing Protocols Classification

Routing protocols can be classified into different groups according to their characteristics. The most commonly used routing protocols are:

■ *RIP* - A distance *vector* interior routing protocol

■ *IGRP* - The *distance vector* interior routing developed by Cisco (deprecated from 12.2 IOS and later)

■ *OSPF* - A link-state interior routing protocol

■ *IS-IS* - A link-state interior routing protocol

■ *EIGRP* - The advanced distance vector interior routing protocol developed by Cisco

■ *BGP* - A path vector exterior routing protocol

Note: IS-IS and BGP are beyond the scope of this course and are covered in the CCNP curriculum.

The classification criteria are explained later in this chapter.

Drag and drop each protocol onto the correct category in the figure.

3.2.2 IGP and EGP

Refer to **Figure** in online course

An autonomous system (AS) - otherwise known as a routing *domain* - is a collection of routers under a common administration. Typical examples are a company's internal network and an Internet service provider's network. Because the Internet is based on the autonomous system concept, two types of routing protocols are required: interior and exterior routing protocols. These protocols are:

- *Interior Gateway Protocols* (IGP) **are used for intra-autonomous system routing - routing inside an autonomous system.**

- **Exterior Gateway Protocols (EGP)** are used for inter-autonomous system routing - routing between autonomous systems.

The figure is a simplified view of the difference between IGPs and EGPs. The autonomous system concept will be explained in more detail later in the chapter.

Characteristics of IGP and EGP Routing Protocols

IGPs are used for routing within a routing domain, those networks within the control of a single organization. An autonomous system is commonly comprised of many individual networks belonging to companies, schools, and other institutions. An IGP is used to route within the autonomous system, and also used to route within the individual networks themselves. For example, CENIC operates an autonomous system comprised of California schools, colleges and universities. CENIC uses an IGP to route within its autonomous system in order to interconnect all of these institutions. Each of the educational institutions also uses an IGP of their own choosing to route within its own individual network. The IGP used by each entity provides best path determination within its own routing domains, just as the IGP used by CENIC provides best path routes within the autonomous system itself. IGPs for IP include RIP, IGRP, EIGRP, OSPF, and IS-IS.

Routing protocols, and more specifically the algorithm used by that routing protocol, use a metric to determine the best path to a network. The metric used by the routing protocol RIP is hop count, which is the number of routers that a packet must traverse in reaching another network. OSPF uses bandwidth to determine the shortest path.

EGPs on the other hand, are designed for use between different autonomous systems that are under the control of different administrations. BGP is the only currently-viable EGP and is the routing protocol used by the Internet. BGP is a *path vector protocol* that can use many different attributes to measure routes. At the ISP level, there are often more important issues than just choosing the fastest path. BGP is typically used between ISPs and sometimes between a company and an ISP. BGP is not part of this course or CCNA; it is covered in CCNP.

Refer to **Packet Tracer Activity** for this chapter

In this activity, the network has already been configured within the autonomous systems. You will configure a default route from AS2 and AS3 (two different companies) to the ISP (AS1) to simulate the Exterior Gateway Routing that would take place from both companies to their ISP. Then you will configure a static route from the ISP (AS1) to AS2 and AS3 to simulate the Exterior Gateway Routing that would take place from the ISP to its 2 customers AS2 and AS3. View the routing table before and after both static routes and default routes are added to observe how the routing table has changed.

Refer to
Figure
in online course

3.2.3 Distance Vector and Link State

Interior Gateway Protocols (IGPs) can be classified as two types:

- Distance vector routing protocols

- *Link-state* routing protocols

Distance Vector Routing Protocol Operation

Distance vector means that routes are advertised as vectors of distance and direction. Distance is defined in terms of a metric such as hop count and direction is simply the next-hop router or exit interface. Distance vector protocols typically use the Bellman-Ford algorithm for the best path route determination.

Some distance vector protocols periodically send complete routing tables to all connected neighbors. In large networks, these routing updates can become enormous, causing significant traffic on the links.

Play the animation to see the operation of distance vector routing protocols.

Although the Bellman-Ford algorithm eventually accumulates enough knowledge to maintain a database of reachable networks, the algorithm does not allow a router to know the exact topology of an internetwork. The router only knows the routing information received from its neighbors.

Distance vector protocols use routers as sign posts along the path to the final destination. The only information a router knows about a remote network is the distance or metric to reach that network and which path or interface to use to get there. Distance vector routing protocols do not have an actual map of the network topology.

Distance vector protocols work best in situations where:

- The network is simple and flat and does not require a special hierarchical design.

- The administrators do not have enough knowledge to configure and troubleshoot link-state protocols.

- Specific types of networks, such as hub-and-spoke networks, are being implemented.

- Worst-case *convergence* times in a network are not a concern.

Distance vector routing protocol functions and operations will be explained in the next chapter. You will also learn about the operations and configuration of the distance vector routing protocols RIP and EIGRP.

Refer to
Figure
in online course

Link-state Protocol Operation

In contrast to distance vector routing protocol operation, a router configured with a *link-state routing protocol* can create a "complete view" or topology of the network by gathering information from all of the other routers. To continue our analogy of sign posts, using a link-state routing protocol is like having a complete map of the network topology. The sign posts along the way from source to destination are not necessary, because all link-state routers are using an identical "map" of the network. A link-state router uses the link-state information to create a topology map and to select the best path to all destination networks in the topology.

Play the animation.

With some distance vector routing protocols, routers send periodic updates of their routing information to their neighbors. Link-state routing protocols do not use periodic updates. After the network has *converged*, a link-state update only sent when there is a change in the topology. For example, the link-state update in the animation is not sent until the 172.16.3.0 network goes down.

Link-state protocols work best in situations where:

- The network design is hierarchical, usually occurring in large networks.

- The administrators have a good knowledge of the implemented link-state routing protocol.

- Fast convergence of the network is crucial.

Link-state routing protocol functions and operations will be explained in later chapters. You will also learn about the operations and configuration of the link-state routing protocol OSPF.

3.2.4 Classful and Classless

Refer to
Figure
in online course

Classful Routing Protocols

Classful routing protocols do not send subnet mask information in routing updates. The first routing protocols such as RIP, were classful. This was at a time when network addresses were allocated based on classes, class A, B, or C. A routing protocol did not need to include the subnet mask in the routing update because the network mask could be determined based on the first octet of the network address.

Classful routing protocols can still be used in some of today's networks, but because they do not include the subnet mask they cannot be used in all situations. Classful routing protocols cannot be used when a network is subnetted using more than one subnet mask, in other words *classful routing protocols* do not support variable length subnet masks (VLSM).

There are other limitations to classful routing protocols including their inability to support *discontiguous* networks. Classful routing protocols, discontiguous networks and VLSM will all be discussed in later chapters.

Classful routing protocols include RIPv1 and IGRP.

Classless Routing Protocols

Classless routing protocols include the subnet mask with the network address in routing updates. Today's networks are no longer allocated based on classes and the subnet mask cannot be determined by the value of the first octet. Classless routing protocols are required in most networks today because of their support for VLSM, discontiguous networks and other features which will be discussed in later chapters.

In the figure, notice that the classless version of the network is using both /30 and /27 subnet masks in the same topology. Also notice that this topology is using a discontiguous design.

Classless routing protocols are RIPv2, EIGRP, OSPF, IS-IS, BGP.

3.2.5 Convergence

Refer to
Figure
in online course

What is Convergence?

Convergence is when all routers' routing tables are at a state of consistency. The network has converged when all routers have complete and accurate information about the network. Convergence time is the time it takes routers to share information, calculate best paths, and update their routing tables. A network is not completely operable until the network has converged; therefore, most networks require short convergence times.

Convergence is both collaborative and independent. The routers share information with each other but must independently calculate the impacts of the topology change on their own routes. Because they develop an agreement with the new topology independently, they are said to converge on this consensus.

Refer to **Packet Tracer Activity** for this chapter

Convergence properties include the speed of propagation of routing information and the calculation of optimal paths. Routing protocols can be rated based on the speed to convergence; the faster the convergence, the better the routing protocol. Generally, RIP and IGRP are slow to converge, whereas EIGRP and OSPF are faster to converge.

In this activity, the network has already been configured with 2 routers, 2 switches and 2 hosts. A new LAN will be added and you will watch the network converge.

3.3 Metrics

3.3.1 Purpose of a Metric

There are cases when a routing protocol learns of more than one route to the same destination. To select the best path, the routing protocol must be able to evaluate and differentiate between the available paths. For this purpose a **metric** is used. A metric is a value used by routing protocols to assign costs to reach remote networks. The metric is used to determine which path is most preferable when there are multiple paths to the same remote network.

Refer to **Figure** in online course

Each routing protocol uses its own metric. For example, RIP uses hop count, EIGRP uses a combination of bandwidth and delay, and Cisco's implementation of OSPF uses bandwidth. Hop count is the easiest metric to envision. The hop count refers to the number of routers a packet must cross to reach the destination network. For R3 in the figure, network 172.16.3.0 is two hops, or two routers away.

Note: The metrics for a particular routing protocol and how they are calculated will be discussed in the chapter for that routing protocol.

3.3.2 Metrics and Routing Protocols

The Metric Parameters

Different routing protocols use different metrics. The metric used by one routing protocol is not comparable to the metric used by another routing protocol. Two different routing protocols might choose different paths to the same destination due to using different metrics.

Play the animation.

Refer to **Figure** in online course

RIP would choose the path with the least amount of hops, whereas OSPF would choose the path with the highest bandwidth.

Metrics used in IP routing protocols include:

- *Hop count* - A simple metric that counts the number of routers a packet must traverse

- *Bandwidth* - Influences path selection by preferring the path with the highest bandwidth

- *Load* - Considers the traffic utilization of a certain link

- *Delay* - Considers the time a packet takes to traverse a path

- *Reliability* - Assesses the probability of a link failure, calculated from the interface error count or previous link failures

- *Cost* - A value determined either by the IOS or by the network administrator to indicate preference for a route. Cost can represent a metric, a combination of metrics or a policy.

Note: At this point, it is not important to completely understand these metrics; they will be explained in later chapters.

Refer to **Figure** in online course

The Metric Field in the Routing Table

The metric for each routing protocol is:

- *RIP:* Hop count - Best path is chosen by the route with the lowest hop count.

- *IGRP and EIGRP:* Bandwidth, Delay, Reliability, and Load - Best path is chosen by the route with the smallest composite metric value calculated from these multiple parameters. By default, only bandwidth and delay are used.

- *IS-IS and OSPF:* Cost - Best path is chosen by the route with the lowest cost. . Cisco's implementation of OSPF uses bandwidth. IS-IS is discussed in CCNP.

Routing protocols determine best path based on the route with the lowest metric.

Refer to the example in the figure The routers are using the RIP routing protocol. The metric associated with a certain route can be best viewed using the `show ip route` command. The metric value is the second value in the brackets for a routing table entry. In the figure, R2 has a route to the 192.168.8.0/24 network that is 2 hops away.

`R 192.168.8.0/24 [120/2] via 192.168.4.1, 00:00:26, Serial0/0/1`

Note: More detailed information about specific routing protocol metrics and how to calculate them will be available in the later chapters describing the individual routing protocols.

3.3.3 Load Balancing

Refer to **Figure** in online course

We have discussed that individual routing protocols use metrics to determine the best route to reach remote networks. But what happens when two or more routes to the same destination have identical metric values? How will the router decide which path to use for packet forwarding? In this case, the router does not choose only one route. **Instead, the router "load balances" between these equal cost paths**. The packets are forwarded using all equal-cost paths.

To see whether load balancing is in effect, check the routing table. **Load balancing is in effect if two or more routes are associated with the same destination.**

Note: Load balancing can be done either per packet or per destination. How a router actually load balances packets between the equal-cost paths is governed by the switching process. The switching process will be discussed in greater detail in a later chapter.

Play the animation.

R2 load balances traffic to PC5 over two equal cost paths.

The `show ip route` command reveals that the destination network 192.168.6.0 is available through 192.168.2.1 (Serial 0/0/0) and 192.168.4.1 (Serial 0/0/1).

`R 192.168.6.0/24 [120/1] via 192.168.2.1, 00:00:24, Serial0/0/0`
`    [120/1] via 192.168.4.1, 00:00:26, Serial0/0/1`

All the routing protocols discussed in this course are capable of automatically load balancing traffic for up to four equal-cost routes by default. EIGRP is also capable of load balancing across unequal-cost paths. This feature of EIGRP is discussed in the CCNP.

3.4 Administrative Distances

3.4.1 Purpose of Administrative Distance

Refer to **Figure** in online course

Multiple Routing Sources

We know that routers learn about adjacent networks that are directly connected and about remote networks by using static routes and dynamic routing protocols. In fact, a router might learn of a route to the same network from more than one source. For example, a static route might have been configured for the same network/subnet mask that was learned dynamically by a dynamic routing protocol, such as RIP. The router must choose which route to install.

Note: You might be wondering about equal cost paths. Multiple routes to the same network can only be installed when they come from the same routing source. For example, for equal cost routes to be installed they both must be static routes or they both must be RIP routes.

Although less common, more than one dynamic routing protocol can be deployed in the same network. In some situations it may be necessary to route the same network address using multiple routing protocols such as RIP and OSPF. Because different routing protocols use different metrics, RIP uses hop count and OSPF uses bandwidth, it is not possible to compare metrics to determine the best path.

So, how does a router determine which route to install in the routing table when it has learned about the same network from more than one routing source?

The Purpose of Administrative Distance

Administrative distance (*AD*) defines the preference of a routing source. Each routing source - including specific routing protocols, static routes, and even directly connected networks - is prioritized in order of most- to least-preferable using an administrative distance value. Cisco routers use the AD feature to select the best path when it learns about the same destination network from two or more different routing sources.

Administrative distance is an integer value from 0 to 255. The lower the value the more preferred the route source. An administrative distance of 0 is the most preferred. Only a directly connected network has an administrative distance of 0, which cannot be changed.

It is possible to modify the administrative distance for static routes and dynamic routing protocols. This is discussed in CCNP.

An administrative distance of 255 means the router will not believe the source of that route and it will not be installed in the routing table.

Note: The term trustworthiness is commonly used when defining administrative distance. The lower the administrative distance value the more trustworthy the route.

Refer to
Figure
in online course

Click show ip route in the figure.

The AD value is the first value in the brackets for a routing table entry. Notice that R2 has a route to the 192.168.6.0/24 network with an AD value of 90.

D 192.168.6.0/24 [90/2172416] via 192.168.2.1, 00:00:24, Serial0/0/0

R2 is running both RIP and EIGRP routing protocols. (Remember: it is not common for routers to run multiple dynamic routing protocols, but is used here to demonstrate how administrative distance works.) R2 has learned of the 192.168.6.0/24 route from R1 through EIGRP updates and from R3 through RIP updates. RIP has an administrative distance of 120, but EIGRP has a lower administrative distance of 90. So, R2 adds the route learned using EIGRP to the routing table and forwards all packets for the 192.168.6.0/24 network to router R1.

Click show ip rip database in the figure.

What happens if the link to R1 becomes unavailable? Then R2 would not have a route to 192.168.6.0. Actually, R2 still has the RIP route information for 192.168.6.0 stored in the RIP database. This can be verified with the **show ip rip database** command. This command shows all RIP routes learned by R2, whether or not the RIP route is installed in the routing table.

3.4.2 Dynamic Routing Protocols

Refer to
Figure
in online course

Click `show ip route` in the figure.

You already know that you can verify these AD values with the **`show ip route`** command.

Click `show ip protocols` in the figure.

The AD value can also be verified with the **`show ip protocols`** command. This command displays all pertinent information about routing protocols operating on the router. We will look at the **`show ip protocols`** command in detail many times during the rest of the course. However, for now notice the highlighted output: R2 has two routing protocols listed and the AD value is called **Distance**.

Click AD Table in the figure.

Notice the different administrative distance values for various routing protocols.

3.4.3 Static Routes

Refer to
Figure
in online course

As you know from Chapter 2, static routes are entered by an administrator who wants to manually configure the best path to the destination. For that reason, static routes have a default AD value of 1. This means that after directly connected networks, which have a default AD value of 0, static routes are the most preferred route source.

There are situations when an administrator will configure a static route to the same destination that is learned using a dynamic routing protocol, but using a different path. The static route will be configured with an AD greater than that of the routing protocol. If there is a link failure in the path used by the dynamic routing protocol, the route entered by the routing protocol is removed from the routing table. The static route will then become the only source and will automatically be added to the routing table. This is known as a floating static route and is discussed in CCNP.

A static route using either a next-hop IP address or an exit interface has a default AD value of 1. However, the AD value is not listed in **`show ip route`** when you configure a static route with the exit interface specified. When a static route is configured with an exit interface, the output shows the network as directly connected via that interface.

Click `show ip route` in the figure.

The static route to 172.16.3.0 is listed as **directly connected**. However, there is no information on what the AD value is. It is a common misconception to assume that the AD value of this route must be 0 because it states "directly connected." However, that is a false assumption. The default AD of any static route, including those configured with an exit interface is 1. Remember, only a directly connected network can have an AD of 0. This can be verified by extending the **`show ip route`** command with the **`[route]`** option. Specifying the **`[route]`** reveals detailed information about the route, including its distance, or AD value.

Click `show ip route 172.16.3.0` in the figure.

The command **`show ip route 172.16.3.0`** reveals that, in fact, the administrative distance is 1.

3.4.4 Directly Connected Networks

Refer to
Figure
in online course

Directly connected networks appear in the routing table as soon as the IP address on the interface is configured and the interface is enabled and operational. The AD value of directly connected networks is 0, meaning that this is the most preferred routing source. There is no better route for a router than having one of its interfaces directly connected to that network. For that reason, the administrative distance of a directly connected network cannot be changed and no other route source can have an administrative distance of 0.

Click `show ip route` in the figure.

The output of the `show ip route` command displays the directly connected networks with no information about the AD value. The output is similar to the output for static routes that point to an exit interface. The only difference is the letter **C** at the beginning of the entry, which indicates that this is a directly connected network.

To see the AD value of a directly connected network, use the `[route]` option.

Click `show ip route 172.16.1.0` in the figure.

The `show ip route 172.16.1.0` command reveals that the distance is 0 for that directly connected route.

Refer to **Packet Tracer Activity** for this chapter

In this activity, you will use version of the `show ip route` command to see details of routing table entries.

3.5 Routing Protocols and Subnetting Activities

3.5.1 Identifying Elements of the Routing Table

Refer to **Figure** in online course

The purpose of this exercise is to practice how to correctly identify the route source, administrative distance, and metric for a given route based on output from the `show ip route` command.

The output is not common for most routing tables. Running more than one routing protocol on the same router is rare. Running three, as shown here, is more of an academic exercise and has value in that it will help you learn to interpret the routing table output.

Drag and drop the appropriate responses to the corresponding space in the table.

- Use the information from the Show IP Route as reference.
- Not all answers are used.
- Some answers are used more than once.

3.5.2 Subnetting Scenario 1

Refer to **Lab Activity** for this chapter

In this activity, you have been given the network address 192.168.9.0/24 to subnet and provide the IP addressing for the network shown in the Topology Diagram.

Refer to **Packet Tracer Activity** for this chapter

Use this Packet Tracer Activity to implement your addressing scheme.

A summary of the instructions are provided within the activity. Use the Lab PDF for more details.

3.5.3 Subnetting Scenario 2

Refer to **Lab Activity** for this chapter

In this activity, you have been given the network address 172.16.0.0/16 to subnet and provide the IP addressing for the network shown in the Topology Diagram.

Refer to **Packet Tracer Activity** for this chapter

Use this Packet Tracer Activity to implement your addressing scheme.

A summary of the instructions are provided within the activity. Use the Lab PDF for more details.

3.5.4 Subnetting Scenario 3

Refer to
Lab Activity
for this chapter

Refer to **Packet Tracer Activity**
for this chapter

In this activity, you have been given the network address 192.168.1.0/24 to subnet and provide the IP addressing for the network shown in the Topology Diagram.

Use this Packet Tracer Activity to implement your addressing scheme.

A summary of the instructions are provided within the activity. Use the Lab PDF for more details.

Summary and Review

Summary

Refer to **Figure** in online course

Dynamic routing protocols are used by routers to automatically learn about remote networks from other routers. In this chapter you were introduced to several different dynamic routing protocols.

You learned that routing protocols can be classified as either classful or classless, either distance vector, link-state, or path vector, and whether a routing protocol is an interior gateway protocol or an exterior gateway protocol. The differences in these classifications will become better understood as you learn more about these routing concepts and protocols in later chapters.

Routing protocols not only discover remote networks, but also have a procedure for maintaining accurate network information. When there is a change in the topology it is the function of the routing protocol to inform other routers about this change.

When there is a change in the network topology, some routing protocols can propagate that information throughout the routing domain faster than other routing protocols. The process of bringing all routing tables to a state of consistency is called convergence. Convergence is when all of the routers in the same routing domain or area have complete and accurate information about the network.

Metrics are used by routing protocols to determine the best path or shortest path to reach a destination network. Different routing protocols may use different metrics. Typically, a lower metric means a better path. Five hops to reach a network is better than 10 hops.

Routers sometimes learn about multiple routes to the same network from both static routes and dynamic routing protocols. When a router learns about a destination network from more than one routing source, Cisco routers use the administrative distance value to determine which source to use. Each dynamic routing protocol has a unique administrative value, along with static routes and directly connected networks. The lower the administrative value, the more preferred the route source. A directly connected network is always the preferred source, followed by static routes and then various dynamic routing protocols.

All of the classifications and concepts in this chapter will be discussed more thoroughly in the rest of the chapters of this course. At the end of this course you may wish to review this chapter to get a review and overview of this information.

Refer to **Figure** in online course

Refer to **Packet Tracer Activity** for this chapter

The Packet Tracer Skills Integration Challenge Activity for this chapter is very similar to the activity you completed at the end of Chapter 2. The scenario is slightly different, allowing you to better practice your skills. In this activity, you build a network from the ground up. Starting with an addressing space and network requirements, you must implement a network design that satisfies the specifications. Then you must implement an effective static routing configuration.

Packet Tracer Skills Integration Instructions (PDF)

To Learn More

Refer to **Figure** in online course

Border Gateway Protocol (BGP) is an inter-autonomous routing protocol - the routing protocol of the Internet. Although BGP is only briefly discussed in this course (it is discussed more fully in CCNP), you might find it interesting to view routing tables of some of the Internet core routers.

Route servers are used to view BGP routes on the Internet. Various web sites provide access to these route server, for example www.traceroute.org. When choosing a route server in a specific autonomous system, you will start a telnet session on that route server. This server is mirroring an Internet core router which is most often a Cisco router.

You can then use the `show ip route` command to view the actual routing table of an Internet router. Use the `show ip route` command followed by the public or global network address of your school, for example `show ip route 207.62.187.0`.

You will not be able to understand much of the information in this output, but these commands should give you a sense of the size of a routing table on a core Internet router.

Go to
the online course
to take the quiz.

Chapter Quiz

Take the chapter quiz to test your knowledge.

Your Chapter Notes

CHAPTER 4

Distance Vector Routing Protocols

Chapter Introduction

Introduction

Refer to
Figure
in online course

The dynamic routing chapters of this course focus on Interior Gateway Protocols (IGPs). As discussed in Chapter 3, IGPs are classified as either distance vector or link-state routing protocols.

This chapter describes the characteristics, operations, and functionality of distance vector routing protocols. There are advantages and disadvantages to using any type of routing protocol. Therefore, the conditions influencing the operation of distance vector protocols and the pitfalls of distance vector protocol operation - along with remedies to overcome such pitfalls - are described. Understanding the operation of distance vector routing is critical to enabling, verifying, and troubleshooting these protocols.

4.1 Introduction to Distance Vector Routing Protocols

4.1.1 Distance Vector Routing Protocols

Refer to
Figure
in online course

Dynamic routing protocols help the network administrator overcome the time-consuming and exacting process of configuring and maintaining static routes. For example, can you imagine maintaining the static routing configurations of the 28 routers shown in the figure? What happens when a link goes down? How do you ensure that *redundant paths* are available? Dynamic routing is the most common choice for large networks like the one shown.

Distance vector routing protocols include RIP, IGRP, and EIGRP.

RIP

Routing Information Protocol (RIP) was originally specified in RFC 1058. It has the following key characteristics:

- Hop count is used as the metric for path selection.

- If the hop count for a network is greater than 15, RIP cannot supply a route to that network.

- Routing updates are broadcast or multicast every 30 seconds, by default.

IGRP

Interior Gateway Routing Protocol (IGRP) is a proprietary protocol developed by Cisco. IGRP has the following key design characteristics:

- Bandwidth, delay, load and reliability are used to create a composite metric.

- Routing updates are broadcast every 90 seconds, by default.

- IGRP is the predecessor of EIGRP and is now obsolete.

EIGRP

Enhanced IGRP (EIGRP) is a Cisco proprietary distance vector routing protocol. EIGRP has these key characteristics:

- It can perform unequal cost load balancing.

- It uses *Diffusing Update Algorithm (DUAL)* to calculate the shortest path.

- There are no periodic updates as with RIP and IGRP. Routing updates are sent only when there is a change in the topology.

4.1.2 Distance Vector Technology

Refer to Figure in online course

The Meaning of Distance Vector

As the name implies, distance vector means that routes are advertised as vectors of distance and direction. Distance is defined in terms of a metric such as hop count and direction is simply the next-hop router or exit interface.

A router using a distance vector routing protocol does not have the knowledge of the entire path to a destination network. Instead the router knows only:

- The direction or interface in which packets should be forwarded and

- The distance or how far it is to the destination network

For example, in the figure, R1 knows that the distance to reach network 172.16.3.0/24 is 1 hop and that the direction is out the interface S0/0/0 toward R2.

Refer to Figure in online course

Operation of Distance Vector Routing Protocols

Some distance vector routing protocols call for the router to periodically broadcast the entire routing table to each of its neighbors. This method is inefficient because the updates not only consume bandwidth but also consume router CPU resources to process the updates.

Distance vector routing protocols share certain characteristics.

Periodic Updates are sent at regular intervals (30 seconds for RIP and 90 seconds for IGRP). Even if the topology has not changed in several days, periodic updates continue to be sent to all neighbors.

Neighbors are routers that share a link and are configured to use the same routing protocol. The router is only aware of the network addresses of its own interfaces and the remote network addresses it can reach through its neighbors. It has no broader knowledge of the network topology. **Routers using distance vector routing are not aware of the network topology.**

Broadcast Updates are sent to 255.255.255.255. Neighboring routers that are configured with the same routing protocol will process the updates. All other devices will also process the update up to Layer 3 before discarding it. Some distance vector routing protocols use multicast addresses instead of broadcast addresses.

Entire Routing Table Updates are sent, with some exceptions to be discussed later, periodically to all neighbors. Neighbors receiving these updates must process the entire update to find pertinent information and discard the rest. Some distance vector routing protocols like EIGRP do not send periodic routing table updates.

4.1.3 Routing Protocol Algorithms

Refer to
Figure
in online course

The Purpose of the Algorithm

At the core of the distance vector protocol is the algorithm. The algorithm is used to calculate the best paths and then send that information to the neighbors.

An algorithm is a procedure for accomplishing a certain task, starting at a given initial state and terminating in a defined end state. Different routing protocols use different algorithms to install routes in the routing table, send updates to neighbors, and make path determination decisions.

The algorithm used for the routing protocols defines the following processes:

- Mechanism for sending and receiving routing information.

- Mechanism for calculating the best paths and installing routes in the routing table.

- Mechanism for detecting and reacting to topology changes.

In the animation, R1 and R2 are configured with a routing protocol. The algorithm sends and receives updates. Both R1 and R2 then glean new information from the update. In this case, each router learns about a new network. The algorithm on each router makes its calculations independently and updates the routing table with the new information. When the LAN on R2 goes down, the algorithm constructs a "triggered" update and sends it to R1. R1 then removes the network from the routing table. Triggered updates will be discusses later in this chapter.

4.1.4 Routing Protocol Characteristics

Refer to
Figure
in online course

Routing Protocols Characteristics

Routing protocols can be compared based on the following characteristics:

- *Time to Convergence* - Time to convergence defines how quickly the routers in the network topology share routing information and reach a state of consistent knowledge. The faster the convergence, the more preferable the protocol. Routing loops can occur when inconsistent routing tables are not updated due to slow convergence in a changing network.

- *Scalability* - Scalability defines how large a network can become based on the routing protocol that is deployed. The larger the network is, the more scalable the routing protocol needs to be.

- *Classless (Use of VLSM) or Classful* - Classless routing protocols include the subnet mask in the updates. This feature supports the use of *Variable Length Subnet Masking (VLSM)* and better route summarization. Classful routing protocols do not include the subnet mask and cannot support VLSM.

- *Resource Usage* - Resource usage includes the requirements of a routing protocol such as memory space, CPU utilization, and link bandwidth utilization. Higher resource requirements necessitate more powerful hardware to support the routing protocol operation in addition to the packet forwarding processes.

- *Implementation and Maintenance* - Implementation and maintenance describes the level of knowledge that is required for a network administrator to implement and maintain the network based on the routing protocol deployed.

The advantages and disadvantages of distance vector routing protocols are shown in the table.

Refer to
Figure
in online course

Routing Protocol Learning Check

In the figure, all the routing protocols discussed in the course are compared based on these characteristics. Although IGRP is no longer supported by the IOS, it is shown here to compare it with the Enhanced version. Also, although the IS-IS routing protocol is covered in the CCNP courses, it is shown here because it is a commonly used interior gateway protocol.

Study the figure, and then click the Reset button to empty the table. Drag and drop the appropriate characteristics to each routing protocol. Based on the information previously discussed, you should be able to identify the advantages and disadvantages of distance vector routing protocols.

4.2 Network Discovery

4.2.1 Cold Start

Refer to
Figure
in online course

When a router *cold starts* or powers up, it knows nothing about the network topology. It does not even know that there are devices on the other end of its links. The only information that a router has is from its own saved configuration file stored in NVRAM. Once a router boots successfully, it applies the saved configuration. As described in Chapter 1 and Chapter 2, if the IP addressing is configured correctly, then the router will initially discover its own directly connected networks.

Initial Network Discovery

In the example in the figure, after a cold start and before the exchange of routing information, the routers initially discover their own directly connected networks and subnet masks. This information is added to their routing tables:

R1

- 10.1.0.0 available through interface FastEthernet 0/0

- 10.2.0.0 available through interface Serial 0/0/0

R2

- 10.2.0.0 available through interface Serial 0/0/0

- 10.3.0.0 available through interface Serial 0/0/1

R3

- 10.3.0.0 available through interface Serial 0/0/1

- 10.4.0.0 available through interface FastEthernet 0/0

Play the animation to watch this initial discovery of connected networks for R1. With this initial information, the routers start to exchange routing information.

4.2.2 Initial Exchange of Routing Information

Refer to
Figure
in online course

If a routing protocol is configured, the routers begin exchanging routing updates. Initially, these updates only include information about their directly connected networks. Upon receiving an update, the router checks it for new information. Any routes that are not currently in its routing table are added.

Initial Exchange

Play the animation to see R1, R2, and R3 start the initial exchange. All three routers send their routing tables to their neighbors, which at this point only contains the directly connected networks. Each router processes updates in the following manner:

R1

- Sends an update about network 10.1.0.0 out the Serial0/0/0 interface
- Sends an update about network 10.2.0.0 out the FastEthernet0/0 interface
- Receives update from R2 about network 10.3.0.0 with a metric of 1
- Stores network 10.3.0.0 in the routing table with a metric of 1

R2

- Sends an update about network 10.3.0.0 out the Serial 0/0/0 interface
- Sends an update about network 10.2.0.0 out the Serial 0/0/1 interface
- Receives an update from R1 about network 10.1.0.0 with a metric of 1
- Stores network 10.1.0.0 in the routing table with a metric of 1
- Receives an update from R3 about network 10.4.0.0 with a metric of 1
- Stores network 10.4.0.0 in the routing table with a metric of 1

R3

- Sends an update about network 10.4.0.0 out the Serial 0/0/1 interface
- Sends an update about network 10.3.0.0 out the FastEthernet0/0
- Receives an update from R2 about network 10.2.0.0 with a metric of 1
- Stores network 10.2.0.0 in the routing table with a metric of 1

After this first round of update exchanges, each router knows about the connected networks of their directly connected neighbors. However, did you notice that R1 does not yet know about 10.4.0.0 and that R3 does not yet know about 10.1.0.0? Full knowledge and a converged network will not take place until there is another exchange of routing information.

4.2.3 Exchange of Routing Information

Refer to
Figure
in online course

At this point the routers have knowledge about their own directly connected networks and about the connected networks of their immediate neighbors. Continuing the journey toward convergence, the routers exchange the next round of periodic updates. Each router again checks the updates for new information.

Next Update

Play the animation to see R1, R2, and R3 send the latest routing table to their neighbors. Each router processes updates in the following manner:

R1

- Sends an update about network 10.1.0.0 out the Serial 0/0/0 interface.
- Sends an update about networks 10.2.0.0 and 10.3.0.0 out the FastEthernet0/0 interface.
- Receives an update from R2 about network 10.4.0.0 with a metric of 2.

- Stores network 10.4.0.0 in the routing table with a metric of 2.

- Same update from R2 contains information about network 10.3.0.0 with a metric of 1. There is no change; therefore, the routing information remains the same.

R2

- Sends an update about networks 10.3.0.0 and 10.4.0.0 out of Serial 0/0/0 interface.

- Sends an update about networks 10.1.0.0 and 10.2.0.0 out of Serial 0/0/1 interface.

- Receives an update from R1 about network 10.1.0.0. There is no change; therefore, the routing information remains the same.

- Receives an update from R3 about network 10.4.0.0. There is no change; therefore, the routing information remains the same.

R3

- Sends an update about network 10.4.0.0 out the Serial 0/0/1 interface.

- Sends an update about networks 10.2.0.0 and 10.3.0.0 out the FastEthernet0/0 interface.

- Receives an update from R2 about network 10.1.0.0 with a metric of 2.

- Stores network 10.1.0.0 in the routing table with a metric of 2.

- Same update from R2 contains information about network 10.2.0.0 with a metric of 1. There is no change; therefore, the routing information remains the same.

Note: Distance vector routing protocols typically implement a technique known as *split horizon*. Split horizon prevents information from being sent out the same interface from which it was received. For example, R2 would not send an update out Serial 0/0/0 containing the network 10.1.0.0 because R2 learned about that network through Serial 0/0/0. This mechanism will be explained in more detail later in this chapter.

4.2.4 Convergence

Refer to **Figure** in online course

The amount of time it takes for a network to converge is directly proportional to the size of that network. In the animation, a branch router in Region 4 (B2-R4) is cold starting. The animation shows the propagation of new routing information as updates are sent between neighboring routers. It takes five rounds of periodic update intervals before most of the branch routers in Regions 1, 2, and 3 learn about the new routes advertised by B2-R4. Routing protocols are compared based on how fast they can propagate this information - their speed to convergence.

The speed of achieving convergence consists of:

- How quickly the routers propagate a change in the topology in a routing update to its neighbors.

- The speed of calculating best path routes using the new routing information collected.

A network is not completely operable until it has converged, therefore, network administrators prefer routing protocols with shorter convergence times.

4.3 Routing Table Maintenance

4.3.1 Periodic Updates: RIPv1 and IGRP

Refer to
Figure
in online course

Maintaining the Routing Table

Many distance vector protocols employ periodic updates to exchange routing information with their neighbors and to maintain up-to-date routing information in the routing table. RIP and IGRP are examples of two such protocols.

In the animation, the routers are periodically sending the routing table to neighbors. The term *periodic updates* refers to the fact that a router sends the complete routing table to its neighbors at a predefined interval. For RIP, these updates are sent every 30 seconds as a broadcast (255.255.255.255) whether or not there has been a topology change. This 30-second interval is a route update timer that also aids in tracking the age of routing information in the routing table.

The age of routing information in a routing table is refreshed each time an update is received. This way information in the routing table can be maintained when there is a topology change. Changes may occur for several reasons, including:

- Failure of a link
- Introduction of a new link
- Failure of a router
- Change of link parameters

Refer to
Figure
in online course

RIP Timers

In addition to the update timer, the IOS implements three additional timers for RIP:

- Invalid
- Flush
- Holddown

Invalid Timer. If an update has not been received to refresh an existing route after 180 seconds (the default), the route is marked as invalid by setting the metric to 16. The route is retained in the routing table until the flush timer expires.

Flush Timer. By default, the flush timer is set for 240 seconds, which is 60 seconds longer than the invalid timer. When the flush timer expires, the route is removed from the routing table.

Holddown Timer. This timer stabilizes routing information and helps prevent routing loops during periods when the topology is converging on new information. Once a route is marked as unreachable, it must stay in holddown long enough for all routers in the topology to learn about the unreachable network. By default, the holddown timer is set for 180 seconds. The holddown timer is discussed in more detail later in this chapter.

Click `show ip route` in the figure.

The timer values can be verified with two commands: `show ip route` and `show ip protocols`. Notice in the output from `show ip route` that each route learned through RIP shows the elapsed time since the last update, expressed in seconds.

Click `show ip protocols` in the figure.

This information is also repeated in the `show ip protocols` output under the heading `Last Update`. The `show ip protocols` command details when this router, R1, is due to send out its next round of updates. It also lists the invalid, holddown, and flush timer default values.

4.3.2 Bounded Updates: EIGRP

Refer to
Figure
in online course

Unlike other distance vector routing protocols, EIGRP does not send periodic updates. Instead, EIGRP sends *bounded updates* about a route when a path changes or the metric for that route changes. When a new route becomes available or when a route needs to be removed, EIGRP sends an update only about that network instead of the entire table. This information is sent only to those routers that need it.

EIGRP uses updates that are:

- Non-periodic because they are not sent out on a regular basis.

- Partial updates sent only when there is a change in topology that influences routing information.

- Bounded, meaning the propagation of partial updates are automatically bounded so that only those routers that need the information are updated.

Note: More details on how EIGRP operates will be presented in Chapter 9.

4.3.3 Triggered Updates

Refer to
Figure
in online course

To speed up the convergence when there is a topology change, RIP uses triggered updates. A triggered update is a routing table update that is sent immediately in response to a routing change. Triggered updates do not wait for update timers to expire. The detecting router immediately sends an update message to adjacent routers. The receiving routers, in turn, generate triggered updates that notify their neighbors of the change.

Triggered updates are sent when one of the following occurs:

- An interface changes state (up or down)

- A route has entered (or exited) the "unreachable" state

- A route is installed in the routing table

Using only triggered updates would be sufficient if there were a guarantee that the wave of updates would reach every appropriate router immediately. However, there are two problems with triggered updates:

- Packets containing the update message can be dropped or corrupted by some link in the network.

- The triggered updates do not happen instantaneously. It is possible that a router that has not yet received the triggered update will issue a regular update at just the wrong time, causing the bad route to be reinserted in a neighbor that had already received the triggered update.

Play the animation to see how a network topology change is propagated through the network. When network 10.4.0.0 becomes unavailable and router 3 becomes aware of that, it sends out the information to its neighbors. The information is then propagated through the network.

4.3.4 Random Jitter

Refer to
Figure
in online course

Issues with Synchronized Updates

When multiple routers transmit routing updates at the same time on multi-access LAN segments (as shown in the animation), the update packets can collide and cause delays or consume too much bandwidth.

Note: Collisions are only an issue with hubs and not with switches.

Sending updates at the same time is known as the synchronization of updates. Synchronization can become a problem with distance vector routing protocols due to their usage of periodic updates. As more routers' timers become synchronized, more collisions of updates and more delays occur in the network. Initially, the updates of routers will not be synchronized. But over time, the timers across a network will become globally synchronized.

The Solution

To prevent the synchronization of updates between routers, the Cisco IOS uses a random variable, called RIP_JITTER, which subtracts a variable amount of time to the update interval for each router in the network. This random jitter, or variable amount of time, ranges from 0% to 15% of the specified update interval. In this way, the update interval varies randomly in a range from 25 to 30 seconds for the default 30-second interval.

4.4 Routing Loops

4.4.1 Definition and Implications

Refer to **Figure** in online course

What is a Routing Loop?

A routing loop is a condition in which a packet is continuously transmitted within a series of routers without ever reaching its intended destination network. A routing loop can occur when two or more routers have routing information that incorrectly indicates that a valid path to an unreachable destination exists.

The loop may be a result of:

- Incorrectly configured static routes

- Incorrectly configured route *redistribution* (redistribution is a process of handing the routing information from one routing protocol to another routing protocol and is discussed in CCNP-level courses)

- Inconsistent routing tables not being updated due to slow convergence in a changing network

- Incorrectly configured or installed discard routes

Distance vector routing protocols are simple in their operations. Their simplicity results in protocol drawbacks like routing loops. Routing loops are less of a problem with link-state routing protocols but can occur under certain circumstances.

Note: The IP protocol has its own mechanism to prevent the possibility of a packet traversing the network endlessly. IP has a Time-to-Live (TTL) field and its value is decremented by 1 at each router. If the TTL is zero, the router drops the packet.

What are the Implications of Routing Loops?

A routing loop can have a devastating effect on a network, resulting in degraded network performance or even a network downtime.

A routing loop can create the following conditions:

- Link bandwidth will be used for traffic looping back and forth between the routers in a loop.

- A router's CPU will be strained due to looping packets.

- A router's CPU will be burdened with useless packet forwarding that will negatively impact the convergence of the network.

- Routing updates may get lost or not be processed in a timely manner. These conditions would introduce additional routing loops, making the situation even worse.

- Packets may get lost in "black holes."

Play the animation to view a possible routing loop scenario in which mechanisms to prevent such loops do not exist.

As you can see, routing loops eat up bandwidth and also router resources, resulting in a slow or even unresponsive network.

There are a number of mechanisms available to eliminate routing loops, primarily with distance vector routing protocols. These mechanisms include:

- Defining a maximum metric to prevent *count to infinity*

- Holddown timers

- Split horizon

- *Route poisoning* or *poison reverse*

- Triggered updates

Triggered updates were discussed in the previous section. The other loop avoidance mechanisms are discussed later in this chapter.

Use the Packet Tracer Activity to experience how a routing loop might occur with misconfigured static routes.

4.4.2 Problem: Count to Infinity

Refer to
Figure
in online course

Count to infinity is a condition that exists when inaccurate routing updates increase the metric value to "infinity" for a network that is no longer reachable. The animation shows what happens to the routing tables when all three routers continue to send inaccurate updates to each other.

4.4.3 Setting a Maximum

Refer to
Figure
in online course

To eventually stop the incrementing of the metric, **"infinity" is defined by setting a maximum metric value**. For example, RIP defines infinity as 16 hops - an "unreachable" metric. Once the routers "count to infinity," they mark the route as unreachable.

4.4.4 Preventing Routing Loops with Holddown Timers

Refer to
Figure
in online course

Earlier you learned that distance vector protocols employ triggered updates to speed up the convergence process. Remember that in addition to triggered updates, routers using distance vector routing protocols also send periodic updates. Let's imagine that a particular network is unstable. The interface resets as **up**, then **down**, then **up** again in rapid succession. The route is flapping. Using triggered updates, the routers might react too quickly and unknowingly create a routing loop. A routing loop could also be created by a periodic update that is sent by the routers during the instability. Holddown timers prevent routing loops from being created by these conditions. Holddown timers also help prevent the count to infinity condition.

Holddown timers are used to prevent regular update messages from inappropriately reinstating a route that may have gone bad. Holddown timers instruct routers to hold any changes that might affect routes for a specified period of time. If a route is identified as **down** or possibly down, any other information for that route containing the same status, or worse, is ignored for a predetermined amount of time (the holddown period). This means that routers will leave a route marked as *unreachable* in that state for a period of time that is long enough for updates to propagate the routing tables with the most current information.

Holddown timers work in the following way:

1. A router receives an update from a neighbor indicating that a network that previously was accessible is now no longer accessible.

2. The router marks the network as possibly down and starts the holddown timer.

3. If an update with a better metric for that network is received from any neighboring router during the holddown period, the network is reinstated and the holddown timer is removed.

4. If an update from any other neighbor is received during the holddown period with the same or worse metric for that network, that update is ignored. Thus, more time is allowed for the information about the change to be propagated.

5. Routers still forward packets to destination networks that are marked as possibly down. This allows the router to overcome any issues associated with intermittent connectivity. If the destination network truly is unavailable and the packets are forwarded, black hole routing is created and lasts until the holddown timer expires.

Play the animation to see an example of the holddown process.

4.4.5 Split Horizon Rule

Refer to **Figure** in online course

Another method used to prevent routing loops caused by slow convergence of a distance vector routing protocol is split horizon. **The split horizon rule says that a router should not advertise a network through the interface from which the update came.**

Applying split horizon to the previous example of route 10.4.0.0 produces the following actions:

- R3 advertises the 10.4.0.0 network to R2.

- R2 receives the information and updates its routing table.

- R2 then advertises the 10.4.0.0 network to R1 out S0/0/0. R2 does not advertise 10.4.0.0 to R3 out S0/0/1, because the route originated from that interface.

- R1 receives the information and updates its routing table.

- Because of split horizon, R1 also does not advertise the information about network 10.4.0.0 back to R2.

Complete routing updates are exchanged, with the exception of routes that violate the split horizon rule. The results look like this:

- R2 advertises networks 10.3.0.0 and 10.4.0.0 to R1.

- R2 advertises networks 10.1.0.0 and 10.2.0.0 to R3.

- R1 advertises network 10.1.0.0 to R2.

- R3 advertises network 10.4.0.0 to R2.

Play the animation to see this process.

Notice that R2 sends different routing updates to R1 and R3.

Note: Split horizon can be disabled by an administrator. Under certain conditions, this has to be done to achieve the proper routing. These conditions are discussed in later courses.

4.4.6 Split Horizon with Poison Reverse or Route Poisoning

Refer to
Figure
in online course

Route Poisoning

Route poisoning is yet another method employed by distance vector routing protocols to prevent routing loops. **Route poisoning is used to mark the route as unreachable in a routing update that is sent to other routers.** Unreachable is interpreted as a metric that is set to the maximum. For RIP, a poisoned route has a metric of 16.

Play the animation to see route poisoning in effect.

The following process occurs:

- Network 10.4.0.0 becomes unavailable due to a link failure.

- R3 poisons the metric with a value of 16 and then sends out a *triggered update* stating that 10.4.0.0 is unavailable.

- R2 processes that update. Because the metric is 16, R2 invalidates the routing entry in its routing table.

- R2 then sends the poison update to R1, indicating that route is unavailable, again by setting the metric value to 16.

- R1 processes the update and invalidates the routing entry for 10.4.0.0 in its routing table.

Route poisoning speeds up the convergence process as the information about 10.4.0.0 spreads through the network more quickly than waiting for the hop count to reach "infinity".

Refer to
Figure
in online course

Split Horizon with Poison Reverse

Poison reverse can be combined with the split horizon technique. The method is called split horizon with poison reverse. **The rule for split horizon with poison reverse states when sending updates out a specific interface, designate any networks that were learned on that interface as unreachable.**

The concept of split horizon with poison reverse is that explicitly telling a router to ignore a route is better than not telling it about the route in the first place.

Play the animation to see an example of the split horizon with poison reverse in effect.

The following process occurs:

- Network 10.4.0.0 becomes unavailable due to a link failure.

- R3 poisons the metric with a value of 16 and then sends out a triggered update stating that 10.4.0.0 is unavailable.

- R2 processes that update, invalidates the routing entry in its routing table, and immediately sends a poison reverse back to R3.

Poison reverse is a specific circumstance that overrides split horizon. It occurs to ensure that R3 is not susceptible to incorrect updates about network 10.4.0.0.

Note: Split horizon is enabled by default. However split horizon with poison reverse may not be the default on all IOS implementations.

4.4.7 IP and TTL

Refer to
Figure
in online course

Time to Live (TTL) is an 8-bit field in the IP header that limits the number of hops a packet can traverse through the network before it is discarded. The purpose of the TTL field is to avoid a situation in which an undeliverable packet keeps circulating on the network endlessly. With TTL, the 8-bit field is set with a value by the source device of the packet. The TTL is decreased by one by every router on the route to its destination. If the TTL field reaches zero before the packet arrives at its destination, the packet is discarded and the router sends an Internet Control Message Protocol (ICMP) error message back to the source of the IP packet.

The animation shows that even in the case of a routing loop packets will not loop endlessly in the network. Eventually the TTL value will be decreased to 0 and the packet will be discarded by the router.

4.5 Distance Vector Routing Protocols today

4.5.1 RIP and EIGRP

Refer to
Figure
in online course

For distance vector routing protocols, there really are only two choices: RIP or EIGRP. The decision about which routing protocol to use in a given situation is influenced by a number of factors including:

- Size of the network
- Compatibility between models of routers
- Administrative knowledge required

RIP

Over the years, RIP has evolved from a classful routing protocol (RIPv1) to a classless routing protocol (RIPv2). RIPv2 is a standardized routing protocol that works in a mixed vendor router environment. Routers made by different companies can communicate using RIP. It is one of the easiest routing protocols to configure, making it a good choice for small networks. However, RIPv2 still has limitations. Both RIPv1 and RIPv2 have a route metric that is based only on hop count and which is limited to 15 hops.

Features of RIP:

- Supports split horizon and split horizon with poison reverse to prevent loops.
- Is capable of load balancing up to six equal cost paths . The default is four equal cost paths.

RIPv2 introduced the following improvements to RIPv1:

- Includes the subnet mask in the routing updates, making it a classless routing protocol.
- Has authentication mechanism to secure routing table updates.
- Supports variable length subnet mask (VLSM).
- Uses multicast addresses instead of broadcast.
- Supports manual route summarization.

EIGRP

Enhanced IGRP (EIGRP) was developed from IGRP, another distance vector protocol. EIGRP is a classless, distance vector routing protocol with features found in link-state routing protocols. However, unlike RIP or OSPF, EIGRP is a proprietary protocol developed by Cisco and only runs on Cisco routers.

EIGRP features include:

- Triggered updates (EIGRP has no periodic updates).

- Use of a *topology table* to maintain all the routes received from neighbors (not only the best paths).

- Establishment of adjacencies with neighboring routers using the EIGRP hello protocol.

- Support for VLSM and manual route summarization. These allow EIGRP to create hierarchically structured large networks.

Advantages of EIGRP:

- Although routes are propagated in a distance vector manner, the metric is based on minimum bandwidth and cumulative delay of the path rather than hop count.

- Fast convergence due to Diffusing Update Algorithm (DUAL) route calculation. DUAL allows the insertion of backup routes into the EIGRP topology table, which are used in case the primary route fails. Because it is a local procedure, the switchover to the backup route is immediate and does not involve the action in any other routers.

- Bounded updates mean that EIGRP uses less bandwidth, especially in large networks with many routes.

- EIGRP supports multiple Network layer protocols through Protocol Dependent Modules, which include support for IP, IPX, and AppleTalk.

4.6 Lab Activities

4.6.1 Lab Activities

Refer to
Lab Activity
for this chapter

In this lab activity, you recreate a network based only on the outputs from the `show ip route` command. Then, to verify your answer you configure the routers and check the actual routing table to the routing table shown in the lab documentation.

Summary and Review

Refer to
Figure
in online course

Summary

One way of classifying routing protocols is by the type of algorithm they use to determine the best path to a destination network. Routing protocols can be classified as distance vector, link state, or path vector. Distance vector means that routes are advertised as vectors of distance and direction. Distance is defined in terms of a metric such as hop count and direction is simply the next-hop router or exit interface.

Distance vector routing protocols include:

- RIPv1
- RIPv2
- IGRP
- EIGRP

Routers that use distance vector routing protocols determine best path to remote networks based on the information they learn from their neighbors. If Router X learns of two paths to the same network, one through Router Y at 7 hops, and another route through Router Z at 10 hops, the router will choose the shorter path using Router Y as the next-hop router. Router X has no knowledge of what the network looks like beyond Routers Y and Z, and can only make its best path decision based on the information sent to it by these two routers. Distance vector routing protocols do not have a map of the topology as do link state routing protocols.

Network discovery is an important process of any routing protocol. Some distance vector routing protocols such as RIP go through a step-by-step process of learning and sharing routing information with their neighbors. As routes are learned from one neighbor, that information is passed on to other neighbors with an increase in the routing metric.

Routing protocols also need to maintain their routing tables to keep them current and accurate. RIP exchanges routing table information with its neighbors every 30 seconds. EIGRP, another distance vector routing protocol, does not send these periodic updates and only sends a "bounded" update when there is a change in the topology and only to those routers that need that information. EIGRP is discussed in a later chapter.

RIP also uses timers to determine when a neighboring router is no longer available, or when some of the routers may not have current routing information. This is typically because the network has not yet converged due to a recent change in the topology. Distance vector routing protocols also use triggered updates to help speed up convergence time.

One disadvantage of distance vector routing protocols is the potential for routing loops. Routing loops can occur when the network is in an unconverged state. Distance vector routing protocols use holddown timers to prevent the router from using another route to a recently down network until all of the routers have had enough time to learn about this change in the topology.

Split horizon and split horizon with poison reverse are also used by routers to help prevent routing loops. The split horizon rule states that a router should never advertise a route through the interface from which it learned that route. Split horizon with poison reverse means that it is better to explicitly state that this router does not have a route to this network by poisoning the route with a metric stating that the route is unreachable.

Distance vector routing protocols are sometime referred to as "routing by rumor", although this can be somewhat of a misnomer. Distance vector routing protocols are very popular with many network administrators as they are typically easily understood and simple to implement. This does

Refer to
Figure
in online course

not necessarily mean link-state routing protocols are any more complicated or difficult to configure. Unfortunately, link-state routing protocols have received this somewhat unwarranted reputation. We will learn in later chapters that link-state routing protocols are as easy to understand and configure as distance vector routing protocols.

Refer to **Packet Tracer Activity** for this chapter

The Packet Tracer Skills Integration Challenge Activity for this chapter is very similar to the activity you completed at the end of Chapter 3. The scenario is slightly different, allowing you to better practice your skills. In this activity, you build a network from the ground up. Starting with an addressing space and network requirements, you must implement a network design that satisfies the specifications. Then implement an effective static routing configuration.

Packet Tracer Skills Integration Instructions (PDF)

To Learn More

Refer to
Figure
in online course

Understanding the distance vector algorithm is not difficult. There are many book and online sources that show how algorithms such as the Bellman-Ford algorithm are used in networking. There are several web sites devoted to explaining how these algorithms work. Seek out some of the resources and familiarize yourself with how this algorithm works.

Here are some suggested resources:

- *Interconnections, Bridges, Routers, Switches, and Internetworking Protocols*, by Radia Perlman
- *Cisco IP Routing*, by Alex Zinin
- *Routing the Internet*, by Christian Huitema

Go to
the online course
to take the quiz.

Quiz

Take the chapter quiz to test your knowledge.

Your Chapter Notes

CHAPTER 5

RIP version 1

Routing Information Protocol

Chapter Introduction

Refer to
Figure
in online course

Over the years, routing protocols have evolved to meet the increasing demands of complex networks. The first protocol used was Routing Information Protocol (RIP). RIP still enjoys popularity because of its simplicity and widespread support.

Understanding RIP is important to your networking studies for two reasons. First, RIP is still in use today. You may encounter a network implementation that is large enough to need a routing protocol, yet simple enough to use RIP effectively. Second, familiarity with many of the fundamental concepts of RIP will help you to compare RIP with other protocols. Understanding how RIP operates and its implementation will make learning other routing protocols easier.

This chapter covers the details of the first version of RIP, including a bit of history, RIPv1 characteristics, operation, configuration, verification, and troubleshooting. Throughout the chapter, you can use Packet Tracer activities to practice what you learn. At the end of the chapter, three hands-on labs and a Packet Tracer Skills Integration Challenge activity are provided to help you integrate RIPv1 into your growing set of networking knowledge and skills.

5.1 RIPv1: Distance Vector, Classful Routing Protocol

5.1.1 Background and Perspective

RIP Historical Impact

Refer to
Figure
in online course

RIP is the oldest of the distance vector routing protocols. Although RIP lacks the sophistication of more advanced routing protocols, its simplicity and continued widespread use is a testament to its longevity. RIP is not a protocol "on the way out." In fact, an IPv6 form of RIP called RIPng (next generation) is now available.

Click the dates in the figure to compare RIP and network protocol development over time.

RIP evolved from an earlier protocol developed at Xerox, called Gateway Information Protocol (GWINFO). With the development of Xerox Network System (*XNS*), GWINFO evolved into RIP. It later gained popularity because it was implemented in the Berkeley Software Distribution (BSD) as a daemon named *routed* (pronounced "route-dee", not "rout-ed"). Various other vendors made their own, slightly different implementations of RIP. Recognizing the need for standardization of the protocol, Charles Hedrick wrote RFC 1058 in 1988, in which he documented the existing protocol and specified some improvements. Since then, RIP has been improved with RIPv2 in 1994 and with RIPng in 1997.

Note: The first version of RIP is often called RIPv1 to distinguish it from RIPv2. However, both versions share many of the same features. When discussing features common to both versions, we will refer to RIP. When discussing features unique to each version, we will use RIPv1 and RIPv2. RIPv2 is discussed in a later chapter.

Links

"RFC 1058: Routing Information Protocol," http://www.ietf.org/rfc/rfc1058.txt

5.1.2 RIPv1 Characteristics and Message Format

Refer to
Figure
in online course

RIP Characteristics

As discussed in Chapter 4, "Distance Vector Routing Protocols," RIP has the following key characteristics:

- RIP is a distance vector routing protocol.

- RIP uses hop count as its only metric for path selection.

- Advertised routes with hop counts greater than 15 are unreachable.

- Messages are broadcast every 30 seconds.

Roll over the fields in the Encapsulated RIPv1 Message to see the encapsulation process.

The data portion of a RIP message is encapsulated into a UDP segment, with both source and destination port numbers set to 520. The IP header and data link headers add broadcast destination addresses before the message is sent out to all RIP configured interfaces.

Refer to
Figure
in online course

RIP Message Format: RIP Header

Three fields are specified in the four byte header portion shown in orange in the figure. The **Command** field specifies the message type, discussed in more detail in the next section. The **Version** field is set to 1 for RIP version 1. The third field is labeled **Must be zero**. "Must be zero" fields provide room for future expansion of the protocol.

RIP Message Format: Route Entry

The route entry portion of the message includes three fields with content: **Address family identifier** (set to 2 for IP unless a router is requesting a full routing table, in which case the field is set to zero), **IP address**, and **Metric**. This route entry portion represents one destination route with its associated metric. One RIP update can contain up to 25 route entries. The maximum datagram size is 504 bytes, not including the IP or UDP headers.

Why are there so many fields set to zero?

RIP was developed before IP and was used for other network protocols (like XNS). BSD also had its influence. Initially, the extra space was added with the intention of supporting larger address spaces in the future. As we will see in Chapter 7, RIPv2 has now used most of these empty fields.

5.1.3 RIP Operation

Refer to
Figure
in online course

RIP Request/Response Process

RIP uses two message types specified in the Command field: **Request message** and **Response message**.

Click Play to view the request/response process.

Each RIP-configured interface sends out a request message on startup, requesting that all RIP neighbors send their complete routing tables. A response message is sent back by RIP-enabled neighbors. When the requesting router receives the responses, it evaluates each route entry. If a route entry is new, the receiving router installs the route in the routing table. If the route is already in the table, the existing entry is replaced if the new entry has a better hop count. The startup router then sends a triggered update out all RIP-enabled interfaces containing its own routing table so that RIP neighbors can be informed of any new routes.

Refer to
Figure
in online course

IP Address Classes and Classful Routing

You may recall from previous studies that IP addresses assigned to hosts were initially divided into 3 classes: class A, class B, and class C. Each class was assigned a default subnet mask, as shown in the figure. Knowing the default subnet mask for each class is important to understanding how RIP operates.

RIP is a classful routing protocol. As you may have realized from the previous message format discussion, RIPv1 does not send subnet mask information in the update. Therefore, a router either uses the subnet mask configured on a local interface, or applies the default subnet mask based on the address class. Due to this limitation, RIPv1 networks cannot be discontiguous nor can they implement VLSM.

IP Addressing is discussed further in Chapter 6, "VLSM and CIDR." You can also visit the links below for a review of the classes.

Links

"Internet Protocol," http://www.ietf.org/rfc/rfc791.txt

"IP Addressing and Subnetting for New Users," http://www.cisco.com/en/US/tech/tk365/technologies_tech_note09186a00800a67f5.shtml

5.1.4 Administrative Distance

Refer to
Figure
in online course

As you know from Chapter 3, "Introduction to Dynamic Routing Protocols," administrative distance (AD) is the trustworthiness (or preference) of the route source. RIP has a default administrative distance of 120. When compared to other interior gateway protocols, RIP is the least-preferred routing protocol. IS-IS, OSPF, IGRP, and EIGRP all have lower default AD values.

Remember, you can check the administrative distance using the `show ip route` or `show ip protocols` commands.

5.2 Basic RIPv1 Configuration
5.2.1 Basic RIPv1 Configuration

Refer to
Figure
in online course

The figure shows the three router topology we used in Chapter 2, "Static Routing". Physically, the topology is the same except that we will not need PCs attached to the LANs. Logically, however, the addressing scheme is different. We are using five class C network addresses.

Click Address Table in the figure to see the interface addressing for each router.

Refer to **Packet
Tracer Activity**
for this chapter

Use the Packet Tracer Activity to configure and activate all the interfaces for the RIP Topology: Scenario A. Detailed instructions are provided within the activity.

5.2.2 Enabling RIP: router rip command

Refer to
Figure
in online course

To enable a dynamic routing protocol, enter the global configuration mode and use the **router** command. As shown in the figure, if you type a space followed by a question mark, a list of all the available routing protocols supported by the IOS displays.

To enter the router configuration mode for RIP, enter **router rip** at the global configuration prompt. Notice that the prompt changes from a global configuration prompt to the following:

R1(config-router)#

This command does not directly start the RIP process. Instead, it provides access to configure routing protocol settings. No routing updates are sent.

If you need to completely remove the RIP routing process from a device, negate the command with **no router rip**. This command stops the RIP process and erases all existing RIP configurations.

5.2.3 Specifying Networks

Refer to
Figure
in online course

By entering the RIP router configuration mode, the router is instructed to run RIP. But the router still needs to know which local interfaces it should use for communication with other routers, as well as which locally connected networks it should advertise to those routers. To enable RIP routing for a network, use the **network** command in the router configuration mode and enter the classful network address for each directly connected network.

Router(config-router)#**network** *directly-connected-classful-network-address*

The **network** command:

- Enables RIP on all interfaces that belong to a specific network. Associated interfaces will now both send and receive RIP updates.

- Advertises the specified network in RIP routing updates sent to other routers every 30 seconds.

Note: If you enter a subnet address, the IOS automatically converts it to a classful network address. For example, if you enter the command **network 192.168.1.32**, the router will convert it to **network 192.168.1.0**.

Refer to
Figure
in online course

In the figure, the **network** command is configured on all three routers for the directly connected networks. Notice that only classful networks were entered.

What happens if you enter a subnet address or interface IP address instead of the classful network address when using the **network** command for RIP configurations?

R3(config)#**router rip**
 R3(config-router)#**network 192.168.4.0**
R3(config-router)#**network 192.168.5.1**

In this example, we entered an interface IP address instead of the classful network address. Notice that the IOS does not give an error message. Instead, the IOS corrects the input and enters the classful network address. This is proven with the verification below.

R3#**show running-config**
 !
 router rip
 network 192.168.4.0
 network 192.168.5.0
 !

Refer to **Packet
Tracer Activity**
for this chapter

Use the Packet Tracer Activity to practice configuring RIP routing on all three routers in the topology. Detailed instructions are provided within the activity.

5.3 Verification and Troubleshooting

5.3.1 Verifying RIP: show ip route

Refer to
Figure
in online course

Powerful Troubleshooting Commands

To verify and troubleshoot routing, first use **show ip route** and **show ip protocols**. If you cannot isolate the problem using these two commands, then use **debug ip rip** to see exactly what is happening. These three commands are discussed in a suggested order that you might use to verify and troubleshoot a routing protocol configuration. Remember, before you configure any routing - whether static or dynamic - make sure all necessary interfaces are "up" and "up" with the **show ip interface brief** command.

Click R1, R2, and R3 to see the routing tables.

The **show ip route** command verifies that routes received by RIP neighbors are installed in a routing table. An **R** in the output indicates RIP routes. Because this command displays the entire routing table, including directly connected and static routes, it is normally the first command used to check for convergence. Routes may not immediately appear when you execute the command because networks take some time to converge. However, once routing is correctly configured on all routers, the **show ip route** command will reflect that each router has a full routing table, with a route to each network in the topology.

Click the Topology button.

As you can see in the figure, there are five networks in the topology. Each router lists five networks in the routing table; therefore, we can say that all three routers are converged because each router has a route to every network shown in the topology.

Refer to
Figure
in online course

Interpreting show ip route Output

Using the information in the figure, let's focus on one RIP route learned by R1 and interpret the output shown in the routing table.

R 192.168.5.0/24 [120/2] via 192.168.2.2, 00:00:23, Serial0/0/0

The listing of routes with an **R** code is a quick way to verify that RIP is actually running on this router. If RIP is not at least partially configured, you will not see any RIP routes.

Next, the remote network address and subnet mask are listed (**192.168.5.0/24**).

The AD value (**120** for RIP) and the distance to the network (**2** hops) is shown in brackets.

The next-hop IP address of the advertising router is listed (R2 at **192.168.2.2**) and how many seconds have passed since the last update (**00:00:23**, in this case).

Finally, the exit interface that this router will use for traffic destined for the remote network is listed (**Serial 0/0/0**).

5.3.2 Verifying RIP: show ip protocols

Refer to
Figure
in online course

Interpreting show ip protocols Output

If a network is missing from the routing table, check the routing configuration using **show ip protocols**. The **show ip protocols** command displays the routing protocol that is currently configured on the router. This output can be used to verify most RIP parameters to confirm that:

- RIP routing is configured

- The correct interfaces send and receive RIP updates

■ The router advertises the correct networks

■ RIP neighbors are sending updates

This command is also very useful when verifying the operations of other routing protocols, as we will see later with EIGRP and OSPF.

Click button 1 in the figure.

The first line of output verifies that RIP routing is configured and running on router R2. As we saw in the previous section, "Basic RIPv1Configuration," at least one active interface with an associated `network` command is needed before RIP routing will start.

Click button 2 in the figure.

These are the timers that show when the next round of updates will be sent out from this router - 23 seconds from now, in the example.

Click button 3 in the figure.

This information relates to filtering updates and redistributing routes, if configured on this router. Filtering and redistribution are both CCNP-level topics.

Click button 4 in the figure.

This block of output contains information about which RIP version is currently configured and which interfaces are participating in RIP updates.

Click button 5 in the figure.

This part of the output shows that router R2 is currently summarizing at the classful network boundary and by default will use up to four equal-cost routes to load balance traffic.

Click button 6 in the figure.

The classful networks configured with the `network` command are listed next. These are the networks that R2 will include in its RIP updates.

Click button 7 in the figure.

Scroll down to see the remaining output. Here, the RIP neighbors are listed as **Routing Information Sources**. **Gateway** is the next-hop IP address of the neighbor that is sending R2 updates. **Distance** is the AD that R2 uses for updates sent by this neighbor. **Last Update** is the seconds since the last update was received from this neighbor.

5.3.3 Verifying RIP: debug ip rip

Refer to
Figure
in online course

Interpreting `debug ip rip` Output

Most RIP configuration errors involve an incorrect `network` statement configuration, a missing `network` statement configuration, or the configuration of discontiguous subnets in a classful environment. As shown in the figure, an effective command used to find issues with RIP updates is the `debug ip rip`. This command displays RIP routing updates as they are sent and received. Because updates are periodic, you need to wait for the next round of updates before seeing any output.

Click button 1 in the figure.

First we see an update coming in from R1 on interface Serial 0/0/0. Notice that R1 only sends one route to the 192.168.1.0 network. No other routes are sent because doing so would violate the split horizon rule. R1 is not allowed to advertise networks back to R2 that R2 previously sent to R1.

Click button 2 in the figure.

The next update that is received is from R3. Again, because of the split horizon rule, R3 only sends one route - the 192.168.5.0 network.

Click button 3 in the figure.

R2 sends out its own updates. First, R2 builds an update to send out the FastEthernet0/0 interface. The update includes the entire routing table except for network 192.168.3.0, which is attached to FastEthernet0/0.

Click button 4 in the figure.

Next, R2 builds an update to send to R3. Three routes are included. R2 does not advertise the network R2 and R3 share nor does it advertise the 192.168.5.0 network because of split horizon.

Click button 5 in the figure.

Finally, R2 builds an update to send to R1. Three routes are included. R2 does not advertise the network that R2 and R1 share, nor does it advertise the 192.168.1.0 network because of split horizon.

Note: If you waited another 30 seconds, you would see all the debug output shown in the figure repeat because RIP sends out periodic updates every 30 seconds.

Click button 6 in the figure.

To stop monitoring RIP updates on R2, enter the `no debug ip rip` command or simply `undebug all`, as shown in figure.

Reviewing this debug output, we can verify that RIP routing is fully operational on R2. But do you see a way that we could optimize RIP routing on R2? Does R2 need to send updates out FastEthernet0/0? We will see in the next topic how we can prevent unnecessary updates.

5.3.4 Passive Interfaces

Refer to
Figure
in online course

Unnecessary RIP Updates Impact Network

As you saw in the previous example, R2 is sending updates out FastEthernet0/0 even though no RIP device exists on that LAN. R2 has no way of knowing this and, as a result, sends an update every 30 seconds. Sending out unneeded updates on a LAN impacts the network in three ways:

1. Bandwidth is wasted transporting unnecessary updates. Because RIP updates are broadcast, switches will forward the updates out all ports.

2. All devices on the LAN must process the update up to the Transport layers, where the receiving device will discard the update.

3. Advertising updates on a broadcast network is a security risk. RIP updates can be intercepted with packet sniffing software. Routing updates can be modified and sent back to the router, corrupting the routing table with false metrics that misdirect traffic.

Stopping Unnecessary RIP Updates

You might think you could stop the updates by removing the 192.168.3.0 network from the configuration using the `no network 192.168.3.0` command, but then R2 would not advertise this LAN as a route in updates sent to R1 and R3. The correct solution is to use the `passive-interface` command, which prevents the transmission of routing updates through a router interface but still allows that network to be advertised to other routers. Enter the `passive-interface` command in router configuration mode.

```
Router(config-router)#passive-interface interface-type interface-number
```
This command stops routing updates out the specified interface. However, the network that the specified interface belongs to will still be advertised in routing updates that are sent out other interfaces.

In the figure, R2 is first configured with the `passive-interface` command to prevent routing updates on FastEthernet0/0 because no RIP neighbors exist on the LAN. The `show ip protocols` command is then used to verify the passive interface. Notice that the interface is no longer listed under **Interface**, but under a new section called **Passive Interface(s)**. Also notice that the network 192.168.3.0 is still listed under **Routing for Networks**, which means that this network is still included as a route entry in RIP updates that are sent to R1 and R3.

All routing protocols support the `passive-interface` command. You will be expected to use the `passive-interface` command when appropriate as part of your normal routing configuration.

Use the Packet Tracer Activity to verify RIP routing and stop RIP updates using the `passive-interface` command. Detailed instructions are provided within the activity.

5.4 Automatic Summarization

5.4.1 Modified Topology: Scenario B

Refer to
Figure
in online course

To aid the discussion of *automatic summarization*, the RIP topology shown in the figure has been modified with the following changes:

Three classful networks are used:

- 172.30.0.0/16
- 192.168.4.0/24
- 192.168.5.0/24

The 172.30.0.0/16 network is subnetted into three subnets:

- 172.30.1.0/24
- 172.30.2.0/24
- 172.30.3.0/24

The following devices are part of the 172.30.0.0/16 classful network address:

- All interfaces on R1
- S0/0/0 and Fa0/0 on R2

The 192.168.4.0/24 network is subnetted as a single subnet 192.168.4.8/30

Refer to
Figure
in online course

Click R1, R2, and R3 to view the configuration details for each router.

Notice that the `no shutdown` and `clock rate` commands are not needed because these commands are still configured from Scenario A. However, because new networks were added, the RIP routing process was completely removed with the `no router rip` command before enabling it again.

Click R1 in the figure.

In the output for R1, notice that both subnets were configured with the `network` command. This configuration is technically incorrect since RIPv1 sends the classful network address in its updates and not the subnet. Therefore, the IOS changed the configuration to reflect the correct, classful configuration, as can be seen with the `show run` output.

Click R2 in the figure.

In the output for R2, notice that the subnet 192.168.4.8 was configured with the **network** command. Again, this configuration is technically incorrect and the IOS changed it to 192.168.4.0 in the running configuration.

Click R3 in the figure.

The routing configuration for R3 is correct. The running configuration matches what was entered in router configuration mode.

Note: On assessment and certification exams, entering a subnet address instead of the classful network address in a **network** command is considered an incorrect answer.

5.4.2 Boundary Routers and Automatic Summarization

Refer to
Figure
in online course

As you know, RIP is a classful routing protocol that automatically summarizes classful networks across major network boundaries. In the figure, you can see that R2 has interfaces in more than one major classful network. This makes R2 a *boundary router* in RIP. Serial 0/0/0 and FastEthernet 0/0 interfaces on R2 are both inside the 172.30.0.0 boundary. The Serial 0/0/1 interface is inside the 192.168.4.0 boundary.

Because boundary routers summarize RIP subnets from one major network to the other, updates for the 172.30.1.0, 172.30.2.0 and 172.30.3.0 networks will automatically be summarized into 172.30.0.0 when sent out R2's Serial 0/0/1 interface.

We will see in the next two sections how boundary routers perform this summarization.

5.4.3 Processing RIP Updates

Refer to
Figure
in online course

Rules for Processing RIPv1 Updates

The following two rules govern RIPv1 updates:

- If a routing update and the interface on which it is received belong to the same major network, the subnet mask of the interface is applied to the network in the routing update.

- If a routing update and the interface on which it is received belong to different major networks, the classful subnet mask of the network is applied to the network in the routing update.

Example of RIPv1 Processing Updates

In the figure, R2 receives an update from R1 and enters the network in the routing table. How does R2 know that this subnet has a /24 (255.255.255.0) subnet mask? It knows because:

- R2 received this information on an interface that belongs to the same classful network (172.30.0.0) as that of the incoming 172.30.1.0 update.

- The IP address for which R2 received the "172.30.1.0 in 1 hops" message was on Serial 0/0/0 with an IP address of 172.30.2.2 and a subnet mask of 255.255.255.0 (/24).

- R2 uses its own subnet mask on this interface and applies it to this and all other 172.30.0.0 subnets that it receives on this interface - in this case, 172.30.1.0.

- The 172.30.1.0 /24 subnet was added to the routing table.

Routers running RIPv1 are limited to using the same subnet mask for all subnets with the same classful network.

As you will learn in later chapters, classless routing protocols like RIPv2 allow the same major (classful) network to use different subnet masks on different subnets, better known as Variable Length Subnet Masking (VLSM).

5.4.4   Sending RIP Updates

Refer to
Figure
in online course

Using Debug to View Automatic Summarization

When sending an update, boundary router R2 will include the network address and associated metric. If the route entry is for an update sent out a different major network, then the network address in the route entry is summarized to the classful or major network address. This is exactly what R2 does for 192.168.4.0 and 192.168.5.0. It sends these classful networks to R1.

R2 also has routes for the 172.30.1.0/24, 172.30.2.0/24 and 172.30.3.0/24 subnets. In R2's routing update to R3 on Serial0/0/1, R2 only sends a summary of the classful network address of 172.30.0.0.

If the route entry is for an update sent within a major network, the subnet mask of the outbound interface is used to determine the network address to advertise. R2 sends the 172.30.3.0 subnet to R1 using the subnet mask on Serial0/0/0 to determine the subnet address to advertise.

R1 receives the 172.30.3.0 update on Serial0/0/0 interface, which has an interface address of 172.30.2.1/24. Since the routing update and interface both belong to the same major network, R1 applies its /24 mask to the 172.30.3.0 route.

Click R1 and R3 Routing Tables in the figure to compare the routing tables.

Notice that R1 has three routes for the 172.30.0.0 major network, which has been subnetted to /24 or 255.255.255.0. R3 has only one route to the 172.30.0.0 network, and the network has not been subnetted. R3 has the major network in its routing table. However, it would be a mistake to assume that R3 does not have full connectivity. R3 will send any packets destined for the 172.30.1.0/24, 172.30.2.0/24, and 172.30.3.0/24 networks to R2 because all three of those networks belong to 172.30.0.0/16 and are reachable through R2.

5.4.5   Advantages and Disadvantages of Automatic Summarization

Refer to
Figure
in online course

Advantages of Automatic Summarization

As we saw with R2 in the previous figure, RIP automatically summarizes updates between classful networks. Because the 172.30.0.0 update is sent out an interface (Serial 0/0/1) on a different classful network (192.168.4.0), RIP sends out only a single update for the entire classful network instead of one for each of the different subnets. This process is similar to what we did when summarized several static routes into a single static route. Why is automatic summarization an advantage?

- Smaller routing updates sent and received, which uses less bandwidth for routing updates between R2 and R3.

- R3 has a single route for the 172.30.0.0/16 network, regardless of how many subnets there are or how it is subnetted. Using a single route results in a faster lookup process in the routing table for R3.

Refer to
Figure
in online course

Is there a disadvantage to automatic summarization? Yes, when there are discontiguous networks configured in the topology.

Disadvantage of Automatic Summarization

As you can see in the figure, the addressing scheme has been changed. This topology will be used to show a main disadvantage with classful routing protocols like RIPv1 - their lack of support for discontiguous networks.

Classful routing protocols do not include the subnet mask in routing updates. Networks are automatically summarized across major network boundaries since the receiving router in unable to determine the mask of the route. This is because the receiving interface may have a different mask than the subnetted routes.

Notice that R1 and R3 both have subnets from the 172.30.0.0/16 major network, whereas R2 does not. Essentially, R1 and R3 are boundary routers for 172.30.0.0/16 because they are separated by another major network, 209.165.200.0/24. This separation creates a discontiguous network, as two groups of 172.30.0.0/24 subnets are separated by at least one other major network. 172.30.0.0/16 is a discontiguous network.

Refer to
Figure
in online course

Discontiguous Topologies do not Converge with RIPv1

The figure shows the RIP configuration for each router based on the topology. The RIPv1 configuration is correct, but it is unable to determine all of the networks in this discontiguous topology. To understand why, remember that a router will only advertise major network addresses out interfaces that do not belong to the advertised route. As a result, R1 will not advertise 172.30.1.0 or 172.30.2.0 to R2 across the 209.165.200.0 network. R3 will not advertise 172.30.100.0 or 172.30.200.0 to R2 across the 209.165.200.0 network. Both routers R1 and R3, however, will advertise the 172.30.0.0 major network address.

What is the result? Without the inclusion of the subnet mask in the routing update, RIPv1 cannot advertise specific routing information that will allow routers to correctly route for the 172.30.0.0/24 subnets.

Click the `show ip route` buttons for R1, R2, and R3 in the figure and review the routes.

- R1 does not have any routes to the LANs attached to R3.

- R3 does not have any routes to the LANs attached to R1.

- R2 has two equal-cost paths to the 172.30.0.0 network.

- R2 will load balance traffic destined for any subnet of 172.30.0.0. This means that R1 will get half of the traffic and R3 will get the other half of the traffic whether or not the destination of the traffic is for one of their LANs.

In Chapter 7, "RIPv2," you will see a version of this topology. It will be used to show the difference between classful and classless routing.

Refer to **Packet
Tracer Activity**
for this chapter

Use the Packet Tracer Activity to implement the Scenario B addressing scheme and explore the advantages and disadvantages of automatic summarization. Detailed instructions are provided within the activity.

5.5 Default Route and RIPv1

5.5.1 Modified Topology: Scenario C

Refer to
Figure
in online course

Adding Internet Access to the Topology

RIP was the first dynamic routing protocol and was used extensively in early implementations between customers and ISPs, as well as between different ISPs. But in today's networks, customers do not necessarily have to exchange routing updates with their ISP. Customer routers that connect to an ISP do not need a listing for every route on the Internet. Instead, these routers have a default route that sends all traffic to the ISP router when the customer router does not have a route to a destination. The ISP configures a static route pointing to the customer router for addresses inside the customer's network.

In scenario C, R3 is the service provider with access to the Internet, as signified by the cloud. R3 and R2 do not exchange RIP updates. Instead, R2 uses a default route to reach the R3 LAN and all other destinations that are not listed in its routing table. R3 uses a summary static route to reach the subnets 172.30.1.0, 172.30.2.0, and 172.30.3.0.

To prepare the topology, we can leave the addressing in place; it is the same as was used in Scenario B. However, we also need to complete the following steps:

Click RIP configuration in the figure.

1. Disable RIP routing for network 192.168.4.0 on R2.

2. Configure R2 with a static default route to send default traffic to R3.

3. Completely disable RIP routing on R3.

4. Configure R3 with a static route to the 172.30.0.0 subnets.

Click the `show ip route` tab in the figure for the corresponding router to see the output.

5.5.2 Propagating the Default Route in RIPv1

Refer to
Figure
in online course

To provide Internet connectivity to all other networks in the RIP routing domain, the default static route needs to be advertised to all other routers that use the dynamic routing protocol. You could configure a static default route on R1 pointing to R2, but this technique is not scalable. With every router added to the RIP routing domain, you would have to configure another static default route. Why not let the routing protocol do the work for you?

In many routing protocols, including RIP, you can use the `default-information originate` command in router configuration mode to specify that this router is to originate default information, by propagating the static default route in RIP updates. In the figure, R2 has been configured with the `default-information originate` command. Notice from the `debug ip rip` output that it is now sending a "quad-zero" static default route to R1.

Click `show ip route` in the figure.

In the routing table for R1, you can see that there is a candidate default route, as denoted by the `R*` code. The static default route on R2 has been propagated to R1 in a RIP update. R1 has connectivity to the LAN on R3 and any destination on the Internet.

Refer to **Packet
Tracer Activity**
for this chapter

Use the Packet Tracer Activity to implement Scenario C with static and default routing and configure R2 to propagate a default route. Detailed instructions are provided within the activity.

5.6 RIPv1 Configuration Labs

5.6.1 Basic RIP Configuration

Refer to
Lab Activity
for this chapter

In this lab, you will work through the configuration and verification commands discussed in this chapter using the same three scenarios. You will configure RIP routing, verify your configurations, investigate the problem with discontiguous networks, observe automatic summarization, and configure and propagate a default route.

Refer to **Packet Tracer Activity** for this chapter

Use Packet Tracer Activity 5.6.1 to repeat a simulation of Lab 5.6.1. Remember, however, that Packet Tracer is not a substitute for a hands-on lab experience with real equipment.

A summary of the instructions is provided within the activity. Use the Lab PDF for more details.

Clicking the Packet Tracer icon will launch Scenario A. All scenarios for this simulation of the hands-on lab can be launched from the links below.

Scenario A

Scenario B

Scenario C

5.6.2 Challenge RIP Configuration

Refer to **Lab Activity** for this chapter

In this lab activity, you will be given a network address that must be subnetted to complete the addressing of the network shown in the Topology Diagram. A combination of RIPv1 and static routing will be required so that hosts on networks that are not directly connected will be able to communicate with each other.

Refer to **Packet Tracer Activity** for this chapter

Use Packet Tracer Activity 5.6.2 to repeat a simulation of Lab 5.6.2. Remember, however, that Packet Tracer is not a substitute for a hands-on lab experience with real equipment.

A summary of the instructions is provided within the activity. Use the Lab PDF for more details.

5.6.3 RIP Troubleshooting

Refer to **Lab Activity** for this chapter

In this lab, you will begin by loading configuration scripts on each of the routers. These scripts contain errors that will prevent end-to-end communication across the network. You will need to troubleshoot each router to determine the configuration errors, and then use the appropriate commands to correct the configurations. When you have corrected all of the configuration errors, all of the hosts on the network should be able to communicate with each other.

Refer to **Packet Tracer Activity** for this chapter

Use Packet Tracer Activity 5.6.3 to repeat a simulation of Lab 5.6.3. Remember, however, that Packet Tracer is not a substitute for a hands-on lab experience with real equipment.

A summary of the instructions is provided within the activity. Use the Lab PDF for more details.

Refer to
Figure
in online course

Summary and Review

Summary

RIP (version 1) is a classful, distance vector routing protocol. RIPv1 was one of the first routing protocols developed for routing IP packets. RIP uses hop count for its metric, with a metric of 16 hops meaning that route is unreachable. As a result, RIP can only be used in networks where there are no more than fifteen routers between any two networks.

RIP messages are encapsulated in a UDP segment, with source and destination ports of 520. RIP routers send their complete routing tables to their neighbors every 30 seconds except for those routes which are covered by the split horizon rule.

RIP is enabled by using the `router rip` command at the global configuration prompt. The `network` command is used to specify which interfaces on the router will be enabled for RIP along with the classful network address for each directly connected network. The `network` command enables the interface to send and receive RIP updates and also advertises that network in RIP updates to other routers.

Refer to
Figure
in online course

The `debug ip rip` command can be used to view the RIP updates that are sent and received by the router. To prevent RIP updates from being sent out an interface, such on a LAN where there are no other routers, the `passive-interface` command is used.

RIP entries are displayed in the routing table with the source code of **R** and have an administrative distance of 120. Default routes are propagated in RIP by configuring a static default route and using the `default-information originate` command in RIP.

RIPv1 automatically summarizes subnets to their classful address when sending an update out an interface that is on a different major network than the subnetted address of the route. Because RIPv1 is a classful routing protocol, the subnet mask is not included in the routing update. When a router receives a RIPv1 routing update, RIP must determine the subnet mask of that route. If the route belongs to the same major classful network as the update, RIPv1 applies the subnet mask of the receiving interface. If the route belongs to a different major classful network than the receiving interface, RIPv1 applies the default classful mask.

Refer to **Packet Tracer Activity**
for this chapter

The `show ip protocols` command can be used to display information for any routing protocol enabled on the router. Regarding RIP, this command displays timer information, status of automatic summarization, which networks are enabled on this router for RIP, and other information.

Because RIPv1 is a classful routing protocol, it does not support discontiguous networks or VLSM. Both of these topics are discussed in Chapter 7, "RIPv2".

The Packet Tracer Skills Integration Challenge Activity for this chapter integrates all the knowledge and skills you acquired in the first two chapters of this course and adds knowledge and skills related to RIPv1.

In this activity, you build a network from the ground up. Starting with an addressing space and network requirements, you must implement a network design that satisfies the specifications. Next, you implement an effective RIPv1 routing configuration with integrated default routing. Detailed instructions are provided within the activity.

Packet Tracer Skills Integration Instructions (PDF)

To Learn More

Refer to
Figure
in online course

RFCs (Request for Comments) are a series of documents submitted to the IETF (Internet Engineering Task Force) to propose an Internet standard or convey new concepts, information or even occasionally even humor. RFC 1058 is the original RFC for RIP written by Charles Hedrick.

RFCs can be accessed from several web sites including www.ietf.org. Read all or parts of RFC 1058. Much of this information will now be familiar to you, along with some additional information as well.

Go to
the online course
to take the quiz.

Quiz

Take the chapter quiz to test your knowledge.

Your Chapter Notes

CHAPTER 6

VLSM and CIDR

Chapter Introduction

Refer to
Figure
in online course

Prior to 1981, IP addresses used only the first 8 bits to specify the network portion of the address, limiting the Internet - then known as ARPANET - to 256 networks. Early on, it became obvious that this was not going to be enough address space.

In 1981, RFC 791 modified the IPv4 32-bit address to allow for three different classes or sizes of the networks: class A, class B, and class C. Class A addresses used 8 bits for the network portion of the address, class B used 16 bits, and class C used 24 bits. This format became known as *classful IP addressing*.

The initial development of classful addressing solved the 256 network limit problem - for a time. A decade later, it became clear that the IP address space was depleting rapidly. In response, the Internet Engineering Task Force (IETF) introduced *Classless Inter-Domain Routing (CIDR)*, which used Variable Length Subnet Masking (VLSM) to help conserve address space.

With the introduction of CIDR and VLSM, ISPs could now assign one part of a classful network to one customer and different part to another customer. This *discontiguous address assignment* by ISPs was paralleled by the development of classless routing protocols. To compare: classful routing protocols always summarize on the classful boundary and do not include the subnet mask in routing updates. Classless routing protocols *do* include the subnet mask in routing updates and are not required to perform summarization. The classless routing protocols discussed in this course are RIPv2, EIGRP and OSPF.

With the introduction of VLSM and CIDR, network administrators had to use additional subnetting skills. VLSM is simply subnetting a subnet. Subnets can be further subnetted in multiple levels, as you will learn in this chapter. In addition to subnetting, it became possible to summarize a large collection of classful networks into an aggregate route, or *supernet*. In this chapter, you will also review route summarization skills.

6.1 Classful and Classless Addressing

6.1.1 Classful IP Addressing

Refer to
Figure
in online course

When the ARPANET was commissioned in 1969, no one anticipated that the Internet would explode out of the humble beginnings of this research project. By 1989, ARPANET had been transformed into what we now call the Internet. Over the next decade, the number of hosts on the Internet grew exponentially, from 159,000 in October 1989, to over 72 million by the end of the millennium. As of January 2007, there were over 433 million hosts on the Internet.

Without the introduction of VLSM and CIDR notation in 1993 (RFC 1519), *Network Address Translator (NAT)* in 1994 (RFC 1631), and *private addressing* in 1996 (RFC 1918), the IPv4 32-bit address space would now be exhausted.

Links:

"ISC Domain Survey: Number of Internet Hosts," https://www.isc.org/solutions/survey/history

Refer to
Figure
in online course

The High Order Bits

IPv4 addresses were initially allocated based on class. In the original specification of IPv4 (RFC 791) released in 1981, the authors established the classes to provide three different sizes of networks for large, medium and small organizations. As a result, class A, B and C addresses were defined with a specific format for the *high order bits*. High order bits are the left-most bits in a 32-bit address.

As shown in the figure:

- Class A addresses begin with a 0 bit. Therefore, all addresses from 0.0.0.0 to 127.255.255.255 belong to class A. The 0.0.0.0 address is reserved for default routing and the 127.0.0.0 address is reserved for loopback testing.

- Class B addresses begin with a 1 bit and a 0 bit. Therefore, all addresses from 128.0.0.0 to 191.255.255.255 belong to class B.

- Class C addresses begin with two 1 bits and a 0 bit. Class C addresses range from 192.0.0.0 to 223.255.255.255.

The remaining addresses were reserved for multicasting and future uses. Multicast addresses begin with three 1s and a 0 bit. Multicast addresses are used to identify a group of hosts that are part of a multicast group. This helps reduce the amount of packet processing that is done by hosts, particularly on broadcast media. In this course, you will see that the routing protocols RIPv2, EIGRP, and OSPF use designated multicast addresses.

IP addresses that begin with four **1** bits were reserved for future use.

Links:

"Internet Protocol," http://www.ietf.org/rfc/rfc791.txt

"Internet Multicast Addresses," http://www.iana.org/assignments/multicast-addresses

Refer to
Figure
in online course

The IPv4 Classful Addressing Structure

The designations of network bits and host bits were established in RFC 790 (released with RFC 791). As shown in the figure, class A networks used the first octet for network assignment, which translated to a 255.0.0.0 classful subnet mask. Because only 7 bits were left in the first octet (remember, the first bit is always 0), this made 2 to the 7th power or 128 networks.

With 24 bits in the host portion, each class A address had the potential for over 16 million individual host addresses. Before CIDR and VLSM, organizations were assigned an entire classful network address. What was one organization going to do with 16 million addresses? Now you can understand the tremendous waste of address space that occurred in the beginning days of the Internet, when companies received class A addresses. Some companies and governmental organizations still have class A addresses. For example, General Electric owns 3.0.0.0/8, Apple Computer owns 17.0.0.0/8, and the U.S. Postal Service owns 56.0.0.0/8. (See the link "Internet Protocol v4 Address Space" below for a listing of all the IANA assignments.)

Class B was not much better. RFC 790 specified the first two octets as network. With the first two bits already established as 1 and 0, 14 bits remained in the first two octets for assigning networks, which resulted in 16,384 class B network addresses. Because each class B network address contained 16 bits in the host portion, it controlled 65,534 addresses. (Remember, 2 addresses were reserved for the network and broadcast addresses.) Only the largest organizations and governments could ever hope to use all 65,000 addresses. Like class A, class B address space was wasted.

To make things worse, class C addresses were often too small! RFC 790 specified the first three octets as network. With the first three bits established as 1 and 1 and 0, 21 bits remained for assigning networks for over 2 million class C networks. But, each class C network only had 8 bits in the host portion, or 254 possible host addresses.

Links:

"A Brief History of the Internet," http://www.isoc.org/internet/history/brief.shtml

"Internet Protocol v4 Address Space," http://www.iana.org/assignments/ipv4-address-space

6.1.2 Classful Routing Protocol

Refer to **Figure** in online course

Example of Classful Routing Updates

Using classful IP addresses meant that the subnet mask of a network address could be determined by the value of the first octet, or more accurately, the first three bits of the address. Routing protocols, such as RIPv1 only needed to propagate the network address of known routes and did not need to include the subnet mask in the routing update. This is because the router receiving the routing update could determine the subnet mask simply by examining the value of the first octet in the network address, or by applying its ingress interface mask for subnetted routes. The subnet mask was directly related to the network address.

Click R1 Update to R2 in the figure.

In the example, R1 knows that subnet 172.16.1.0 belongs to the same major classful network as the outgoing interface. Therefore, it sends a RIP update to R2 containing subnet 172.16.1.0. When R2 receives the update, it applies the receiving interface subnet mask (/24) to the update and adds 172.16.1.0 to the routing table.

Click R2 Update to R3 in the figure.

When sending updates to R3, R2 summarizes subnets 172.16.1.0/24, 172.16.2.0/24, and 172.16.3.0/24 into the major classful network 172.16.0.0. Because R3 does not have any subnets that belong to 172.16.0.0, it will apply the classful mask for a class B network, /16.

6.1.3 Classless IP Addressing

Refer to **Figure** in online course

The Move Towards Classless Addressing

By 1992, members of the IETF (Internet Engineering Task Force) had serious concerns about the exponential growth of the Internet and the limited scalability of Internet routing tables. They were also concerned with the eventual exhaustion of 32-bit IPv4 address space. The depletion of the class B address space was occurring so fast that within two years there would be no more class B addresses available (RFC 1519). This depletion was occurring because every organization that requested and obtained approval for IP address space received an entire classful network address - either a class B with 65,534 host addresses or a class C with 254 host addresses. One fundamental cause of this problem was the lack of flexibility. No class existed to serve a mid-sized organization that needed thousands of IP addresses but not 65,000.

In 1993, IETF introduced Classless Inter-Domain Routing, or CIDR (RFC 1517). CIDR allowed for:

- More efficient use of IPv4 address space

- Prefix aggregation, which reduced the size of routing tables

To CIDR-compliant routers, address class is meaningless. The network portion of the address is determined by the network subnet mask, also known as the *network prefix*, or prefix length (/8, /19, etc.). The network address is no longer determined by the class of the address.

ISPs could now more efficiently allocate address space using any prefix length, starting with /8 and larger (/8, /9, /10, etc.). ISPs were no longer limited to a /8, /16, or /24 subnet mask. Blocks of IP addresses could be assigned to a network based on the requirements of the customer, ranging from a few hosts to hundreds or thousands of hosts.

Refer to
Figure
in online course

CIDR and Route Summarization

CIDR uses Variable Length Subnet Masks (VLSM) to allocate IP addresses to subnets according to individual need rather than by class. This type of allocation allows the network/host boundary to occur at any bit in the address. Networks can be further divided or subnetted into smaller and smaller subnets.

Just as the Internet was growing at an exponential rate in the early 1990s, so were the size of routing tables that were maintained by Internet routers under classful IP addressing. CIDR allowed for *prefix aggregation*, which you already know as route summarization. Recall from Chapter 2, "Static Routing" that you can create one static route for multiple networks. Internet routing tables were now able to benefit from the same type of aggregation of routes. The ability for routes to be summarized as a single route helps reduce the size of Internet routing tables.

In the figure, notice that ISP1 has four customers, each with a variable amount of IP address space. However, all of the customer address space can be summarized into one advertisement to ISP2. The 192.168.0.0/20 summarized or aggregated route includes all the networks belonging to Customers A, B, C, and D. This type of route is known as a supernet route. A supernet summarizes multiple network addresses with a mask less than the classful mask.

Propagating VLSM and supernet routes requires a classless routing protocol, because the subnet mask can no longer be determined by the value of the first octet. The subnet mask now needs to be included with the network address. Classless routing protocols include the subnet mask with the network address in the routing update.

Links:

"Classless Inter-Domain Routing (CIDR): an Address Assignment and Aggregation Strategy," http://www.ietf.org/rfc/rfc1519.txt

"Internet Protocol v4 Address Space," http://www.iana.org/assignments/ipv4-address-space

6.1.4 Classless Routing Protocol

Refer to
Figure
in online course

Classless routing protocols include RIPv2, EIGRP, OSPF, IS-IS, and BGP. These routing protocols include the subnet mask with the network address in their routing updates. Classless routing protocols are necessary when the mask cannot be assumed or determined by the value of the first octet.

For example, the networks 172.16.0.0/16, 172.17.0.0/16, 172.18.0.0/16 and 172.19.0.0/16 can be summarized as 172.16.0.0/14.

If R2 sends the 172.16.0.0 summary route without the /14 mask, R3 only knows to apply the default classful mask of /16. In a classful routing protocol scenario, R3 is unaware of the 172.17.0.0/16, 172.18.0.0/16 and 172.19.0.0/16 networks.

Note: Using a classful routing protocol, R2 can send these individual networks without summarization, but the benefits of summarization are lost.

Classful routing protocols cannot send supernet routes because the receiving router will apply the default classful to the network address in the routing update. If our topology contained a classful routing protocol, then R3 would only install 172.16.0.0/16 in the routing table.

Note: When a supernet route is in a routing table, for example, as a static route, a classful routing protocol will not include that route in its updates.

With a classless routing protocol, R2 will advertise the 172.16.0.0 network along with the /14 mask to R3. R3 will then be able to install the supernet route 172.16.0.0/14 in its routing table giving it reachability to the 172.16.0.0/16, 172.17.0.0/16, 172.18.0.0/16 and 172.19.0.0/16 networks.

6.2 VLSM

6.2.1 VLSM in Action

In a previous course, you learned how Variable Length Subnet Masking (VLSM) allows the use of different masks for each subnet. After a network address is subnetted, those subnets can be further subnetted. **As you most likely recall, VLSM is simply subnetting a subnet. VLSM can be thought of as** *sub-subnetting***.**

Click Play to view the animation.

The figure shows the network 10.0.0.0/8 that has been subnetted using the subnet mask of /16, which makes 256 subnets.

```
10.0.0.0/16
 10.1.0.0/16
 10.2.0.0/16
 .
 .
 .
10.255.0.0/16
```

Any of these /16 subnets can be subnetted further. For example, in the figure, the 10.1.0.0/16 subnet is subnetted again using the /24 mask, and results in the following additional subnets.

```
10.1.1.0/24
 10.1.2.0/24
 10.1.3.0/24
 .
 .
 .
10.1.255.0/24
```

The 10.2.0.0/16 subnet is also subnetted again with a /24 mask. The 10.3.0.0/16 subnet is subnetted again with the /28 mask, and the 10.4.0.0/16 subnet is subnetted again with the /20 mask.

Individual host addresses are assigned from the addresses of "sub-subnets". For example, the figure shows the 10.1.0.0/16 subnet divided into /24 subnets. The 10.1.4.10 address would now be a member of the more specific subnet 10.1.4.0/24.

6.2.2 VLSM and IP Addresses

Another way to view the VLSM subnets is to list each subnet and its sub-subnets. In the figure, the 10.0.0.0/8 network is the starting address space. It is subnetted with a /16 mask on the first round of subnetting. You already know that borrowing 8 bits (going from /8 to /16) creates 256 subnets. With classful routing, that is as far as you can go. You can only choose one mask for all your networks. With VLSM and classless routing, you have more flexibility to create additional network addresses and use a mask that fits your needs.

Click 10.1.0.0/16 in the figure.

For subnet 10.1.0.0/16, 8 more bits are borrowed again, to create 256 subnets with a /24 mask. This mask will allow 254 host addresses per subnet. The subnets ranging 10.1.0.0/24 to 10.1.255.0/24 are subnets of the subnet 10.1.0.0/16.

Click 10.2.0.0/16 in the figure.

Subnet 10.2.0.0/16 is also further subnetted with a /24 mask. The subnets ranging from 10.2.0.0/24 to 10.2.255.0/24 are subnets of the subnet 10.2.0.0/16.

Click 10.3.0.0/16 in the figure.

Subnet 10.3.0.0/16 is further subnetted with a /28 mask. This mask will allow 14 host addresses per subnet. Twelve bits are borrowed, creating 4,096 subnets ranging from 10.3.0.0/28 to 10.3.255.240/28.

Click 10.4.0.0/16 in the figure.

Subnet 10.4.0.0/16 is further subnetted with a /20 mask. This mask will allow 4094 host addresses per subnet. Four bits are borrowed, creating 16 subnets ranging from 10.4.0.0/20 to 10.4.240.0/20. These /20 subnets are big enough to subnet even further, allowing more networks.

6.3 CIDR

6.3.1 Route Summarization

Refer to
Figure
in online course

As you previously learned, route summarization also known as route aggregation, is the process of advertising a *contiguous* set of addresses as a single address with a less-specific, shorter subnet mask. Remember that CIDR is a form of route summarization and is synonymous with the term *supernetting*.

You should already be familiar with route summarization that is done by classful routing protocols like RIPv1. RIPv1 summarizes subnets to a single major network classful address when sending the RIPv1 update out an interface that belongs to another major network. For example, RIPv1 will summarize 10.0.0.0/24 subnets (10.0.0.0/24 through 10.255.255.0/24) as 10.0.0.0/8.

CIDR ignores the limitation of classful boundaries, and allows summarization with masks that are less than that of the default classful mask. This type of summarization helps reduce the number of entries in routing updates and lowers the number of entries in local routing tables. It also helps reduce bandwidth utilization for routing updates and results in faster routing table lookups.

The figure shows a single static route with the address 172.16.0.0 and the mask 255.248.0.0 summarizing all of the 172.16.0.0/16 to 172.23.0.0/16 classful networks. Although 172.22.0.0/16 and 172.23.0.0/16 are not shown in the graphic, these are also included in the summary route. Notice that the /13 mask (255.248.0.0) is less than the default classful mask /16 (255.255.0.0).

Note: You may recall that a supernet is always a route summary, but a route summary is not always a supernet.

It is possible that a router could have both a specific route entry and a summary route entry covering the same network. Let us assume that router X has a specific route for 172.22.0.0/16 using Serial 0/0/1 and a summary route of 172.16.0.0/13 using Serial0/0/0. Packets with the IP address of 172.22.n.n match both route entries. These packets destined for 172.22.0.0 would be sent out the Serial0/0/1 interface because there is a more specific match of 16 bits, than with the 13 bits of the 172.16.0.0/13 summary route.

6.3.2 Calculating Route Summarization

Refer to
Figure
in online course

Calculating route summaries and supernets is identical to the process that you already learned in Chapter 2, "Static Routing." Therefore, the following example is presented as a quick review.

Summarizing networks into a single address and mask can be done in three steps. Let's look at the following four networks:

- 172.20.0.0/16

- 172.21.0.0/16

- 172.22.0.0/16

- 172.23.0.0/16

Click Step 1 in the figure.

The first step is to list the networks in binary format. The figure shows all four networks in binary.

Click Step 2 in the figure.

The second step is to count the number of left-most matching bits to determine the mask for the summary route. You can see in the figure that the first 14 left-most matching bits match. This is the prefix, or subnet mask, for the summarized route: /14 or 255.252.0.0.

Click Step 3 in the figure.

The third step is to copy the matching bits and then add zero bits to determine the summarized network address. The figure shows that the matching bits with zeros at the end results in the network address 172.20.0.0. The four networks - 172.20.0.0/16, 172.21.0.0/16, 172.22.0.0/16, and 172.23.0.0/16 - can be summarized into the single network address and prefix 172.20.0.0/14.

The activities in the next section offer you an opportunity to practice designing and troubleshooting VLSM addressing schemes. You will also practice creating and troubleshooting route summarizations.

6.4 VLSM and Route Summarization Activity

6.4.1 Basic VLSM Calculation and Addressing Design Activity

Refer to
Lab Activity
for this chapter

In this activity, you will use the network address 192.168.1.0/24 to subnet and provide the IP addressing for a given topology. VLSM will be used so that the addressing requirements can be met using the 192.168.1.0/24 network.

Refer to **Packet
Tracer Activity**
for this chapter

You can use Packet Tracer Activity 6.4.1 to complete this activity. A summary of the instructions is provided within the activity, but you should use the Activity PDF on the previous page for more details.

6.4.2 Challenge VLSM Calculation and Addressing Design Activity

Refer to
Lab Activity
for this chapter

In this activity, you will use the network address 172.16.0.0/16 to subnet and provide the IP addressing for a given topology. VLSM will be used so that the addressing requirements can be met using the 172.16.0.0/16 network.

Refer to Packet Tracer Activity for this chapter

You can use Packet Tracer Activity 6.4.2 to complete this activity. A summary of the instructions is provided within the activity, but you should use the Activity PDF on the previous page for more details.

6.4.3 Troubleshooting a VLSM Addressing Design Activity

Refer to Lab Activity for this chapter

In this activity, the network address 172.16.128.0/17 was used to provide the IP addressing for a network. VLSM has been used to subnet the address space **incorrectly**. You will need to troubleshoot the addressing that was assigned to each subnet to determine where errors are present and determine the correct addressing assignments where needed.

Refer to Packet Tracer Activity for this chapter

You can use Packet Tracer Activity 6.4.3 to complete this activity. A summary of the instructions is provided within the activity, but you should use the Activity PDF on the previous page for more details.

6.4.4 Basic Route Summarization Activity

Refer to Lab Activity for this chapter

In this activity, you are given a network with subnetting and address assignments already completed. Your task is to determine summarized routes that can be used to reduce the number of entries in routing tables.

Refer to Packet Tracer Activity for this chapter

You can use Packet Tracer Activity 6.4.4 to complete this activity. A summary of the instructions is provided within the activity, but you should use the Activity PDF on the previous page for more details.

6.4.5 Challenge Route Summarization Activity

Refer to Lab Activity for this chapter

In this activity, you are given a network with subnetting and address assignments already completed. Your task is to determine summarized routes that can be used to reduce the number of entries in routing tables.

Refer to Packet Tracer Activity for this chapter

You can use Packet Tracer Activity 6.4.5 to complete this activity. A summary of the instructions is provided within the activity, but you should use the Activity PDF on the previous page for more details.

6.4.6 Troubleshooting Route Summarization Activity

Refer to Lab Activity for this chapter

In this activity, the LAN IP addressing is already completed for the network. VLSM was used to subnet the address space. The summary routes are **incorrect**. You will need to troubleshoot the summary routes that have been assigned to determine where errors are present and determine the correct summary routes.

Refer to Packet Tracer Activity for this chapter

You can use Packet Tracer Activity 6.4.6 to complete this activity. A summary of the instructions is provided within the activity, but you should use the Activity PDF on the previous page for more details.

Summary and Review

Summary

Refer to
Figure
in online course

CIDR (Classless Inter-Domain Routing) was introduced in 1993 replacing the previous generation of IP address syntax, classful networks. CIDR allowed for more efficient use of IPv4 address space and prefix aggregation, known as route summarization or supernetting.

With CIDR, address classes (class A, class B, class C) became meaningless. The network address was no longer determined by the value of the first octet, but assigned prefix length (subnet mask). Address space, the number of hosts on a network, could now be assigned a specific prefix depending upon the number of hosts needed for that network.

CIDR allows for supernetting. A supernet is a group of major network addresses summarized as a single network address with a mask less than that of the default classful mask.

CIDR uses VLSM (Variable Length Subnet Masks) to allocate IP addresses to subnetworks according to need rather than by class. VLSM allows for subnets to be further divided or subnetted into even smaller subnets. Simply put, VLSM is just subnetting a subnet.

Propagating CIDR supernets or VLSM subnets require a classless routing protocol. A classless routing protocol includes the subnet mask along with the network address in the routing update.

Determining the summary route and subnet mask for a group of networks can be done in three easy steps. The first step is to list the networks in binary format. The second step is to count the number of left-most matching bits. This will give you the prefix length or subnet mask for the summarized route. The third step is to copy the matching bits and then add zero bits to the rest of the address to determine the summarized network address. The summarized network address and subnet mask can now be used as the summary route for this group of networks. Summary routes can be used by both static routes and classless routing protocols. Classful routing protocols can only summarize routes to the default classful mask.

Classless routing protocols and their ability to support CIDR supernet, VLSM, and discontiguous networks is described in the following chapters.

Refer to
Figure
in online course

Refer to **Packet
Tracer Activity**
for this chapter

The Packet Tracer Skills Integration Challenge Activity for this chapter is a moderately complex VLSM design scenario. You will create an addressing scheme based on requirements specified in the instructions, then you will build the network and configure the routers. Because you have not yet learned classful routing protocols, you will be shown two commands that will make your RIP network converge in a classless manner. Finally, you configure a summary route.

Packet Tracer Skills Integration Instructions (PDF)

To Learn More

Refer to
Figure
in online course

RFC 1519 Classless Inter-Domain Routing (CIDR)

RFCs (Request for Comments) are a series of documents submitted to the IETF (Internet Engineering Task Force) to propose an Internet standard or convey new concepts, information or even occasionally even humor. RFC 1519 is the RFC for Classless Inter-Domain Routing (CIDR).

RFCs can be accessed from several web sites including www.ietf.org. Read all or parts of RFC 1519 to learn more about the introduction of CIDR to the Internet community.

Internet Core Routers

In the To Learn More section of Chapter 3 (Introduction to Dynamic Routing Protocols), you accessed route servers to display BGP routes on the Internet. One such site is www.traceroute.org.

Access one of the route servers and using the `show ip route` command, view the actual routing table of an Internet router. Notice how many routes there are on an Internet core router. As of March 2007, there were over 200,000 routes. Many of these are summarized routes and supernets. Use the command `show ip route 207.62.187.0` to view one such supernet.

CAIDA

An interesting web site is CAIDA, the Cooperative Assocation for Internet Data Analysis, www. caida.org. CAIDA "provides tools and analyses promoting the engineering and maintenance of a robust, scalable global Internet infrastructure." There are several sponsors for CAIDA including Cisco Systems. Although much of this information may seem beyond your understanding, you will begin to recognize many of these terms and concepts.

Go to
the online course
to take the quiz.

Chapter Quiz

Take the chapter quiz to test your knowledge.

Your Chapter Notes

CHAPTER 7

RIPv2

Chapter Introduction

Refer to
Figure
in online course

RIP Version 2 (RIPv2) is defined in RFC 1723. It is the first classless routing protocol discussed in this course. The figure places RIPv2 in its proper perspective with other routing protocols. Although RIPv2 is a suitable routing protocol for some environments, it has lost popularity when compared to other routing protocols such as EIGRP, OSPF, and IS-IS, which offer more features and are more scalable.

While it may be less popular than other routing protocols, both versions of RIP are still appropriate in some situations. Although RIP lacks the capabilities of many of the later protocols, its sheer simplicity and widespread use in multiple operating systems makes it an ideal candidate for smaller, homogeneous networks where multi-vendor support is necessary - especially within UNIX environments.

Because you will need to understand RIPv2 - even if you do not use it - this chapter will focus on the differences between a classful routing protocol (RIPv1) and a classless routing protocol (RIPv2) rather than on the details of RIPv2. The main limitation of RIPv1 is that it is a classful routing protocol. As you know, classful routing protocols do not include the subnet mask with the network address in routing updates, which can cause problems with discontiguous subnets or networks that use Variable-Length Subnet Masking (VLSM). Because RIPv2 is a classless routing protocol, subnet masks are included in the routing updates, making RIPv2 more compatible with modern routing environments.

RIPv2 is actually an enhancement of RIPv1's features and extensions rather than an entirely new protocol. Some of these enhanced features include:

- Next-hop addresses included in the routing updates
- Use of multicast addresses in sending updates
- Authentication option available

Like RIPv1, RIPv2 is a distance vector routing protocol. Both versions of RIP share the following features and limitations:

- Use of holddown and other timers to help prevent routing loops.
- Use of split horizon or split horizon with poison reverse to also help prevent routing loops.
- Use of triggered updates when there is a change in the topology for faster convergence.
- Maximum hop count limit of 15 hops, with the hop count of 16 signifying an unreachable network.

7.1 RIPv1 Limitations

7.1.1 Lab Topology

The figure shows the topology and addressing scheme used in this chapter. This scenario is similar to the routing domain with three routers that was used at the end of Chapter 5, "RIP version 1." Remember that both the R1 and R3 routers have subnets that are part of the 172.30.0.0/16 major classful network (class B). Also remember that R1 and R3 are connected to R2 using subnets of the 209.165.200.0/24 major classful network (class C). This topology is discontiguous and will not converge because 172.30.0.0/16 is divided by the 209.165.200.0/24.

Click R1, R2, and R3 to see the starting configuration for each router.

Summary Route

The topology shows that R2 has a static summary route to the 192.168.0.0/16 network. The configuration of this summary route will be displayed later in this section.

Refer to
Figure
in online course

The concept and configuration of static summary routes was discussed in Chapter 2, "Static Routing." We can inject static route information into routing protocol updates. This is called redistribution and will also be discussed later in this section. For now, understand that this summary route will cause problems with RIPv1 because 192.168.0.0/16 is not a major classful address and includes all of the /24 versions of 192.168.0.0/16, as shown in the topology.

Finally, notice that the R1 and R3 routers contain VLSM networks and are sharing address space from the 172.30.0.0/16 major classful network. Next, we will look at the VLSM addressing scheme.

VLSM

Review the VLSM addressing scheme in the figure. As shown in the top chart, both R1 and R3 have had the 172.30.0.0/16 network subnetted into /24 subnets. Four of these /24 subnets are assigned: two to R1 (172.30.1.0/24 and 172.30.2.0/24) and two to R3 (172.30.100.0/24 and 172.30.110.0/24).

Refer to
Figure
in online course

In the bottom chart, we have taken the 172.30.200.0/24 subnet and subnetted it again, using the first four bits for subnets and the last four bits for hosts. The result is a 255.255.255.240 mask or /28. Subnet 1 and Subnet 2 are assigned to R3. This means that the subnet 172.30.200.0/24 can no longer be used even though the remaining /28 subnets can be used.

RFC 1918 Private Addresses

You should already be familiar with RFC 1918 and the reasoning behind private addressing. All the examples in the curriculum use private IP addresses for the inside addressing example.

The RFC 1918-compliant addresses are shown in the table. But when IP traffic is routed across WAN links through an ISP, or when inside users need to access outside sites, a public IP address must be used.

Refer to
Figure
in online course

Cisco Example IP Addresses

You may have noticed that the WAN links between R1, R2, and R3 are using public IP addresses. Although these IP addresses are not private addresses according to RFC 1918, Cisco has acquired some public address space to use for example purposes.

The addresses shown in the figure are all valid public IP addresses that are routable on the Internet. Cisco has set these addresses aside for educational purposes. Therefore, this course and future courses will use these addresses when there is a need to use public addresses.

In the figure, R1, R2, and R3 are connected using the 209.165.200.224/27 Cisco public address space. Because WAN links need only two addresses, 209.165.200.224/27 is subnetted with a /30 mask. In the topology, subnet 1 is assigned to the WAN link between R1 and R2. Subnet 2 is assigned to the WAN link between R2 and R3.

Refer to
Figure
in online course

Loopback Interfaces

Notice that R3 is using loopback interfaces (Lo0, Lo1, and Lo2). A loopback interface is a software-only interface that is used to emulate a physical interface. Like other interfaces, it can be assigned an IP address. Loopback interfaces are also used by other routing protocols, such as OSPF, for different purposes. These uses will be discussed in Chapter 11 OSPF.

In a lab environment, loopback interfaces are useful in creating additional networks without having to add more physical interfaces on the router. A loopback interface can be pinged and the subnet can be advertised in routing updates. Therefore, loopback interfaces are ideal for simulating multiple networks attached to the same router. In our example, R3 does not need four LAN interfaces to demonstrate multiple subnets and VLSM. Instead, we use loopback interfaces.

Links

"Internet Assigned Numbers Authority," http://www.iana.org/

"Configuring Logical Interfaces," http://www.cisco.com/en/US/docs/ios/12_2/interface/configuration/guide/icflogin.html

7.1.2 RIPv1 Topology Limitations

Refer to
Figure
in online course

Static Routes and Null Interfaces

To configure the static supernet route on R2, the following command is used:

```
R2(config)#ip route 192.168.0.0 255.255.0.0
Null0
```

Remember that route summarization allows a single high-level route entry to represent many lower-level routes, thereby reducing the size of routing tables. The static route on R2 uses a /16 mask to summarize all 256 networks ranging from 192.168.0.0/24 to 192.168.255.0/24.

The address space represented by the static summary route 192.168.0.0/16 does not actually exist. In order to simulate this static route, we use a *null interface* as the exit interface. You do not need to enter any commands to create or configure the null interface. It is always up but does not forward or receive traffic. Traffic sent to the null interface is discarded. For our purposes, the null interface will serve as the exit interface for our static route. Remember from Chapter 2, "Static Routing," that a static route must have an active exit interface before it will be installed in the routing table. Using the null interface will allow R2 to advertise the static route in RIP even though networks belonging to the summary 192.168.0.0/16 do not actually exist.

Route Redistribution

The second command that needs to be entered is the **redistribute static** command:

```
R2(config-router)#
redistribute static
```

Redistribution involves taking the routes from one routing source and sending those routes to another routing source. In our example topology, we want the RIP process on R2 to redistribute our static route (192.168.0.0/16) by importing the route into RIP and then sending it to R1 and R3 using the RIP process. We will see if this is indeed happening and if not, why not.

Links

"Configuring Logical Interfaces," http://www.cisco.com/en/US/docs/ios/12_2/interface/configuration/guide/icflogin.html

Refer to
Figure
in online course

Verifying and Testing Connectivity

To test whether or not the topology has full connectivity, we first verify that both serial links on R2 are up using the **show ip interface brief** as shown in the figure for R2 Links. If a link is down, the Status field or the Protocol field (or both fields) will display **down** in the command output. If a link is up, both fields will display **up**, as shown here. R2 has direct connectivity to R1 and R3 across the serial links.

But can R2 ping LANs on R1 and R3? Are there any connectivity problems with a classful routing protocol and the discontiguous subnets of 172.30.0.0? Let's test the communications between the routers using **ping**.

Click R2 Pings in the figure.

This output shows R2 attempting to ping the 172.30.1.1 interface on R1 and the 172.30.100.1 interface on R3. Whenever R2 pings any of the 172.30.0.0 subnets on R1 or R3, only about 50% of the ICMP messages are successful.

Click R1 Pings in the figure.

This output shows that R1 is able to ping 10.1.0.1 but is unsuccessful when attempting to ping the 172.30.100.1 interface on R3.

Click R3 Pings in the figure.

This output shows that R3 is able to ping 10.1.0.1 but is unsuccessful when attempting to ping the 172.30.1.1 interface on R1.

As you can see, there is an obvious problem when trying to communicate with the 172.30.0.0 discontiguous subnets. In the following sections we will examine routing tables and routing updates to further investigate this problem and attempt to resolve it.

> Refer to **Packet Tracer Activity** for this chapter

Use the Packet Tracer Activity to practice your router configuration skills, including RIPv1 configurations.

7.1.3 RIPv1: Discontiguous Networks

> Refer to **Figure** in online course

You already know that RIPv1 is a classful routing protocol. As you can see in the RIPv1 message format, It does not include the subnet masks in its routing updates. Therefore, RIPv1 cannot support discontiguous networks, VLSM, or Classless Inter-Domain Routing (CIDR) supernets. However, might there be room to expand the RIPv1 message format to include the subnet mask so that we could actually have a discontiguous network configuration? How would you change the format of this message in the figure to include the subnet mask?

> Refer to **Figure** in online course

Because the subnet mask is not included in the update, RIPv1 and other classful routing protocols must summarize networks at major network boundaries. As you can see in the figure, RIPv1 on both the R1 and R3 routers will summarize their 172.30.0.0 subnets to the classful major network address of 172.30.0.0 when sending routing updates to R2. From the perspective of R2, both updates have an equal cost of 1 hop to reach network 172.30.0.0/16. As you will see, R2 installs both paths in the routing table.

Examining the Routing Tables

> Refer to **Figure** in online course

As you have seen, R2 gets inconsistent results when attempting to ping an address on one of the 172.30.0.0 subnets.

Click R2 Routes in the figure.

Notice that R2 has two equal cost routes to the 172.30.0.0/16 network. This is because both R1 and R3 are sending R2 a RIPv1 update for the 172.30.0.0/16 classful network with a metric of 1 hop. Because R1 and R3 automatically summarized the individual subnets, R2's routing table only contains the major classful network address of 172.30.0.0/16.

We can examine the contents of the routing updates as the updates are sent and received with **debug ip rip** command.

Click R2 Debug 1 in the figure.

The output from this command shows that R2 is receiving two 172.30.0.0 equal cost routes with a metric of 1 hop. R2 is receiving one route on Serial 0/0/0 from R1 and the other route on Serial 0/0/1 from R3. Notice that the subnet mask is not included with the network address in the update.

What about R1 and R3? Are they receiving each other's 172.30.0.0 subnets?

Click R1 Routes in the figure.

Here we see that R1 has its own 172.30.0.0 routes: 172.30.2.0/24 and 172.30.1.0/24. But R1 does not send R2 those subnets. R3 has a similar routing table. Both R1 and R3 are boundary routers and are only sending the summarized 172.30.0.0 network to R2 in their RIPv1 routing updates. As a result, R2 only knows about the 172.30.0.0/16 classful network and is unaware of any 172.30.0.0 subnets.

Click R2 Debug 2 in the figure.

Notice in the `debug ip rip` output for R2 that it is not including the 172.30.0.0 network in its updates to either R1 or R3. Why not? Because the split horizon rule is in effect. R2 learned about 172.30.0.0/16 on both the Serial 0/0/0 and Serial 0/0/1 interfaces. Because R2 learned about the 172.30.0.0 on these interfaces, it does not include that network in updates it sends out these same interfaces.

7.1.4 RIPv1: No VLSM Support

Refer to
Figure
in online course

Because RIPv1 does not send the subnet mask in routing updates, it cannot support VLSM. R3 router is configured with VLSM subnets, all of which are members of the class B network 172.30.0.0/16:

- 172.30.100.0/**24** (FastEthernet 0/0)
- 172.30.110.0/**24** (Loopback 0)
- 172.30.200.16/**28** (Loopback 1)
- 172.30.200.32/**28** (Loopback 2)

As we saw with the 172.30.0.0/16 updates to R2 by R1 and R3, RIPv1 either summarizes the subnets to the classful boundary or uses the subnet mask of the outgoing interface to determine which subnets to advertise.

Click on the Topology in the figure.

To demonstrate how RIPv1 uses the subnet mask of the outgoing interface, R4 is added to the topology connected to R3 through the FastEthernet0/0 interface on the 172.30.100.0/24 network.

Click Router Output in the figure.

Refer to the `debug ip rip` in the figure. Notice that the only 172.30.0.0 subnet that is sent to the R4 router is 172.30.110.0. Also, notice that R3 is sending the full 172.30.0.0 major classful network out Serial 0/0/1.

Why is RIPv1 on R3 not including the other subnets, 172.30.200.16/28 and 172.30.200.32/28, in updates to R4? Those subnets do not have the same subnet mask as FastEthernet 0/0. This is why all subnets must use the same subnet mask when a classful routing protocol is implemented in the network.

A more detailed explanation

R3 needs to determine which 172.30.0.0 subnets to include in the updates leaving its FastEthernet 0/0 interface with the IP address 172.30.100.1/24. It will only include those 172.30.0.0 routes in its routing table with the same mask as the exit interface. Since the interface is 172.30.100.1 with a /24 mask, it will only include 172.30.0.0 subnets with a /24 mask. The only one that meets this condition is 172.30.110.0.

The other 172.30.0.0 subnets, 172.30.200.16/28 and 172.30.200.32/28, are not included because the /28 masks do not match the /24 mask of the outgoing interface. The receiving router, R4, can only apply its own /24 interface mask to RIPv1 route advertisements with 172.30.0.0 subnets. R4 would apply the wrong mask of /24 to these subnets with /28 masks.

7.1.5 RIPv1: No CIDR Support

Refer to **Figure** in online course

The 192.168.0.0/16 Static Route

So far, most of this information should be familiar to you from Chapter 5, "RIP version 1." However, there is one issue that we have not yet addressed.

Click R2 Routing in the figure.

We configured a static route to the 192.168.0.0/16 network on R2 and instructed RIP to include that route in its updates using the `redistribute static` command, as shown in the figure. This static route is a summary of the 192.168.0.0/24 subnets ranging from 192.168.0.0/24 to 192.168.255.0/24.

```
R2(config)#ip route 192.168.0.0 255.255.0.0 Null0
```
Click R2 Routes in the figure.

We can see that the static route is included in R2's routing table.

Click R1 Routes in the figure.

Looking at the routing table for R1, we notice that R1 is not receiving this 192.168.0.0/16 route in its RIP updates from R2, although we might expect that it should.

Click R2 Debug in the figure.

Using `debug ip rip` on R2, we notice that RIPv1 does not include the 192.168.0.0/16 route in its RIP updates to either R1 or R3. Can you think why this route is not included? Look at the route 192.168.0.0/16. What is the class of the route? Class A, B, or C? What is the mask used in the static route? Does it match the class? Is the mask in the static route less than the classful mask?

We configured the static route 192.168.0.0 with a /16 mask. This is fewer bits than the classful class C mask of /24. Because the mask does not match the class or a subnet of the class, RIPv1 will not include this route in its updates to other routers.

RIPv1 and other classful routing protocols cannot support CIDR routes that are summarized routes with a smaller subnet mask than the classful mask of the route. RIPv1 ignores these supernets in the routing table and does not include them in updates to other routers. This is because the receiving router would only be able to apply the larger classful mask to the update and not the shorter /16 mask.

Note: If the 192.168.0.0 static route were configured with a /24 mask or greater, this route would be included in the RIP updates. The receiving routers would apply the classful /24 mask to this update.

Refer to **Packet Tracer Activity** for this chapter

Use the Packet Tracer Activity in Simulation mode to see that updates are not sent across classful network boundaries with RIPv1. In RealTime mode, verify non-convergence with the `show ip route`, `ping`, and `debug ip rip`.

7.2 Configuring RIPv2

7.2.1 Enabling and Verifying RIPv2

Comparing RIPv1 and RIPv2 Message Formats

RIPv2 is defined in RFC 1723. Like version 1, RIPv2 is encapsulated in a UDP segment using port 520 and can carry up to 25 routes. Although RIPv2 has the same basic message format as RIPv1, two significant extensions are added.

The first extension in the RIPv2 message format is the subnet mask field that allows a 32 bit mask to be included in the RIP route entry. As a result, the receiving router no longer depends upon the subnet mask of the inbound interface or the classful mask when determining the subnet mask for a route.

The second significant extension to the RIPv2 message format is the addition of the Next Hop address. The Next Hop address is used to identify a better next-hop address - if one exists - than the address of the sending router. If the field is set to all zeros (0.0.0.0), the address of the sending router is the best next-hop address. Detailed information about how the Next Hop address is used is beyond the scope of this course. However, an example can be found in RFC 1722 or *Routing TCP/IP Volume 1* by Jeff Doyle.

Links

"RFC 1723: RIP Version 2," http://www.ietf.org/rfc/rfc1723.txt

Version 2

By default, when a RIP process is configured on a Cisco router, it is running RIPv1. However, even though the router only sends RIPv1 messages, it can interpret both RIPv1 and RIPv2 messages. A RIPv1 router will just ignore the RIPv2 fields in the route entry.

Click R2 RIPv1 in the figure.

The `show ip protocols` command verifies that R2 is configured for RIPv1 but receives RIP messages for both versions.

Click RIPv2 Configs in the figure.

Notice that the `version 2` command is used to modify RIP to use version 2. This command should be configured on all routers in the routing domain. The RIP process will now include the subnet mask in all updates, making RIPv2 a classless routing protocol.

Click R2 RIPv2 in the figure.

As you can see from the output, when a router is configured for version 2, only RIPv2 messages are sent and received.

Click Revert to RIPv1 in the figure.

The default behavior of RIPv1 can be restored by using the command `no version` in the router configuration mode. However, the command `version 1` can also be used so that only RIPv1 messages are sent and received.

7.2.2 Auto-summary and RIPv2

Examining the Routing Tables

Because RIPv2 is a classless routing protocol, you might expect to see the individual 172.30.0.0 subnets in the routing tables. However, when we examine the routing table for R2 in the figure, we still see the summarized 172.30.0.0/16 route with same two equal cost paths. Routers R1 and R3 still do not include the 172.30.0.0 subnets of the other router.

Click R1 Routes in the figure.

The only difference so far between RIPv1 and RIPV2 is that R1 and R3 each have a route to the 192.168.0.0/16 supernet. This route was the static route configured on R2 and redistributed by RIP.

Click R1 Debug 1 in the figure.

So, what is happening? To examine which RIPv2 routes are being sent and received, we will use `debug ip rip`. The figure shows the `debug ip rip` output for R1. Notice that RIPv2 is sending both the network address and subnet mask:

```
RIP: sending v2 update to 224.0.0.9 via Serial0/0 (209.165.200.230)
 172.30.0.0/16 via 0.0.0.0, metric 1, tag 0
```

However, notice that the route sent is the summarized classful network address, 172.30.0.0/16, and not the individual 172.30.1.0/24 and 172.30.2.0/24 subnets.

Click Auto-summary in the figure.

By default, RIPv2 automatically summarizes networks at major network boundaries, just like RIPv1. Both R1 and R3 routers are still summarizing their 172.30.0.0 subnets to the class B address of 172.30.0.0 when sending updates out their interfaces on the 209.165.200.228 and 209.165.200.232 networks, respectively. The command `show ip protocols` verifies that "automatic summarization is in effect."

Click R1 Debug 2 in the figure.

The only change resulting from the `version 2` command is that R2 is now including the 192.168.0.0/16 network in its updates. This is because RIPv2 includes the 255.255.0.0 mask with the 192.168.0.0 network address in the update. Both R1 and R3 will now receive this redistributed static route via RIPv2 and enter it into their routing tables.

Note: Remember, the 192.168.0.0/16 route could not be distributed with RIPv1 because the subnet mask was less than the classful mask. Because the mask is not included in RIPv1 updates, there was no way for the RIPv1 router to determine what that mask should be. Therefore, the update was never sent.

7.2.3 Disabling Auto-Summary in RIPv2

Refer to **Figure** in online course

As you can see in the figure, to modify the default RIPv2 behavior of automatic summarization, use the command `no auto-summary` in the router configuration mode. This command is not valid with RIPv1. Even though the Cisco IOS will let you configure `no auto-summary` for RIPv1, the command has no effect. You must also configure version 2 before the Cisco IOS will change the way it sends RIP updates.

Once automatic summarization has been disabled, RIPv2 will no longer summarize networks to their classful address at boundary routers. RIPv2 will now include all subnets and their appropriate masks in its routing updates. The command `show ip protocols` can be used to verify that "automatic network summarization is not in effect."

7.2.4 Verifying RIPv2 Updates

Refer to **Figure** in online course

Now that we are using the classless routing protocol RIPv2 and we have also disabled automatic summarization, what should we expect to see in the routing tables?

In the figure, the routing table for R2 now contains the individual subnets for 172.30.0.0/16. Notice that there is no longer a single summary route with two equal cost paths. Each subnet and mask has its own specific entry, along with the exit interface and next-hop address to reach that subnet.

Click R1 Routes in the figure.

The routing table for R1 contains all of the subnets for 172.30.0.0/16, including those subnets from R3.

Click R3 Routes in the figure.

The routing table for R3 contains all of the subnets for 172.30.0.0/16, including those subnets from R1. This network is converged.

Click R2 Debug in the figure.

We can verify that the classless routing protocol RIPv2 is indeed sending and receiving the subnet mask information in the routing updates using **debug ip rip**. Notice that each route entry now includes the slash notation for the subnet mask.

We can also see that an update on one interface has its metric incremented before it is sent out another interface. For example, the update that was received on Serial 0/0/1 for the 172.30.100.0/24 network with 1 hop is sent out other interfaces, such as Serial 0/0/0, with a metric of 2, or 2 hops.

```
RIP: received v2 update from 209.165.200.234 on Serial0/0/1
  172.30.100.0/24 via 0.0.0.0 in
1 hops
 RIP: sending v2 update to 224.0.0.9 via Serial0/0/0 (209.165.200.229)
  172.30.100.0/24 via 0.0.0.0,
metric 2, tag 0
```

Notice also that the updates are sent using the multicast address 224.0.0.9. RIPv1 sends updates as a broadcast 255.255.255.255. There are several advantages to using a multicast address. Details about multicast addressing are beyond the scope of this course; in general, however, multicasts can take up less bandwidth on the network. In addition, multicasting updates require less processing by devices that are not RIP-enabled. Under RIPv2, any device that is not configured for RIP will discard the frame at the Data Link layer. With broadcast updates under RIPv1 configurations, all devices on a broadcast network like Ethernet must process a RIP update all the way up to the Transport layer, where the device finally discovers that the packet is destined for a process that does not exist.

Refer to **Packet Tracer Activity** for this chapter

Use the Packet Tracer Activity to configure RIPv2, disable automatic summarization, and verify your configurations.

7.3 VLSM and CIDR

7.3.1 RIPv2 and VLSM

Refer to **Figure** in online course

Because classless routing protocols like RIPv2 can carry both the network address and the subnet mask, they do not need to summarize these networks to their classful addresses at major network boundaries. Therefore, classless routing protocols support VLSM. Routers using RIPv2 no longer need to use the inbound interface's mask to determine the subnet mask in the route advertisement. The network and the mask are explicitly included in each and every routing update.

In networks that use a VLSM addressing scheme, a classless routing protocol is essential to propagate all of the networks along with their correct subnet masks. Looking at the output from **debug ip rip** for R3 in the figure, we can see that RIPv2 include the networks and their subnet masks in its routing updates.

Also notice in the figure that we have once again added the R4 router in the topology. Remember, with RIPv1, R3 would only send R4 the 172.30.0.0 routes that had the same mask as the FastEthernet 0/0 exit interface. Because the interface is 172.30.100.1 with a /24 mask, RIPv1 only included 172.30.0.0 subnets with a /24 mask. The only route that met this condition was 172.30.110.0.

However, with RIPv2, R3 can now include all of the 172.30.0.0 subnets in its routing updates to R4, as shown in the debug output in the figure. This is because RIPv2 can include the proper subnet mask with the network address in the update.

7.3.2 RIPv2 and CIDR

Refer to **Figure** in online course

One of the goals of Classless Inter-Domain Routing (CIDR) as stated by RFC 1519 is "to provide a mechanism for the aggregation of routing information." This goal includes the concept of supernetting. A supernet is a block of contiguous classful networks that is addressed as a single network. On the R2 router, we configured a supernet - a static route to a single network that is used to represent multiple networks or subnets.

Supernets have masks that are smaller than the classful mask (/16 here, instead of the classful /24). For the supernet to be included in a routing update, the routing protocol must have the capability of carrying that mask. In other words, it must be a classless routing protocol, like RIPv2.

The static route on R2 does include a mask which is less than the classful mask:

```
R2(config)#ip route 192.168.0.0 255.255.0.0 Null0
```
In a classful environment, the 192.168.0.0 network address would be associated with the class C mask /24, or 255.255.255.0. In today's networks, we no longer associate network addresses with classful masks. In this example, the 192.168.0.0 network has a /16, or 255.255.0.0, mask. This route could represent a series of 192.168.0.0/24 networks or any number of different address ranges. The only way this route can be included in a dynamic routing update is with a classless routing protocol that includes the /16 mask.

Click R2 Debug in the figure.

Using **debug ip rip** we can see that this CIDR supernet is included in the routing update sent by R2. Automatic summarization does not have to be disabled on RIPv2 or any classless routing protocol in order for supernets to be included in the updates.

Click R1 Routes in the figure.

The routing table for R1 shows that it has received the supernet route from R2.

7.4 Verifying and Troubleshooting RIPv2

7.4.1 Verification and Troubleshooting Commands

Refer to **Figure** in online course

There are several ways to verify and troubleshoot RIPv2. Many of the same commands used for RIPv2 can be used to verify and troubleshoot other routing protocols.

It is always best to begin with the basics:

1. Make sure all of the links (interfaces) are up and operational.

2. Check the cabling.

3. Check to make sure you have the correct IP address and subnet mask on each interface.

4. Remove any unnecessary configuration commands that are no longer necessary or have been replaced by other commands.

Click show ip route in the figure.

This is the first command to use to check for network convergence. As you examine the routing table, it is important to look for the routes that you expect to be in the routing table as well as for those that should not be in the routing table.

Click show ip interface brief in the figure.

If a network is missing from the routing table, often it is because an interface is down or incorrectly configured. The **show ip interface brief** command quickly verifies the status of all interfaces.

Click show ip protocols in the figure.

The **show ip protocols** command verifies several critical items, including verifying that RIP is enabled, the version of RIP, the status of automatic summarization, and the networks that were included in the network statements. The Routing Information Sources listed at the bottom of the output are the RIP neighbors from which this router is currently receiving updates.

Click debug ip rip in the figure.

As demonstrated throughout the chapter, **debug ip rip** is an excellent command to use to examine the contents of the routing updates that are sent and received by a router. There may be times when a route is being received by a router but is not being added to the routing table. One reason for this could be that a static route is also configured for the same network being advertised. By default, a static route has a lower administrative distance than any dynamic routing protocol and will take precedence in being added to the routing table.

Click ping in the figure.

An easy way to verify round-trip connectivity is with the **ping** command. If end-to-end connectivity is not successful, begin by pinging the local interfaces. If successful, ping the router interfaces on the directly connected networks. If that is also successful, continue pinging interfaces on each successive router. Once a ping is unsuccessful, examine both routers and all the routers in-between to determine where and why the ping is failing.

Click show running-config in the figure.

The **show running-config** can be used to verify all the commands currently configured. Usually, other commands are more efficient and provide more information than a simple listing of the current configuration. However, the **show running-config** command is useful in determining if anything obvious was forgotten or misconfigured.

7.4.2 Common RIPv2 issues

Refer to
Figure
in online course

When troubleshooting issues specific to RIPv2, there are several areas to examine.

Version

A good place to begin troubleshooting a network that is running RIP is to verify that version 2 is configured on all routers. Although RIPv1 and RIPv2 are compatible, RIPv1 does not support discontiguous subnets, VLSM, or CIDR supernet routes. It is always better to use the same routing protocol on all routers unless there is a specific reason not to do so.

Network Statements

Another source of problems might be incorrect or missing network statements. Remember, the network statement does two things:

- It enables the routing protocol to send and receive updates on any local interfaces that belong to that network.

- It includes that network in its routing updates to its neighboring routers.

A missing or incorrect network statement will result in missed routing updates and routing updates not being sent or received on an interface.

Automatic Summarization

If there is a need or expectation for sending specific subnets and not just summarized routes, make sure that automatic summarization has been disabled.

7.4.3 Authentication

Refer to **Figure** in online course

Most routing protocols send their routing updates and other routing information using IP (in IP packets). IS-IS is the notable exception and is discussed in CCNP courses. A security concern of any routing protocol is the possibility of accepting invalid routing updates. The source of these invalid routing updates could be an attacker maliciously attempting to disrupt the network or trying to capture packets by tricking the router into sending its updates to the wrong destination. Another source of invalid updates could be a misconfigured router. Or perhaps a host is attached to the network and - unknown to its user - the host is running the routing protocol of the local network.

For example, in the figure, R1 is propagating a default route to all other routers in this routing domain. However, someone has mistakenly added router R4 to the network, which is also propagating a default route. Some of the routers may forward default traffic to R4 instead of to the real gateway router, R1. These packets could be "black holed" and never seen again.

Whatever the reason, it is good practice to authenticate routing information transmitted between routers. RIPv2, EIGRP, OSPF, IS-IS, and BGP can be configured to authenticate routing information. This practice ensures routers will only accept routing information from other routers that have been configured with the same password or authentication information. Note: Authentication does not encrypt the routing table.

Note: Because RIP has given way to more popular routing protocols, detailed configuration features for authentication in RIPv2 are not discussed in this chapter. Instead, configuring routing protocols to use authentication will be discussed in a later course with other security issues.

Refer to **Packet Tracer Activity** for this chapter

Use the Packet Tracer Activity to see how unintentional routing updates can corrupt the routing table.

7.5 RIPv2 Configuration Labs

7.5.1 Basic RIPv2 Configuration

Refer to **Lab Activity** for this chapter

In this lab, you will work with a *discontiguous network* that is subnetted using VLSM. As you have seen throughout this chapter and Chapter 5, "RIP version 1", this can be an issue when the routing protocol used does not include enough information to distinguish the individual subnets. To solve this problem, you will configure RIPv2 as the classless routing protocol to provide subnet mask information in the routing updates.

Refer to **Packet Tracer Activity** for this chapter

Use the Packet Tracer Activity to repeat a simulation of Lab 7.5.1. Remember, however, that Packet Tracer is not a substitute for a hands-on lab experience with real equipment.

A summary of the instructions is provided within the activity. Use the Lab PDF for more details.

7.5.2 Challenge RIPv2 Configuration

Refer to
Lab Activity
for this chapter

In this lab activity, you are given a network address that must be subnetted using VLSM to complete the addressing of the network. A combination of RIP version 2 and static routing will be required so that hosts on networks that are not directly connected will be able to communicate with each other and the Internet.

Refer to **Packet
Tracer Activity**
for this chapter

Use the Packet Tracer Activity to repeat a simulation of Lab 7.5.2. Remember, however, that Packet Tracer is not a substitute for a hands-on lab experience with real equipment.

A summary of the instructions is provided within the activity. Use the Lab PDF for more details.

7.5.3 RIPv2 Troubleshooting

Refer to
Lab Activity
for this chapter

In this lab, you begin by loading configuration scripts on each of the routers. These scripts contain errors that will prevent end-to-end communication across the network. After loading the corrupted scripts, troubleshoot each router to determine the configuration errors, and then use the appropriate commands to correct the configurations. When you have corrected all of the configuration errors, all of the hosts on the network should be able to communicate with each other.

Refer to **Packet
Tracer Activity**
for this chapter

Use the Packet Tracer Activity to repeat a simulation of Lab 7.5.3. Remember, however, that Packet Tracer is not a substitute for a hands-on lab experience with real equipment.

A summary of the instructions is provided within the activity. Use the Lab PDF for more details.

Summary and Review

Summary

Refer to
Figure
in online course

RIPv2 is a classless, distance vector routing protocol, that is defined in RFC 1723. Because RIPv2 is a classless routing protocol, it includes the subnet mask with the network addresses in the routing updates. As with other classless routing protocols, RIPv2 supports CIDR supernets, VLSM and discontiguous networks.

We saw that classful routing protocols like RIPv1 can not support discontiguous networks because they automatically summarize at major network boundaries. A router that receives routing updates from multiple routers advertising the same classful summary route cannot determine which subnets belong to which summary route. This inability leads to unexpected results including misrouted packets.

The default version of RIP is version 1. The command **version 2** is used to modify RIP to RIPv2.

Similar to RIPv1, RIPv2 automatically summarizes at major network boundaries. However, with RIPv2 automatic summarization can be disabled with the **no auto-summary** command. Automatic summarization must be disabled to support discontiguous networks. RIPv2 also supports CIDR supernets and VLSM because the specific subnet mask is included with the network address in every routing update. You can use the **debug ip rip** command to view the RIP update sending the subnet mask with the network address as part of the route entry.

The **show ip protocols** command will display that RIP is now sending and receiving version 2 updates and whether or not automatic summarization is in effect.

Refer to
Figure
in online course

The Packet Tracer Skills Integration Challenge Activity integrates all the knowledge and skills you acquired in previous chapters of this course and prior courses. Skills related to the discussion of RIPv2 are also included. In this activity, you build a network from the ground up.

Refer to **Packet
Tracer Activity**
for this chapter

Starting with an addressing space and network requirements, you must implement a network design that satisfies the specifications, then implement an effective RIPv2 routing configuration with integrated default routing. Detailed instructions are provided within the activity.

Packet Tracer Skills Integration Instructions (PDF)

To Learn More

Refer to
Figure
in online course

RFC 1723 RIP version 2

RFCs (Request for Comments) are a series of documents submitted to the IETF (Internet Engineering Task Force) to propose an Internet standard or convey new concepts, information or even occasionally even humor. RFC 1723 is the RFC for RIP version 2.

RFCs can be accessed from several web sites including www.ietf.org. Read all or parts of RFC 1723 to learn more about this classless routing protocol.

Packet Tracer

Use Packet Tracer to create two discontiguous classful networks. Each discontiguous network should have several routers and subnets, one using VLSM. Between the two groups of discontiguous networks, add another router linking the two discontiguous networks. Be sure to use a different major network between this router and each of the two discontiguous networks.

Use this scenario to examine the issues with RIPv1 and how RIPv2 can be used to solve these routing issues.

Go to
the online course
to take the quiz.

Chapter Quiz

Take the chapter quiz to test your knowledge.

Your Chapter Notes

CHAPTER 8

The Routing Table: A Closer Look

Chapter Introduction

Refer to
Figure
in online course

In previous chapters, we examined the routing table using the `show ip route` command. We saw how directly connected, static, and dynamic routes are added and deleted from the routing table.

As a network administrator, it is important to know the routing table in depth when troubleshooting network issues. Understanding the structure and lookup process of the routing table will help you diagnose *any* routing table issue - regardless of your level of familiarity with a particular routing protocol. For example, you may encounter a situation in which the routing table has all of the routes you would expect to see, but packet forwarding is not performing as expected. Knowing how to step through the lookup process of a destination IP address for a packet will give you the ability to determine if the packet is being forwarded as expected, if and why the packet is being sent elsewhere, or if the packet has been discarded.

In this chapter, we will take a closer look at the routing table. The first part of the chapter focuses on the structure of Cisco's IP routing table. We will examine the format of the routing table and learn about level 1 and level 2 routes. The second part of the chapter analyzes the lookup process of the routing table. We will discuss classful routing behavior, as well as classless routing behavior, which uses the `no ip classless` and `ip classless` commands.

Many of the details regarding the structure and lookup process of the Cisco IP routing table have been omitted from this chapter. If you are interested in reading more about this subject and the inner workings of the Cisco IOS as it pertains to routing, see *Cisco IP Routing,* by Alex Zinin (ISBN 0-201-60473-6).

Note: This book is *not* a beginner's book on routing protocols - it is a thorough examination of the protocols, processes, and algorithms used by the Cisco IOS.

8.1 The Routing Table Structure

8.1.1 Lab Topology

Refer to
Figure
in online course

In this chapter, we will be using a simple three router network, as shown in the figure. R1 and R2 share a common 172.16.0.0/16 network with 172.16.0.0/24 subnets. R2 and R3 are connected by the 192.168.1.0/24 network. Notice that R3 also has a 172.16.4.0/24 subnet that is disconnected, or discontiguous, from the 172.16.0.0 network that R1 and R2 share. The effects of this discontiguous subnet will be examined later in this chapter when we look at the route lookup process.

Click R1 and R3 in the figure.

The interface configurations for R1 and R3 are also shown in the figure. In a later section, we will configure the interfaces for R2.

8.1.2 Routing Table Entries

Refer to
Figure
in online course

The sample routing table in the figure consists of route entries from the following sources:

- Directly connected networks

- Static routes

- Dynamic routing protocols

The source of the route does not affect the structure of the routing table. The figure shows a sample routing table with directly connected, static, and dynamic routes. Notice that the 172.16.0.0/24 subnets have a combination of all three types of routing sources.

Note: The routing table hierarchy in Cisco IOS was originally implemented with the classful routing scheme. Although the routing table incorporates both classful and classless addressing, the overall structure is still built around this classful scheme.

8.1.3 Level 1 Routes

Refer to
Figure
in online course

Routers R1 and R3 already have their interfaces configured with the appropriate IP addresses and subnet masks. We will now configure the interfaces for R2 and use **debug ip routing** to view the routing table process that is used to add these entries.

The figure shows what happens as the Serial 0/0/1 interface for R2 is configured with the 192.168.1.1/24 address. As soon as **no shutdown** is entered, the output from **debug ip routing** shows that this route has been added to the routing table.

Refer to
Figure
in online course

In the figure, **show ip route** displays the directly connected network in the routing table that we just added to R2.

The Cisco IP routing table is not a flat database. The routing table is actually a hierarchical structure that is used to speed up the lookup process when locating routes and forwarding packets. Within this structure, the hierarchy includes several levels. For simplicity, we will discuss all routes as one of two levels: level 1 or level 2.

Refer to
Figure
in online course

Let's learn about level 1 and level 2 routes by reviewing the routing table entry in more detail.

`C 192.168.1.0/24 is directly connected, Serial0/0/1`

A level 1 route is a route with a subnet mask equal to or less than the classful mask of the network address. 192.168.1.0/24 is a level 1 network route, because the subnet mask is equal to the network's classful mask. /24 is the classful mask for class C networks, such as the 192.168.1.0 network.

A level 1 route can function as a:

- *Default route* - A default route is a static route with the address 0.0.0.0/0.

- *Supernet route* - A supernet route is a network address with a mask less than the classful mask.

- *Network route* - A network route is a route that has a subnet mask equal to that of the classful mask. A network route can also be a parent route. Parent routes will be discussed in the next section.

The source of the level 1 route can be a directly connected network, static route, or a dynamic routing protocol.

Refer to
Figure
in online course

Ultimate Route

The level 1 route 192.168.1.0/24 can be further defined as an *ultimate route*. An ultimate route is a route that includes:

- either a next-hop IP address (another path)

- and/or an exit interface

The directly connected network 192.168.1.0/24 is a level 1 network route because it has a subnet mask that is the same as its classful mask. This same route is also an ultimate route because it contains the exit interface Serial 0/0/1.

```
C 192.168.1.0/24 is directly connected,
Serial0/0/1
```
We will see in the next topic that level 2 routes are also ultimate routes.

8.1.4 Parent and Child Routes: Classful Networks

In the previous topic, we saw a level 1 network route that was also an ultimate route. Now let's take a look at another type of level 1 network route, a parent route. The figure shows the configuration of the 172.16.3.1/24 interface on R2 and the output from the **show ip route** command. Notice that there are actually two additional entries in the routing table. One entry is the parent route and the other entry is the child route. Why are there two entries instead of one?

Click Parent and Child in the figure.

When the 172.16.3.0 subnet was added to the routing table, another route, 172.16.0.0, was also added. The first entry, 172.16.0.0/24, does not contain any next-hop IP address or exit interface information. This route is known as a *level 1 parent route*.

A level 1 parent route is a network route that does not contain a next-hop IP address or exit interface for any network. A parent route is actually a heading that indicates the presence of level 2 routes, also known as *child routes*. A level 1 parent route is automatically created any time a subnet is added to the routing table. In other words, a parent route is created whenever a route with a mask greater than the classful mask is entered into the routing table. The subnet is the level 2 child route of the parent route. In this case, the level 1 parent route that was automatically created is:

```
172.16.0.0/24 is subnetted, 1 subnets
```
A level 2 route is a route that is a subnet of a classful network address. Like a level 1 route, the source of a level 2 route can be a directly connected network, a static route, or a dynamic routing protocol. In this case, the level 2 route is the actual subnet route that was added to the network when we configured the FastEthernet 0/0 interface:

```
C 172.16.3.0 is directly connected, FastEthernet0/0
```
Note: Remember that the routing table hierarchy in Cisco IOS has a classful routing scheme. A level 1 parent route is the classful network address of the subnet route. This is the case even if a classless routing protocol is the source of the subnet route.

Click Play to view the animation.

Let's analyze the routing table entries for both the level 1 parent route and the level 2 child route (subnet).

Level 1 Parent Route

This parent route contains the following information:

- `172.16.0.0` - The classful network address for our subnet. Remember, the Cisco IP routing table is structured in a classful manner.

- `/24` - The subnet mask for all of the child routes. If the child routes have variable length subnet masks (VLSM), the subnet mask will be excluded from the parent route and included with the individual child routes. This will be shown in a later section.

- is subnetted, 1 subnet - This part of the route specifies that this is a parent route and in this case has one child route, that is, 1 subnet.

Level 2 Child Route

The second entry, 172.16.3.0, is the actual route for our directly connected network. This is a level 2 route, also known as a child route, and contains the following information:

- C - The route code for directly connected network.

- 172.16.3.0 - The specific route entry.

- is directly connected - Along with the route code of C, this specifies that this is a directly connected network with an administrative distance of 0.

- FastEthernet0/0 - The exit interface for forwarding packets that match this specific route entry.

The level 2 child route is the specific route entry for the 172,16.3.0/24 subnet. Notice that the subnet mask is not included with the subnet, the level 2 child route. The subnet mask for this child route (subnet) is the /24 mask included in its parent route, 172.16.0.0.

Level 2 child routes contain the route source and the network address of the route. **Level 2 child routes are also considered ultimate routes because they will contain the next-hop IP address and/or exit interface.**

Refer to
Figure
in online course

The figure shows the configuration of the Serial 0/0/0 interface on R2.

Click 2 and 3 in the figure.

The routing table shows two child routes for the same 172.16.0.0/24 parent route. Both 172.16.2.0 and 172.16.3.0 are members of the same parent route, because they are both members of the 172.16.0.0/16 classful network.

Refer to
Figure
in online course

Because both child routes have the same subnet mask, the parent route still maintains the /24 mask, but now shows 2 subnets. The role of the parent route will be examined when we discuss the route lookup process.

Note: If there is only a single level 2 child route and that route is removed, the level 1 parent route will be automatically deleted. A level 1 parent route exists only when there is at least one level 2 child route.

8.1.5 Parent and Child Routes: Classless Networks

Refer to
Figure
in online course

For this discussion, we will use the topology shown in the figure. Using RouterX with the VLSM configuration shown, we can examine the effect of VLSM on the routing table. RouterX has three directly connected networks. All three subnets belong to the classful network 172.16.0.0/16 and are therefore level 2 child routes.

Click 2, 3, and 4 in the figure.

Notice that our child routes do not share the same subnet mask, as was in the case in the classful example. In this case, we are implementing a network addressing scheme with VLSM.

Click 1 in the figure.

Whenever there are two or more child routes with different subnet masks belonging to the same classful network, the routing table presents a slightly different view, which states that this parent network is **variably subnetted**.

Although the parent/child relationship uses a classful structure to display networks and their subnets, this format can be used with both classful and classless addressing. **Regardless of the ad-**

dressing scheme used by the network (classless or classful), the routing table will use a classful scheme.

Refer to **Figure** in online course

Click Play to view the animation.

There are several distinct differences with this parent route and its child routes compared to the classful example discussed earlier. First, the parent route of 172.16.0.0 now contains the classful mask /16. In the classful example earlier, the classful mask was not displayed.

Also notice that the parent route states that the child routes are `"variably subnetted"`. Like the classful example, the parent route displays the number of subnets, but now it also includes the number of different masks of the child routes.

The final difference between classful and classless networks exists in the child routes. Each child route now contains the subnet mask for that specific route. In the non-VLSM example, both child routes shared the same subnet mask and the parent displayed their common subnet mask. With VLSM, the various subnet masks are displayed with the specific child routes.

The parent route contains the following information:

- **172.16.0.0** - The parent route, the classful network address associated with all child routes.

- **/16** - The classful subnet mask of the parent route.

- **variably subnetted** - States that the child routes are variably subnetted and that there are multiple masks for this classful network.

- **3 subnets, 2 masks** - Indicates the number of subnets and the number of different subnet masks for the child routes under this parent route.

Using one of the child routes as an example, we can see the following information:

- **C** - The route code for a directly connected network.

- **172.16.1.4** - The specific route entry.

- **/30** - The subnet mask for this specific route.

- **is directly connected** - Along with the route code of C, specifies that this is a directly connected network with an administrative distance of 0.

- **Serial0/0/0** - The exit interface for forwarding packets that match this specific route entry.

So, why does Cisco use the classful routing table format? We will understand the answer to this in the following sections when the route lookup process is discussed.

8.2 Routing Table Lookup Process

8.2.1 Steps in the Route Lookup Process

Refer to **Figure** in online course

In this topology, RIPv1, a classful routing protocol, is now configured. Notice that we have specifically chosen a classful routing protocol with our discontiguous 172.16.0.0 subnets. The reason for this will become evident in a later section.

Click the buttons in the figure to review the RIP configuration and resulting routing tables.

As you would expect with this addressing scheme and a classful routing protocol, there are reachability problems. Neither R1 nor R2 has a route to 172.16.4.0. Also, R3 does not have routes to subnets 172.16.1.0/24, 172.16.2.0/24, or 172.16.3.0/24.

Let's examine in more depth how the routers determine the best routes to use when sending packets and why classful routing protocols do not work with discontiguous designs. We will consider:

1. What happens when a router receives an IP packet, examines the IP destination address, and looks that address up in the routing table?

2. How does the router decide which route in the routing table is the best match?

3. What effect does the subnet mask have on the routing table lookup process?

4. How does the router decide whether or not to use a supernet or default route if a better match is not found?

Let's begin to answer these questions by examining the steps in the route lookup process.

Refer to
Figure
in online course

The Route Lookup Process

Follow these steps in the figure to see the route lookup process. Don't worry about fully understanding the steps right now. You will better understand this process when we examine a few examples in the following sections.

Click Step 1.

The router examines level 1 routes, including network routes and supernet routes, for the best match with the destination address of the IP packet.

Click Step 1a.

If the best match is a level 1 ultimate route - a classful network, supernet, or default route - this route is used to *forward the packet.*

Click Step 1b.

If the best match is a level 1 parent route, proceed to Step 2.

Click Step 2.

The router examines child routes (the subnet routes) of the parent route for a best match.

Click Step 2a.

If there is a match with a level 2 child route, that subnet will be used to *forward the packet.*

Click Step 2b.

If there is not a match with any of the level 2 child routes, proceed to Step 3. Click Step 3. Is the router implementing classful or classless routing behavior?

Click Step 3a.

Classful routing behavior: If *classful* routing behavior is in effect, terminate the lookup process and *drop the packet.*

Click Step 3b.

Classless routing behavior: If *classless* routing behavior is in effect, continue searching level 1 supernet routes in the routing table for a match, including the default route, if there is one.

Click Step 4.

If there is now a lesser match with a level 1 supernet or default routes, the router uses that route to *forward the packet.*

Click Step 5.

If there is not a match with any route in the routing table, the router *drops the packet.*

Classful and classless routing behavior will be discussed in more detail in a later section.

Note: A route referencing only a next-hop IP address and not an exit interface must be resolved to a route with an exit interface. A recursive lookup is performed on the next-hop IP address until the route is resolved to an exit interface.

8.2.2 Longest Match: Level 1 Network Routes

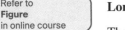

Longest Match

The term best match was used in the previous route lookup discussion. What is meant by the best match? Best match is also referred to as longest match.

First of all, what is a match? For there to be a match between the destination IP address of a packet and a route in the routing table, a minimum number of left-most bits must match between the IP address of the packet and the route in the routing table. The subnet mask of the route in the routing table is used to determine the minimum number of left-most bits that must match. (Remember, an IP packet only contains the IP address and not the subnet mask.)

The best match or longest match is the route in the routing table that has the most number of left-most matching bits with the destination IP address of the packet. **The route with the most number of equivalent left-most bits, or the longest match, is always the preferred route.**

For example, in the figure we have a packet destined for 172.16.0.10. Many possible routes *could* match this packet. Three possible routes are shown that *do* match this packet: 172.16.0.0/12, 172.16.0.0/18, and 172.16.0.0/26. Of the three routes, 172.16.0.0/26 has the longest match. Remember, for any of these routes to be considered a match there must be at least the number of matching bits indicated by the subnet mask of the route.

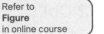

Example: Level 1 Ultimate Route

The subnet mask that is used to determine the longest match is not always obvious. Let's examine this concept in more detail, using several examples.

Click Play to view the animation.

In this example, PC1 sends a ping to 192.168.1.2, the interface on R3. R1 receives the packet.

Click Route Info and then R1 Routing Table in the figure.

Remember the first part of Step 1 in the route lookup process? The figure demonstrates this step.

Click Step 1 in the figure.

The router first examines level 1 routes for the best match. In our example, there is a match between the destination IP address 192.168.1.2 and the level 1 ultimate route of 192.168.1.0/24.

Click Step 1a in the figure.

```
R 192.168.1.0/24 [120/1] via 172.16.2.2, 00:00:25,
Serial0/0/0
```
R1 uses this route and forwards the packet out interface Serial 0/0/0.

Why is there a match with the 192.168.1.0/24 level 1 route and not with one of the 172.16.0.0 subnets? This may seem obvious. We say, "Of course the router will use 192.168.1.0/24." But the lookup process is comparing 32 bit addresses with 32 bit route entries, looking for the longest match.

The algorithm used by the IOS to search the routing table is beyond the scope of this chapter. What is important is to understand why a route entry matches or doesn't match the packet's destination IP address.

Why is there not a match with any of the 172.16.0.0/24 subnets in the routing table?

The 172.16.0.0/24 is a parent route of three subnets or child routes. Before a child route is examined for a match, there must be at least a match between the destination IP address of the packet and the **classful address** of the parent route, or 172.16.0.0/16.

Do at least 16 of the left-most bits of the parent route match the first 16 bits of the packet's destination IP address of 192.168.1.2? The answer, **no**, is obvious to us. But in the figure, you will see that the router actually checks the first bit and finds a match. The router then moves to the second bit. Because there is not a match, the lookup process will search other route entries.

Now let's see how the router finds a match between the packet's destination IP address of 192.168.1.2 and the next route in the routing table, 192.168.1.0/24, an ultimate route.

```
R 192.168.1.0/24 [120/1] via 172.16.2.2, 00:00:25, Serial0/0/0
```

The route, 192.168.1.0, is a level 1 ultimate route and, therefore, it also contains the subnet mask, /24. In the figure, notice that at least the first 24 left-most bits match.

Not only does the minimum of 24 bits match, but a total of 30 bits match, as shown in the figure. Is this important? As we will see later, there can be situations in which there are multiple potential routes with different subnet masks in the routing table for the same destination IP address. Which one is the preferred route? The one with the most number of matching bits, the longest match.

In this example, there is a match between the destination IP address 192.168.1.0 and the level 1 ultimate route 192.168.1.0/24. Because there is not a longer, more specific match, the packet is forwarded out the exit interface Serial 0/0/0.

Note: Remember that the route lookup process will need to do a recursive lookup on any route that references only a next-hop IP address and not an exit interface. For a review of recursive lookups, refer to Chapter 2, "Static Routing."

8.2.3 Longest Match: Level 1 Parent and Level 2 Child Routes

Let's examine what happens when there is a match with a level 1 parent route.

Click Route Info in the figure.

As shown in the figure, a parent route does not include a next-hop address or an exit interface but is only a "header" for its level 2 child routes, the subnets.

The subnet mask for the child routes - /24 in the figure - is displayed in the parent route, 172.16.0.0, for subnets that use the same subnet mask.

Before any level 2 child routes are examined for a match, there must first be a match between the classful address of the level 1 parent route and the destination IP address of the packet.

Example: Level 1 Parent Route and Level 2 Child Routes

In the example in the figure, PC1 sends a ping to PC2 at 172.16.3.10. R1 receives the packet and begins to search the routing table for a route.

Click Step 1b in the figure.

The first match that occurs is with the level 1 parent route, 172.16.0.0. Remember, with non-VLSM subnets the classful mask of the parent is not displayed. Before any child routes (subnets) are examined for a match, there must first be a match with the classful address of the parent route.

Because the first route entry is a level 1 parent route that matches the destination address (Step 1b of the route lookup process), the route lookup process moves to Step 2.

Click Step 2 in the figure.

Because there is a match with the parent route, the level 2 child routes will be examined for a match. However, this time the actual subnet mask of /24 is used for the minimum number of left-most bits that must match.

Click Step 2a in the figure.

The route lookup process searches the child routes for a match. In this case, there must be a minimum of 24 bits that match.

Refer to
Figure
in online course

Let's see how the router finds a match with one of the level 2 child routes.

First, the router examines the parent route for a match. In this example, the first 16 bits of the IP address must match that of the parent route. The left-most 16 bits must match because that is the classful mask of the parent route, /16.

If there is a match with the parent route, then the router checks the 172.16.1.0 route. Child routes are only examined when there is a match with the classful mask of the parent.

Click 2 in the figure.

Checking the first subnet, 172.16.1.0, the 23rd bit does not match; therefore, this route is rejected because the first 24 bits do not match.

Click 3 in the figure.

Next, the router checks the 172.16.2.0/24 route. Because the 24th bit does not match, this route is also rejected. All 24 bits must match.

Click 4 in the figure.

The router checks the last child route for 172.16.3.0/24 and finds a match. The first 24 bits do match. The routing table process will use this route, 172.16.3.0/24, to forward the packet with the destination IP address of 172.16.3.10 out the exit interface of Serial 0/0/0.

```
R 172.16.3.0 [120/1] via 172.16.2.2, 00:00:25, Serial0/0/0
```
What happens if the router does not have a route? Then it discards the packet.

Refer to
Figure
in online course

Example: Route Lookup Process with VLSM

What about our RouterX topology, which is using a VLSM addressing scheme? How does this change the lookup process?

Click 1 in the figure.

Using VSLM does not change the lookup process. With VLSM, the /16 classful mask is displayed with the level 1 parent route (172.16.0.0/16 in the figure).

Click 2, 3, and 4 in the figure.

As with non-VLSM networks, if there is a match between the packet's destination IP address and the classful mask of the level 1 parent route, the level 2 child routes will be searched.

The only difference with VLSM is that child routes display their own specific subnet masks. These subnet masks are used to determine the number of left-most bits that must match the packet's destination IP address. For example, for there to be a match with the 172.16.1.4 child route, a minimum of 30 left-most bits must match because the subnet mask is /30.

8.3 Routing Behavior

8.3.1 Classful and Classless Routing Behavior

Refer to
Figure
in online course

The next step in the route lookup process (Step 3) looks at *routing behavior*. Routing behavior influences the process of searching for the preferred route using the **no ip classless** or **ip classless** commands.

Classless and classful routing *behaviors* are not the same as classless and classful routing *protocols*. Classful and classless routing *protocols* affect how the routing table is populated. Classful and classless routing *behaviors* determine how the routing table is searched after it is populated. In the figure, the routing sources (including classful and classless routing protocols) are the inputs used to populate the routing table. The routing behavior, specified by the **ip classless** or **no ip classless** commands, determines how the route lookup process will proceed at Step 3.

As you can see, routing protocols and routing behaviors are completely independent of each other. The routing table could be populated with routes from a *classless routing protocol* like RIPv2 yet implement *classful routing behavior* because the **no ip classless** command is configured.

Refer to
Figure
in online course

Topology Changes

In Chapter 7, "RIPv2," we learned that classful routing protocols like RIPv1 do not support discontiguous networks. Even though our current topology has discontiguous networks, we can configure static routes to reach those networks.

Click R2 Configuration in the figure.

First, we add a static "quad-zero" route on R2 for sending default traffic to R3. We then add the **default-information originate** command to the RIP routing process so that R2 will send R1 the default route. This will allow R1 and R2 the capability of reaching all other networks, including 172.16.4.0/24 on R3. Finally, we enter the command **no network 192.168.1.0** because we no longer want to exchange RIP updates with R3.

Click R3 Configuration in the figure.

To finish our configuration, we remove RIP routing on R3 and add a static route on R3 for sending traffic for the major network 172.16.0.0/16, which does not have a longer match in the routing table, to R2.

We are not going to test the connectivity at this time. Connectivity will be tested in the following sections.

8.3.2 Classful Routing Behavior: no ip classless

Refer to
Figure
in online course

We now focus on Step 3 in the route lookup process. Namely, what happens after Step 2b when there is not a match with any of the level 2 child routes of the parent. Later, you will see a specific example.

As you recall from the previous section, in Steps 1 and 2, the router examines level 1 and child routes looking for the best match with the IP packet's destination address. Let's assume there is no match and resume our review of the route lookup process with Step 3.

Click through Steps 3 and 3a in the figure to review how classful routing behavior impacts the route lookup process.

Click Step 3 in the figure.

Is the router implementing classful or classless routing behavior?

Click Step 3a in the figure.

If *classful* routing behavior is in effect, terminate the lookup process and *drop the packet*.

Note: Under classful routing behavior, the process never goes to Step 4.

Refer to
Figure
in online course

Prior to IOS 11.3, **no ip classless** was the default behavior for Cisco routers. The command **no ip classless** means that the route lookup process uses classful routing table lookups by default. This will be explained in the following sections.

The commands **no ip classless** and **ip classless** are global configuration commands and can be viewed by typing **show running-config**. In IOS versions 11.3 and later, the command **ip classless** is the default, implementing a classless route lookup process.

What is the effect of classful routing behavior when all the routers are configured with the **no ip classless** command?

```
R1(config)#no ip classless
 R2(config)#no ip classless
R3(config)#no ip classless
```

Let's examine what happens when the router is performing classful routing behavior - that is, when the **no ip classless** command is configured.

8.3.3 Classful Routing Behavior - Search Process

Refer to
Figure
in online course

In our routing table lookup process, Step 3a states that when classful routing behavior is in effect (**no ip classless**) the process will not continue searching level 1 routes in the routing table. If a packet doesn't match a child route for the parent network route, then the router drops the packet. Let's see an example.

Example: R2 operating with Classful Routing Behavior

In this example, R2 receives a packet destined for PC3 at 172.16.4.10.

Click R2 Routing Table and Parent in the figure.

The routing process searches the routing table and finds a 16-bit match with the parent route 172.16.0.0, as shown in the figure. According to Step 1b of the routing process, if a match is made in the parent route, the child routes are checked.

Now let's look at the actual bit-matching process that is taking place as the child routes are checked.

Click 1, 2, and 3 in the figure.

Notice that none of the 24 left-most bits of the child routes matches the destination IP address of 172.16.4.10. At most, only 21 bits match. There is no match with the level 2 child routes.

Refer to
Figure
in online course

So what happens next? Router R2 drops the packet.

Click No Matches in the figure.

Because router R2 is using classful routing behavior, **no ip classless***, the router will not search beyond the child routes for a lesser match.*

Click Drop Packet in the figure.

The routing table process will not use the default route, 0.0.0.0/0, or any other route.

A common error is to assume that a default route will *always* be used if the router does not have a better route. In our example, R2's default route is not examined nor used, although it is a match. This is often a very surprising result when a network administrator does not understand the difference between classful and classless routing behavior.

Note: We will also see another example in Chapter 9 EIGRP where understanding the routing table lookup process will assist you in troubleshooting why a default route does not get used - even with classless routing behavior.

Why does classful routing behavior perform like this? The *general* idea of classful routing behavior comes from the time when all networks were of a classful nature. At the beginning of the Internet's growth, an organization received a class A, class B, or class C major network address. Once an organization had a classful IP major network address, that organization would also administer all of the subnets for that classful address. All routers belonging to the organization would know about all of the subnets for the major network. If a subnet was not in the routing table, then the subnet did not exist. As you learned in Chapter 6, "VLSM and CIDR," IP addresses are no longer allocated based on class.

8.3.4 Classless Routing Behavior: ip classless

Refer to
Figure
in online course

Starting with IOS 11.3, Cisco changed the default routing behavior from classful to classless. The **ip classless** command is configured by default. The **show running-config** command displays the routing behavior. Classless routing behavior means that the routing process no longer assumes that all subnets for a major classful network can only be reached within the child routes of the parent. Classless routing behavior works well for discontiguous networks and CIDR supernets.

In this section, we will examine the effect of classless routing behavior. All routers are configured with the **ip classless** command.

```
R1(config)#ip classless
 R2(config)#ip classless
R3(config)#ip classless
```

We will discuss what happens to a packet when there is a match with a level 1 parent route but there is not a match with any of the level 2 child routes or subnets. This takes us to Step 3b, Classless routing behavior.

Refer to
Figure
in online course

As you recall from the routing table process, in Steps 1 and 2, the routing table process examines level 1 and level 2 child routes looking for the best match with the IP packet's destination address. Let's assume there is no match and resume our review of the route lookup process with Step 3.

The Route Lookup Process:

Follow these steps in the figure to see the route lookup process:

Click Step 3.

Is the router implementing classful or classless routing behavior?

Click Step 3a.

Classful routing behavior: If *classful* routing behavior is in effect, terminate the lookup process and *drop the packet*.

Click Step 3b.

Classless routing behavior: If *classless* routing behavior is in effect, continue searching level 1 supernet routes in the routing table for a match, including the default route, if there is one.

Click Step 4.

If there is now a lesser match with a level 1 supernet or default routes, the router uses that route to *forward the packet*.

Click Step 5.

If there is not a match with any route in the routing table, the router *drops the packet*.

8.3.5 Classless Routing Behavior - Search Process

Refer to
Figure
in online course

Let's revisit our sample topology and look at the bit matching that happens when classless routing behavior (`ip classless`) is in effect.

Example: R2 Operating with Classless Routing Behavior

Click R2 Routing Table and Parent in the figure.

Again, R2 receives a packet destined for PC3 at 172.16.4.10. Just as it did with the classful routing behavior, the router searches the routing table and finds a 16-bit match with the parent route 172.16.0.0, as shown in the figure. According to Step1b of the routing process, if there is a match with a parent route, then the child routes are checked.

Click 1, 2, 3 in the figure.

As before, none of the 24 left-most bits of the child routes matches the destination IP address of 172.16.4.10. At most, only 21 bits match. There is no match with the level 2 child routes.

Refer to
Figure
in online course

Because we are using classless routing behavior (`ip classless`), the router continues searching the routing table, beyond this parent route and its child routes. The routing process will continue to search the routing table for a route with a subnet mask fewer than the 16 bits of the previous parent route. In other words, the router will now continue to search the other routes in the routing table where there may be fewer bits that match, but still a match.

Click Network Route in the figure.

The 192.168.1.0

/24 route does not have 24 left-most bits that match the destination IP address.

```
C 192.168.1.0/24 is directly connected, Serial0/0/1
```
Click Default Route in the figure.

How about the default route? How many bits need to match?

```
S* 0.0.0.0/
0 is directly connected, Serial0/0/1
```
The mask is /0, which means that zero or no bits need to match. A default route will be the lowest-bit match. In classless routing behavior, if no other route matches, the default route will match.

Click Forward Packet in the figure.

In this case the router will use the default route, because it is the best match. The packet will be forwarded out the Serial 0/0/1 interface.

Classful Route on R3

Click R3 Routing Table in the figure.

What does R3 do with return traffic back to PC2 at 172.16.2.10? In the figure, you'll see that in the routing table for R3, both the 172.16.4.0/24 subnet route and the 172.16.0.0/16 classful network route are level 2 child routes of the 172.16.0.0/16 parent route. Whenever there are routes for both the subnets of a classful network and a route for the classful network route itself, the classful route is considered a level 2 child route, just like the subnets.

In this case, R3 uses the 172.16.0.0/16 child route and forwards the traffic out Serial 0/0/1 back to R2.

Refer to
Figure
in online course

Classful vs. Classless Routing Behavior in the Real World

Remember that classful and classless routing *behaviors* are independent from classful and classless routing *protocols*. A router could be configured with classful routing behavior (`no ip class-`

less) and a classless routing protocol, such as RIPv2. A router could also be configured with classless routing behavior (**ip classless**) and a classful routing protocol, such as RIPv1.

In today's networks, it is recommended to use classless routing behavior so that supernet and default routes can be used whenever needed.

8.4 Routing Table Labs

8.4.1 Investigating the Routing Table Lookup Process

Refer to **Lab Activity** for this chapter

In this lab, you will be able to investigate classless and classful routing behavior.

Refer to **Packet Tracer Activity** for this chapter

In this Packet Tracer activity, you will be able to investigate classless and classful routing behavior.

8.4.2 The show ip route Challenge Lab

Refer to **Lab Activity** for this chapter

In this lab activity, you will determine the topology of a network using the outputs from the **show ip route** command. You must draw a topology diagram and determine the interface addressing on each router. Then you must build and configure the network based on the outputs. The DTE and DCE assignment is at your discretion. When complete, the outputs from your network must match those given below.

Refer to **Packet Tracer Activity** for this chapter

In this lab activity, you will determine the topology of a network using the outputs from the **show ip route** command.

You must draw a topology diagram and determine the interface addressing on each router. Next, you must build and configure the network based on the outputs. The DTE and DCE assignment is at your discretion. When complete, the outputs from your network must match those given below.

Summary and Review

Refer to
Figure
in online course

Summary

Understanding the structure and lookup process of the routing table can be an important tool in verifying and troubleshooting networks. Knowing which routes should be included and which routes should not be included in the routing table is a critical skill when troubleshooting routing issues.

The Cisco IP routing table is structured in a classful manner, which means that it uses to the default, classful addresses, to organize the route entries. The source of a routing entry can be a directly connected network, static route, or a route learned dynamically from a routing protocol.

In this chapter, you learned that there are level 1 and level 2 routes. A level 1 route can be either an ultimate route or a parent route. A level 1 ultimate route is a route with a subnet mask equal to, or less than the default classful mask of the network; and either a next hop address or an exit interface. For example, a route learned through RIP with the network address of 192.168.1.0 and a /24 network mask is a level 1 ultimate route. These routes are displayed in the routing table as a single route entry, such as:

```
R 192.168.1.0/24 [120/1] via 172.16.2.2, 00:00:25, Serial0/0/0
```

Another type of level 1 route is a parent route. A level 1 parent route is automatically created when a subnet route is added to the routing table. The subnet route is known as a level 2 child route. The parent route is a header for level 2 child routes. Here is an example of a level 1 parent route and a level 2 child route:

```
 172.16.0.0/24 is subnetted, 1 subnets
R 172.16.1.0 [120/1] via 172.16.2.1, 00:00:07, Serial0/0/0
```

The subnet mask of the child routes are displayed in the parent route unless VLSM is used. With VLSM, the parent route displays the default classful mask and the subnet mask is included with the individual VLSM route entries.

You were also introduced to the routing table lookup process in this chapter. When a packet is received by the router, it looks for the longest match with one of the routes in the routing table. The longest match is the route with the largest number of left-most bits that match between the destination IP address of the packet and the network address of the route in the routing table. The subnet mask associated with the network address in the routing table defines the minimum number of bits that must match for that route to be a match.

Before examining any level 2 child routes (subnets) for a match there must first be a match with the level 1 parent route. The classful mask of the parent determines how many bits must match the parent route. If there is a match with the parent route, then the child routes will be searched for a match.

What happens when there is a match with the parent route but none of the child routes? If the router is using classful routing behavior, no other routes will be searched and the packet will be discarded. Classful routing behavior was the default routing behavior on Cisco routers prior to IOS 11.3. Classful routing behavior can be implemented using the **no ip classless** command.

Starting with IOS 11.3 classless routing behavior became the default. If there is a match with a parent route but none of the child routes, the routing table process will continue to search other routes in the routing table including a default route should one exist. Classless routing behavior is implemented by using the **ip classless** command.

Routes to networks get added to the routing table from various sources including directly connected networks, static routes, classful routing protocols and classless routing protocols. The lookup process, classful or classless routing behavior, is independent of the source of the route. A routing table may have routes learned from a classful routing protocol such as RIPv1, but uses classless routing behavior, **no ip classless**, for the lookup process.

Refer to
Figure
in online course

Packet Tracer Skills Integration Instructions (PDF)

To Learn More

An excellent source on the routing table structure and the lookup process is Alex Zinin's book, *Cisco IP Routing*, which goes into more detail than was discussed in this chapter.

Refer to **Packet
Tracer Activity**
for this chapter

Cisco IP Routing, Chapter 4: Routing Table Maintenance includes:

- Comparison of Route Sources

- Representation of Routing Information and Interfaces

- Routing Table Structure

- Route Source Selection

Refer to
Figure
in online course

- Routing Table Initialization

- Asynchronous Table Maintenance

- Route Resolvability

- Dynamic Route Processing

- Static Route Processing

- Manual Routing Table Clearance

- Default Route Selection

Go to
the online course
to take the quiz.

Chapter Quiz

Take the chapter quiz to test your knowledge.

Your Chapter Notes

CHAPTER 9

EIGRP

Chapter Introduction

Refer to
Figure
in online course

Enhanced Interior Gateway Routing Protocol (EIGRP) is a distance vector, classless routing protocol that was released in 1992 with IOS 9.21. As its name suggests, EIGRP is an enhancement of Cisco IGRP (Interior Gateway Routing Protocol). Both are Cisco proprietary protocols and only operate on Cisco routers.

The main purpose in Cisco's development of EIGRP was to create a classless version of IGRP. EIGRP includes several features that are not commonly found in other distance vector routing protocols like RIP (RIPv1 and RIPv2) and IGRP. These features include:

- Reliable Transport Protocol (RTP)
- Bounded Updates
- Diffusing Update Algorithm (DUAL)
- Establishing Adjacencies
- Neighbor and Topology Tables

Although EIGRP may *act* like a link-state routing protocol, it is still a distance vector routing protocol.

Note: The term *hybrid* routing protocol is sometimes used to define EIGRP. However, this term is misleading because EIGRP is not a hybrid between distance vector and link-state routing protocols - it is solely a distance vector routing protocol. Therefore, Cisco is no longer using this term to refer to EIGRP.

In this chapter, you will learn how to configure EIGRP and verify your EIGRP configuration with new show commands. You will also learn the formula used by EIGRP to calculate this composite metric.

Unique to EIGRP is its Reliable Transport Protocol (RTP) which provides reliable and unreliable delivery of EIGRP packets. In addition, EIGRP establishes relationships with directly connected routers that are also enabled for EIGRP. Neighbor relationships are used to track the status of these neighbors. RTP and the tracking of neighbor adjacencies set the stage for the EIGRP workhorse, the Diffusing Update Algorithm (DUAL).

As the computational engine that drives EIGRP, DUAL resides at the center of the routing protocol, guaranteeing *loop-free* paths and backup paths throughout the routing domain. You will learn exactly how DUAL selects a route to install in the routing table and what DUAL does with potential backup routes.

Like RIPv2, EIGRP can operate with classful or classless routing behavior. You will learn how to disable automatic summarization and then how to manually summarize networks to reduce the size of routing tables. Finally, you will learn how to use default routing with EIGRP.

9.1 Introduction to EIGRP

9.1.1 EIGRP: An Enhanced Distance Vector Routing Protocol

Refer to
Figure
in online course

Although EIGRP is described as an enhanced distance vector routing protocol, it is still a distance vector routing protocol. This can sometimes be a source of confusion. In order to appreciate enhancements of EIGRP and eliminate any confusion, we must first look at its predecessor, IGRP.

Roots of EIGRP: IGRP

Cisco developed the proprietary IGRP in 1985, in response to some of the limitations of RIPv1, including the use of the hop count metric and the maximum network size of 15 hops.

Instead of hop count, both IGRP and EIGRP use metrics composed of bandwidth, delay, reliability, and load. By default, both routing protocols use only bandwidth and delay. However, because IGRP is a classful routing protocol that uses the Bellman-Ford algorithm and periodic updates, its usefulness is limited in many of today's networks.

Therefore, Cisco enhanced IGRP with a new algorithm, DUAL and other features. The commands for both IGRP and EIGRP are similar, and in many cases identical. This allows for easy migration from IGRP to EIGRP. Cisco discontinued IGRP starting with IOS 12.2(13)T and 12.2(R1s4)S.

Although discussed in more detail throughout this chapter, let us examine some of the differences between a traditional distance vector routing protocol such as RIP and IGRP, and the enhanced distance vector routing protocol, EIGRP.

The figure summarizes the main differences between a traditional distance vector routing protocol, such as RIP, and the enhanced distance vector routing protocol EIGRP.

The Algorithm

Traditional distance vector routing protocols all use some variant of the Bellman-Ford or Ford-Fulkerson algorithm. These protocols, such as RIP and IGRP, age out individual routing entries, and therefore need to periodically send routing table updates.

EIGRP uses the Diffusing Update Algorithm (DUAL). Although still a distance vector routing protocol, EIGRP with DUAL implements features not found in traditional distance vector routing protocols. EIGRP does not send periodic updates and route entries do not age out. Instead, EIGRP uses a lightweight Hello protocol to monitor connection status with its neighbors. Only changes in the routing information, such as a new link or a link becoming unavailable cause a routing update to occur. EIGRP routing updates are still vectors of distances transmitted to directly connected neighbors.

Path Determination

Traditional distance vector routing protocols such as RIP and IGRP keep track of only the preferred routes; the best path to a destination network. If the route becomes unavailable, the router waits for another routing update with a path to this remote network.

EIGRP's DUAL maintains a topology table separate from the routing table, which includes both the best path to a destination network and any backup paths that DUAL has determined to be loop-free. Loop-free means that the neighbor does not have a route to the destination network that passes through this router.

Later in this chapter, you will see that for a route to be considered as a valid loop-free backup path by DUAL, it must meet a requirement known as the feasibility condition. Any backup path that meets this condition is guaranteed to be loop-free. Because EIGRP is a distance vector routing protocol, it is possible that there might be loop-free backup paths to a destination network that do not meet the feasibility condition. These paths are therefore *not* included in the topology table as a valid loop-free backup path by DUAL.

If a route becomes unavailable, DUAL will search its topology table for a valid backup path. If one exists, that route is immediately entered into the routing table. If one does not exist, DUAL performs a network discovery process to see if there happens to be a backup path that did not meet the requirement of the feasibility condition. This process is discussed more thoroughly later in this chapter.

Convergence

Traditional distance vector routing protocols such as RIP and IGRP use periodic updates. Due to the unreliable nature of periodic updates, traditional distance vector routing protocols are prone to routing loops and the count-to-infinity problem. RIP and IGRP use several mechanisms to help avoid these problems including holddown timers, which cause long convergence times.

EIGRP does not use holddown timers. Instead, loop-free paths are achieved through a system of route calculations (diffusing computations) that are performed in a coordinated fashion among the routers. The detail of how this is done is beyond the scope of this course, but the result is faster convergence than traditional distance vector routing protocols.

9.1.2 EIGRP Message Format

Refer to
Figure
in online course

Roll over the fields in the Encapsulated EIGRP Message to see the encapsulation process.

The data portion of an EIGRP message is encapsulated in a packet. This data field is called Type/Length/Value or TLV. As shown in the figure, the types of TLVs relevant to this course are EIGRP Parameters, IP Internal Routes, and IP External Routes. The components of the TLV data field are discussed further on the next page.

The EIGRP packet header is included with every EIGRP packet, regardless of its type. The EIGRP packet header and TLV are then encapsulated in an IP packet. In the IP packet header, the protocol field is set to 88 to indicate EIGRP, and the destination address is set to the multicast 224.0.0.10. If the EIGRP packet is encapsulated in an Ethernet frame, the destination MAC address is also a multicast address: 01-00-5E-00-00-0A.

Refer to
Figure
in online course

Note: In the following discussion of EIGRP messages, many fields are beyond the scope of this course. All fields are shown to provide an accurate picture of the EIGRP message format. However, only the fields relevant to the CCNA candidate are discussed.

Click EIGRP Packet Header in the figure.

Every EIGRP message includes the header. Important fields for our discussion include the Opcode field and the Autonomous System Number field. Opcode specifies the EIGRP packet type:

- Update

- Query

- Reply

- Hello

The *Autonomous System (AS)* Number specifies the EIGRP routing process. Unlike RIP, Cisco routers can run multiple instances of EIGRP. The AS number is used to track multiple instances of EIGRP.

EIGRP packet types are discussed later in this chapter.

Click TLV: EIGRP Parameters in the figure.

The EIGRP parameters message includes the weights that EIGRP uses for its composite metric. By default, only bandwidth and delay are weighted. Both are equally weighted, therefore, the K1 field for bandwidth and the K3 field for delay are both set to 1. The other K values are set to zero. Metric calculations are further discussed later in this chapter.

The Hold Time is the amount of time the EIGRP neighbor receiving this message should wait before considering the advertising router to be down. Hold Time is discussed in more detail later in this chapter.

Click TLV: IP Internal in the figure.

The IP Internal message is used to advertise EIGRP routes within an autonomous system. Important fields for our discussion include: the metric fields (Delay and Bandwidth), the subnet mask field (Prefix Length), and the Destination field.

Delay is calculated as the sum of delays from source to destination in units of 10 microseconds. Bandwidth is the lowest configured bandwidth of any interface along the route.

The subnet mask is specified as the prefix length or the number of network bits in the subnet mask. For example, the prefix length for the subnet mask 255.255.255.0 is 24 because 24 is the number of network bits.

The Destination field stores the address of the destination network. Although only 24 bits are shown in this figure, this field varies based on the value of the network portion of the 32-bit network address. For example, the network portion of 10.1.0.0/16 is 10.1. Therefore, the Destination field stores the first 16 bits. Because the *minimum* length of this field is 24 bits, the remainder of the field is padded with zeros. If a network address is longer than 24 bits (192.168.1.32/27, for example), then the Destination field is extended for another 32 bits (for a total of 56 bits) and the unused bits are padded with zeros.

Click TLV: IP External in the figure.

The IP External message is used when external routes are imported into the EIGRP routing process. In this chapter, we will import or redistribute a default static route into EIGRP. Notice that the bottom half of the IP External TLV includes all the fields used by the IP Internal TLV.

Note: Some EIGRP literature may incorrectly state that the Maximum Transmission Unit (MTU) is one of the metrics used by EIGRP. MTU is *not* a metric used by EIGRP. The MTU is included in the routing updates but it is not used to determine the routing metric.

9.1.3 Protocol Dependent Modules (PDM)

Refer to
Figure
in online course

EIGRP has the capability for routing several different protocols including IP, IPX, and AppleTalk using protocol-dependent modules (PDM). PDMs are responsible for the specific routing tasks for each Network layer protocol.

For example:

- The IP-EIGRP module is responsible for sending and receiving EIGRP packets that are encapsulated in IP and for using DUAL to build and maintain the IP routing table. As you can see in the figure, EIGRP uses different EIGRP packets and maintains separate neighbor, topology, and routing tables for each Network layer protocol.

■ The IPX EIGRP module is responsible for exchanging routing information about IPX networks with other IPX EIGRP routers. IPX EIGRP and Appletalk EIGRP are not included in this course.

9.1.4 RTP and EIGRP Packet Types

Refer to
Figure
in online course

Reliable Transport Protocol (RTP) is the protocol used by EIGRP for the delivery and reception of EIGRP packets. EIGRP was designed as a Network layer independent routing protocol; therefore, it cannot use the services of UDP or TCP because IPX and Appletalk do not use protocols from the TCP/IP protocol suite. The figure shows conceptually how RTP operates.

Although "Reliable" is part of its name, RTP includes both reliable delivery and unreliable delivery of EIGRP packets, similar to TCP and UDP, respectively. Reliable RTP requires an acknowledgement to be returned by the receiver to the sender. An unreliable RTP packet does not require an acknowledgement.

RTP can send packets either as a unicast or a multicast. Multicast EIGRP packets use the reserved multicast address of 224.0.0.10.

Refer to
Figure
in online course

EIGRP Packet Types

EIGRP uses five different packet types, some in pairs.

Click Hello in the figure.

Hello packets are used by EIGRP to discover neighbors and to form adjacencies with those neighbors. EIGRP hello packets are multicasts and use unreliable delivery. EIGRP Hello packets are discussed in a later section.

Click Update and ACK in the figure.

Update packets are used by EIGRP to propagate routing information. Unlike RIP, EIGRP does not send periodic updates. Update packets are sent only when necessary. EIGRP updates contain only the routing information needed and are sent only to those routers that require it. EIGRP update packets use reliable delivery. Update packets are sent as a multicast when required by multiple routers, or as a unicast when required by only a single router. In the figure, because the links are point-to-point, the updates are sent as unicasts.

Acknowledgement (ACK) packets are sent by EIGRP when reliable delivery is used. RTP uses reliable delivery for EIGRP update, query, and reply packets. EIGRP acknowledgement packets contain a nonzero acknowledgment number and always are sent by using a unicast address.

In the figure, R2 has lost connectivity to the LAN attached to its FastEthernet interface. R2 immediately sends an Update to R1 and R3 noting the downed route. R1 and R3 respond with an acknowledgement.

Click Query and Reply in the figure.

Query and reply packets are used by DUAL when searching for networks and other tasks. Queries and replies use reliable delivery. Queries use multicast, whereas replies are always sent as unicast. DUAL is discussed in a later section. Query and reply packets are discussed in more detail in CCNP.

In the figure, R2 has lost connectivity to the LAN and it sends out queries to all EIGRP neighbors searching for any possible routes to the LAN. Because queries use reliable delivery, the receiving router must return an EIGRP acknowledgement. (To keep this example simple, acknowledgements were omitted in the graphic.)

All neighbors must send a reply regardless of whether or not they have a route to the downed network. Because replies also use reliable delivery, routers such as R2, must send an acknowledgement.

Note: You may be wondering why R2 would send out a query for a network it knows is down. Actually, only the interface attached to the network is down. Another router could be attached to the same LAN. Therefore, R2 queries for such a router before completely removing the network from its database.

9.1.5 Hello Protocol

Refer to
Figure
in online course

Before any EIGRP packets can be exchanged between routers, EIGRP must first discover its neighbors. EIGRP neighbors are other routers running EIGRP on shared, directly connected networks.

EIGRP routers discover neighbors and establish adjacencies with neighbor routers using the Hello packet. On most networks EIGRP Hello packets are sent every 5 seconds. On multipoint non-broadcast multiaccess networks (NBMA) such as X.25, Frame Relay, and ATM interfaces with access links of T1 (1.544 Mbps) or slower, Hellos are unicast every 60 seconds. An EIGRP router assumes that as long as it is receiving Hello packets from a neighbor, the neighbor and its routes remain viable.

Holdtime tells the router the maximum time the router should wait to receive the next Hello before declaring that neighbor as unreachable. By default, the *hold time* is three times the Hello interval, or 15 seconds on most networks and 180 seconds on low speed NBMA networks. If the hold time expires, EIGRP will declare the route as down and DUAL will search for a new path by sending out queries.

9.1.6 EIGRP Bounded Updates

Refer to
Figure
in online course

EIGRP uses the term *partial* or *bounded* when referring to its update packets. Unlike RIP, EIGRP does not send periodic updates. Instead, EIGRP sends its updates only when the metric for a route changes.

The term *partial* means that the update only includes information about the route changes. EIGRP sends these incremental updates when the state of a destination changes, instead of sending the entire contents of the routing table.

The term *bounded* refers to the propagation of partial updates sent only to those routers that are affected by the change. The partial update is automatically "bounded" so that only those routers that need the information are updated.

By sending only the routing information that is needed and only to those routers that need it, EIGRP minimizes the bandwidth required to send EIGRP packets.

9.1.7 DUAL: An Introduction

Refer to
Figure
in online course

Diffusing Update Algorithm (DUAL) is the convergence algorithm used by EIGRP instead of the Bellman-Ford or Ford Fulkerson algorithms used by other distance vector routing protocols, like RIP. DUAL is based on research conducted at SRI International, using calculations that were first proposed by E.W. Dijkstra and C.S. Scholten. The most prominent work with DUAL has been done by J.J. Garcia-Luna-Aceves.

Routing loops, even temporary ones, can be extremely detrimental to network performance. Distance vector routing protocols such as RIP prevent routing loops with *hold-down timers* and split horizon. Although EIGRP uses both of these techniques, it uses them somewhat differently; the primary way that EIGRP prevents routing loops is with the DUAL algorithm.

Click Play to view the basic operation of DUAL.

The DUAL algorithm is used to obtain loop-freedom at every instant throughout a route computation. This allows all routers involved in a topology change to synchronize at the same time. Routers that are not affected by the topology changes are not involved in the recomputation. This method provides EIGRP with faster convergence times than other distance vector routing protocols.

The decision process for all route computations is done by the DUAL Finite State Machine. In general terms, a finite state machine (FSM) is a model of behavior composed of a finite number of states, transitions between those states, and events or actions that create the transitions.

The DUAL FSM tracks all routes, uses its metric to select efficient, loop-free paths, and selects the routes with the least cost path to insert into the routing table. The DUAL FSM will be discussed in more detail later in this chapter.

Because recomputation of the DUAL algorithm can be processor-intensive, it is advantageous to avoid recomputation whenever possible. Therefore, DUAL maintains a list of backup routes it has already determined to be loop-free. If the primary route in the routing table fails, the best backup route is immediately added to the routing table.

9.1.8 Administrative Distance

> Refer to
> **Figure**
> in online course

As you know from Chapter 3, "Introduction to Dynamic Routing Protocols," administrative distance (AD) is the trustworthiness (or preference) of the route source. EIGRP has a default administrative distance of 90 for internal routes and 170 for routes imported from an external source, such as default routes. When compared to other interior gateway protocols (IGPs), EIGRP is the most preferred by the Cisco IOS because it has the lowest administrative distance.

Notice in the figure that EIGRP has a third AD value, of 5, for summary routes. Later in this chapter, you will learn how to configure EIGRP summary routes.

9.1.9 Authentication

> Refer to
> **Figure**
> in online course

Like other routing protocols, EIGRP can be configured for authentication. RIPv2, EIGRP, OSPF, IS-IS, and BGP can all be configured to encrypt and authenticate their routing information.

It is good practice to authenticate transmitted routing information. This practice ensures that routers will only accept routing information from other routers that have been configured with the same password or authentication information.

Note: Authentication does not encrypt the router's routing table.

As stated in previous chapters, configuring routing protocols to use authentication will be discussed in a later course.

9.2 Basic EIGRP Configuration

9.2.1 EIGRP Network Topology

> Refer to
> **Figure**
> in online course

The figure shows our topology from previous chapters, but now includes the addition of the ISP router. Notice that both the R1 and R2 routers have subnets that are part of the 172.16.0.0/16 classful network, a class B address. The fact that 172.16.0.0 is a class B address is only relevant because EIGRP automatically summarizes at classful boundaries, similar to RIP.

Click R1, R2, and R3 to see each router's starting configuration.

Notice that the ISP router does not physically exist in our configurations. The connection between R2 and ISP is represented with a *loopback interface* on router R2. Remember from Chapter 7, "RIPv2," that a loopback interface can be used to represent an interface on a router that does not have any actual connection to a physical link on the network. Loopback addresses can be verified with the `ping` command and included in routing updates.

Note: Loopback interfaces also have specific uses with some routing protocols, as we will see in Chapter 11, OSPF.

9.2.2 Autonomous Systems and Process IDs

Refer to
Figure
in online course

Autonomous System

An autonomous system (AS) is a collection of networks under the administrative control of a single entity that presents a common routing policy to the Internet. In the figure, companies A, B, C, and D are all under the administrative control of ISP1. ISP1 "presents a common routing policy" for all of these companies when advertising routes to ISP2.

The guidelines for the creation, selection, and registration of an autonomous system are described in RFC 1930. AS numbers are assigned by the Internet Assigned Numbers Authority (IANA), the same authority that assigns IP address space. You learned about IANA and its Regional Internet Registries (RIRs) in a previous course. The local RIR is responsible for assigning an AS number to an entity from its block of assigned AS numbers. Prior to 2007, AS numbers were 16-bit numbers, ranging from 0 to 65535. Now 32-bit AS numbers are assigned, increasing the number of available AS numbers to over 4 billion.

Who needs an autonomous system number? Usually ISPs (Internet Service Providers), Internet backbone providers, and large institutions connecting to other entities that also have an AS number. These ISPs and large institutions use the exterior gateway routing protocol Border Gateway Protocol, or BGP, to propagate routing information. BGP is the only routing protocol that uses an actual autonomous system number in its configuration.

The vast majority of companies and institutions with IP networks do not need an AS number because they come under the control of a larger entity such as an ISP. These companies use interior gateway protocols such as RIP, EIGRP, OSPF, and IS-IS to route packets within their own networks. They are one of many independent and separate networks within the autonomous system of the ISP. The ISP is responsible for the routing of packets within its autonomous system and between other autonomous systems.

Refer to
Figure
in online course

Process ID

Both EIGRP and OSPF use a process ID to represent an instance of their respective routing protocol running on the router.

```
Router(config)#router eigrp autonomous-system
```
Although EIGRP refers to the parameter as an "autonomous-system" number, it actually functions as a process ID. This number is *not* associated with an autonomous system number discussed previously and can be assigned any 16-bit value.

```
Router(config)#router eigrp 1
```
In this example, the number 1 identifies this particular EIGRP process running on this router. In order to establish neighbor adjacencies, EIGRP requires all routers in the same routing domain to be configured with the same process ID. Typically, only a single process ID of any routing protocol would be configured on a router.

Note: RIP does not use process IDs; therefore, it can only support a single instance of RIP. Both EIGRP and OSPF can support multiple instances of each routing protocol, although this type of multiple routing protocol implementation is not usually needed or recommended.

9.2.3 The router eigrp command

Refer to
Figure
in online course

The **router eigrp** *autonomous-system* global configuration command enables EIGRP. The autonomous system parameter is a number chosen by the network administrator between 1 and 65535. The number chosen is the process ID number and is important because all routers in this EIGRP routing domain must use the same process ID number (*autonomous-system* number).

Click Router Output in the figure.

As you can see from the topology and router output in the figure, we will enable EIGRP on all three routers using the process ID of 1.

9.2.4 The network Command

Refer to
Figure
in online course

The network command in EIGRP has the same function as in other IGP routing protocols:

- Any interface on this router that matches the network address in the **network** command will be enabled to send and receive EIGRP updates.

- This network (or subnet) will be included in EIGRP routing updates.

Click Router Output in the figure.

The **network** command is used in router configuration mode.

`Router(config-router)#`**network** *network-address*

The *network-address* is the classful network address for this interface. The figure shows the network commands configured for R1 and R2. R3 will be configured on the next page. In the figure, a single classful network statement is used on R1 to include both 172.16.1.0/24 and 172.16.3.0/30 subnets:

`R1(config-router)#`**network 172.16.0.0**

When EIGRP is configured on R2, DUAL sends a notification message to the console stating that a neighbor relationship with another EIGRP router has been established. This new *adjacency* happens automatically because both R1 and R2 are using the same **eigrp 1** routing process and both routers are now sending updates on the 172.16.0.0 network.

`R2(config-router)#`**network 172.16.0.0**

```
 %DUAL-5-NBRCHANGE:
 IP-EIGRP 1: Neighbor 172.16.3.1 (Serial0/0) is up: new adjacency
```

Refer to
Figure
in online course

The network Command with a Wildcard Mask

By default, when using the network command and a classful network address such as 172.16.0.0, all interfaces on the router that belong to that classful network address will be enabled for EIGRP. However, there may be times when the network administrator does not want to include all interfaces within a network when enabling EIGRP. To configure EIGRP to advertise specific subnets only, use the *wildcard-mask* option with the **network** command:

`Router(config-router)#`**network** *network-address* [*wildcard-mask*]

Think of a *wildcard mask* as the inverse of a subnet mask. The inverse of subnet mask 255.255.255.252 is 0.0.0.3. To calculate the inverse of the subnet mask, subtract the subnet mask from 255.255.255.255:

```
 255.255.255.255
 - 255.255.255.252
 Subtract the subnet mask
 — — — — — — — -
 0. 0. 0. 3
 Wildcard mask
```

Click Router Output in the figure.

In the figure, R2 is configured with the subnet 192.168.10.8 and the wildcard mask 0.0.0.3.

```
R2(config-router)#network 192.168.10.8 0.0.0.3
```

Some IOS versions will also let you simply enter the subnet mask. For example, you might enter the following:

```
R2(config-router)#network 192.168.10.8 255.255.255.252
```

However, the IOS will then convert the command to the wildcard mask format, as can be verified with the **show run** command:

```
R2#show run
 <some output omitted>
 !
 router eigrp 1
 network 172.16.0.0
 network 192.168.10.8
0.0.0.3
 auto-summary
!
```

The figure also shows the configuration for R3. As soon as the classful network 192.168.10.0 is configured, R3 establishes adjacencies with both R1 and R2.

9.2.5 Verifying EIGRP

Refer to
Figure
in online course

Before any updates can be sent or received by EIGRP, routers must establish adjacencies with their neighbors. EIGRP routers establish adjacencies with neighbor routers by exchanging EIGRP Hello packets.

Use the **show ip eigrp neighbors** command to view the neighbor table and verify that EIGRP has established an adjacency with its neighbors. For each router, you should be able to see the IP address of the adjacent router and the interface that this router uses to reach that EIGRP neighbor. In the figure, we can verify that all routers have established the necessary adjacencies. Each router has two neighbors listed in the neighbor table.

The output from the **show ip eigrp neighbor** command includes:

- **H column -** Lists the neighbors in the order they were learned.

- **Address -** The IP address of the neighbor.

- **Interface -** The local interface on which this Hello packet was received.

- **Hold -** The current hold time. Whenever a Hello packet is received, this value is reset to the maximum hold time for that interface and then counts down to zero. If zero is reached, the neighbor is considered "down".

- **Uptime -** Amount of time since this neighbor was added to the neighbor table.

    - **SRTT** (Smooth Round Trip Timer) and **RTO** (Retransmit Interval) - Used by RTP to manage reliable EIGRP packets. SRTT and RTO are discussed further in CCNP courses.

  - **Queue Count -** Should always be zero. If more than zero, then EIGRP packets are waiting to be sent. Queue count is discussed further in CCNP courses.

  - **Sequence Number -** Used to track updates, queries, and reply packets. Sequence numbers are discussed further in CCNP courses.

The **show ip eigrp neighbors** command is very useful for verifying and troubleshooting EIGRP. If a neighbor is not listed after adjacencies have been established with a router's neighbors, check the local interface to make sure it is activated with the **show ip interface brief** command. If the interface is active, try pinging the IP address of the neighbor. If the ping fails, it means that the neighbor interface is down and needs to be activated. If the ping is successful and EIGRP still does not see the router as a neighbor, examine the following configurations:

- Are both routers configured with the same EIGRP process ID?

- Is the directly connected network included in the EIGRP network statements?

- Is the **passive-interface** command configured to prevent EIGRP Hello packets on the interface?

As with RIP, the **show ip protocols** command can be used to verify that EIGRP is enabled. The **show ip protocols** command displays different types of output specific to each routing protocol. We will examine some of these details in later sections.

Click Router Output in the figure.

Notice that the output specifies the process ID used by EIGRP:

```
Routing Protocol is "
eigrp 1"
```

Remember, the process ID must be the same on all routers for EIGRP to establish neighbor adjacencies and share routing information.

EIGRP's internal and external administrative distances are also displayed:

```
Distance:
internal 90 external 170
```

9.2.6 Examining the Routing Table

Another way to verify that EIGRP and other functions of the router are configured properly is to examine the routing tables with the **show ip route** command.

Click R1, R2, and R3 in the figure.

By default, EIGRP automatically summarizes routes at the major network boundary. We can disable the automatic summarization with the **no auto-summary** command, just as we did in RIPv2. We will examine this in more detail in a later section.

Notice that EIGRP routes are denoted in the routing table with a **D**, which stands for DUAL.

Remember, because EIGRP is a classless routing protocol (includes the subnet mask in the routing update), it supports VLSM and CIDR. We can see in the routing table for R1 that the 172.16.0.0/16 parent network is variably subnetted with three child routes using either a /24 or /30 mask.

Introducing the Null0 Summary Route

The figure shows the routing table for R2 with two entries highlighted. Notice that EIGRP has automatically included a summary route to Null0 for the classful networks 192.168.10.0/24 and 172.16.0.0/16.

Remember from Chapter 7, "RIPv2," that Null0 is not an actual interface. Notice that the summary routes are sourced from Null0 - this is because these routes are used for advertisement purposes. The 192.168.10.0/24 and 172.16.0.0/16 routes do not actually represent a path to reach the parent networks. If a packet does not match one of the level 2 child routes, it is sent to the Null0 interface. In other words, if the packet matches the level 1 parent - the classful network address - but none of the subnets, the packet is discarded.

Note: EIGRP automatically includes a null0 summary route as a child route whenever both of following conditions exist:

- There is at least one subnet that was learned via EIGRP.

- Automatic summarization is enabled.

We will see that the null0 summary route is removed when automatic summary is disabled.

Refer to
Figure
in online course

R3 Routing Table

The routing table for R3 shows that both R1 and R2 are automatically summarizing the 172.16.0.0/16 network and sending it as a single routing update. R1 and R2 are not propagating the individual subnets because of automatic summarization. We will turn off automatic summarization later. Because R3 is getting two equal cost routes for 172.16.0.0/16 from both R1 and R2, both routes are included in the routing table.

Refer to **Packet
Tracer Activity**
for this chapter

Use the Packet Tracer Activity to configure and verify basic EIGRP routing.

9.3 EIGRP Metric Calculation

9.3.1 EIGRP Composite Metric and the K Values

Refer to
Figure
in online course

EIGRP uses the following values in its composite metric to calculate the preferred path to a network:

- Bandwidth

- Delay

- Reliability

- Load

Note: As mentioned earlier in this chapter, although MTU is included in the routing table updates, it is not a routing metric used by EIGRP or IGRP. By default, only bandwidth and delay are used to calculate the metric. Cisco recommends that reliability and load are not used unless the administrator has an explicit need to do so.

The Composite Metric

The figure shows the composite metric formula used by EIGRP. The formula consists of values K1 through K5, known as EIGRP metric weights. By default, K1 and K3 are set to 1, and K2, K4, and K5 are set to 0. The result is that only the bandwidth and delay values are used in the computation of the default composite metric.

The default K values can be changed with the EIGRP router command:

```
Router(config-router)#metric weights tos k1 k2 k3 k4 k5
```
Note: Modifying the metric weights is beyond the scope of this course, but their relevance is important in establishing neighbors and is discussed in a later section. The **tos** (Type of Service) value is left over from IGRP and was never implemented. The **tos** value is always set to 0.

Refer to
Figure
in online course

Verifying the K Values

The **show ip protocols** command is used to verify the K values. The command output for R1 is shown in the figure. Notice that the K values on R1 are set to the default. Again, changing these values to other than the default is not recommended unless the network administrator has a very good reason to do so.

9.3.2 EIGRP Metrics

Refer to
Figure
in online course

Examining the Metric Values

You now know the defaults for the K values. By using the `show interface` command we can examine the *actual* values used for bandwidth, delay, reliability, and load in the computation of the routing metric.

Click Router Output in the figure.

The output in the figure shows the values used in the composite metric for the Serial 0/0/0 interface on R1.

```
 MTU 1500 bytes,
BW 1544 Kbit, DLY 20000 usec,

reliability 255/255, txload 1/255, rxload 1/255
```
Bandwidth

The bandwidth metric (1544 Kbit) is a static value used by some routing protocols such as EIGRP and OSPF to calculate their routing metric. The bandwidth is displayed in Kbit (kilobits). Most serial interfaces use the default bandwidth value of 1544 Kbit or 1,544,000 bps (1.544 Mbps). This is the bandwidth of a T1 connection. However, some serial interfaces use a different default bandwidth value. Always verify bandwidth with the `show interface` command.

The value of the bandwidth may or may not reflect the actual physical bandwidth of the interface. *Modifying the bandwidth value does not change the actual bandwidth of the link.* If actual bandwidth of the link differs from the default bandwidth value, then you should modify the bandwidth value, as we will see in a later section.

Refer to
Figure
in online course

Delay

Delay is a measure of the time it takes for a packet to traverse a route. The delay (DLY) metric is a static value based on the type of link to which the interface is connected and is expressed in microseconds. Delay is not measured dynamically. In other words, the router does not actually track how long packets are taking to reach the destination. The delay value, much like the bandwidth value, is a default value that can be changed by the network administrator.

```
 MTU 1500 bytes, BW 1544 Kbit,
DLY 20000 usec,
 reliability 255/255, txload 1/255, rxload 1/255
```

The table in the figure shows the default delay values for various interfaces. Notice that the default value is 20,000 microseconds for Serial interfaces and 100 microseconds for FastEthernet interfaces.

Refer to
Figure
in online course

Reliability

Reliability (`reliability`) is a measure of the probability that the link will fail or how often the link has experienced errors. Unlike delay, Reliability is measured dynamically with a value between 0 and 255, with 1 being a minimally reliable link and 255 one hundred percent reliable. Reliability is calculated on a 5-minute weighted average to avoid the sudden impact of high (or low) error rates.

Reliability is expressed as a fraction of 255 - the higher the value, the more reliable the link. So, 255/255 would be 100 percent reliable, whereas a link of 234/255 would be 91.8 percent reliable.

Remember: By default, EIGRP does not use reliability in its metric calculation.

Load

Load (`load`) reflects the amount of traffic utilizing the link. Like reliability, load is measured dynamically with a value between 0 and 255. Similar to reliability, load is expressed as a fraction of

255. However, in this case a lower load value is more desirable because it indicates less load on the link. So, 1/255 would be a minimally loaded link. 40/255 is a link at 16 percent capacity, and 255/255 would be a link that is 100 percent saturated.

Load is displayed as both an outbound, or transmit, load value (txload) and an inbound, or receive, load value (rxload). This value is calculated on a 5-minute weighted average to avoid the sudden impact of high (or low) channel usage.

Remember: By default, EIGRP does not use load in its metric calculation.

9.3.3 Using the bandwidth Command

Refer to **Figure** in online course

On most serial links, the bandwidth metric will default to 1544 Kbits. Because both EIGRP and OSPF use bandwidth in default metric calculations, a correct value for bandwidth is very important to the accuracy of routing information. But what do you do if the actual bandwidth of the link does not match the default bandwidth of the interface?

Click Configure Bandwidth in the figure.

Use the interface command **bandwidth** to modify the bandwidth metric:

```
Router(config-if)#bandwidth kilobits
```
Use the interface command **no bandwidth** to restore the default value.

In the figure, the link between R1 and R2 has a bandwidth of 64 kbps, and the link between R2 and R3 has a bandwidth of 1024 kbps. The figure shows the configurations used on all three routers to modify the bandwidth on the appropriate serial interfaces.

Click Verify Bandwidth in the figure.

We can verify the change using the **show interface** command. It is important to modify the bandwidth metric on both sides of the link to ensure proper routing in both directions.

Note: A common misconception for students new to networking and the Cisco IOS is to assume that the **bandwidth** command will change the physical bandwidth of the link. As stated in the previous section, the **bandwidth** command only modifies the bandwidth metric used by routing protocols such as EIGRP and OSPF. Sometimes, a network administrator will change the bandwidth value in order have more control over the chosen outgoing interface.

9.3.4 Calculating the EIGRP Metric

Refer to **Figure** in online course

The figure shows the composite metric used by EIGRP. Using the default values for K1 and K3, we can simplify this calculation to: the slowest bandwidth (or minimum bandwidth) plus the cumulative sum of all of the delays.

In other words, by examining the bandwidth and delay values for all of the outgoing interfaces of the route, we can determine the EIGRP metric. First, determine the link with the slowest bandwidth. That bandwidth is used for the **(10,000,000/bandwidth) * 256** portion of the formula. Next, determine the delay value for each outgoing interface on the way to the destination. Sum the delay values and divide by 10 (**sum of delay/10**) and then multiply by 256 (*** 256**). Add the bandwidth and sum of delay values to obtain the **EIGRP metric**.

The routing table output for R2 shows that the route to 192.168.1.0/24 has an EIGRP metric of 3,014,400. Let's see exactly how EIGRP calculated this value.

Refer to **Figure** in online course

Bandwidth

Click Bandwidth Calculation in the figure.

Because EIGRP uses the slowest bandwidth in its metric calculation, we can find the slowest bandwidth by examining each interface between R2 and the destination network 192.168.1.0. The Serial 0/0/1 interface on R2 has a bandwidth of 1,024 Kbps or 1,024,000 bps. The FastEthernet 0/0 interface on R3 has a bandwidth of 100,000 Kbps or 100 Mbps. Therefore, the slowest bandwidth is 1024 Kbps and is used in the calculation of the metric.

EIGRP takes the *reference bandwidth* value of 10,000,000 and divides it by the bandwidth value in kbps. This will result in higher bandwidth values receiving a lower metric and lower bandwidth values receiving a higher metric.

10,000,000 is divided by 1024. If the result is not a whole number, then the value is rounded down. In this case, 10,000,000 divided by 1024 equals 9765.625. The .625 is dropped before multiplying by 256. The bandwidth portion of the composite metric is 2,499,840.

Delay

Using the same outgoing interfaces we can also determine the delay value.

Click Delay Calculation in the figure.

EIGRP uses the cumulative sum of delay metrics of all of the outgoing interfaces. The Serial 0/0/1 interface on R2 has a delay of 20000 microseconds. The FastEthernet 0/0 interface on R3 has a delay of 100 microseconds.

Each delay value is divided by 10 and then summed. 20,000/10 + 100/10 results in a value of 2,010. This result is then multiplied by 256. The delay portion of the composite metric is 514,560.

Adding Bandwidth and Delay

Click EIGRP Metric in the figure.

Simply add the two values together, 2,499,840 + 514,560, to obtain the EIGRP metric of 3,014,400. This value matches the value shown in the routing table for R2. This is a result of the slowest bandwidth and the sum of the delays

Refer to **Packet Tracer Activity** for this chapter

Use the Packet Tracer Activity to investigate EIGRP's metric calculations.

9.4 DUAL

9.4.1 DUAL Concepts

Refer to **Figure** in online course

As stated in a previous section, DUAL (Diffusing Update Algorithm) is the algorithm used by EIGRP. This section will discuss how DUAL determines the best loop-free path and loop-free backup paths.

DUAL uses several terms which will be discussed in more detail throughout this section:

- Successor
- *Feasible Distance (FD)*
- *Feasible Successor (FS)*
- Reported Distance (RD) or Advertised Distance (AD)
- Feasible Condition or *Feasibility Condition (FC)*

These terms and concepts are at the center of DUAL's loop avoidance mechanism. Let's examine them in more depth.

9.4.2 Successor and Feasible Distance

Refer to
Figure
in online course

A *successor* is a neighboring router that is used for packet forwarding and is the least-cost route to the destination network. The IP address of a successor is shown in a routing table entry right after the word via.

Feasible distance (FD) is the lowest calculated metric to reach the destination network. FD is the metric listed in the routing table entry as the second number inside the brackets. As with other routing protocols this is also known as the metric for the route.

Click Router Output in the figure.

Examining the routing table for R2 in the figure, we can see that EIGRP's best path for the 192.168.1.0/24 network is through router R3 and that the feasible distance is 3014400-the same metric that we calculated in the last topic:

```
D 192.168.1.0/24 [90/
3014400] via
192.168.10.10, 00:00:31, Serial0/0/1
```

Other successors and feasible distances are also shown in the figure. Can you answer the following questions?

What is the IP address of the successor for network 172.16.1.0/24?

Answer: 172.16.3.1, which is R1.

What is the feasible distance to 172.16.1.0/24?

Answer: 40514560.

9.4.3 Feasible Successors, Feasibility Condition and Reported Distance

Refer to
Figure
in online course

One of the reasons DUAL can converge quickly after a change in the topology is because it can use backup paths to other routers known as *feasible successors* without having to recompute DUAL.

Click Feasible Successor in the figure.

A *feasible successor* (FS) is a neighbor who has a loop-free backup path to the same network as the successor by satisfying the feasibility condition. In our topology, would R2 consider R1 to be a feasible successor to network 192.168.1.0/24? In order to be a feasible successor, R1 must satisfy the *feasibility condition* (FC). Let's examine what that means.

Click Feasibility Condition in the figure.

The feasibility condition (FC) is met when a neighbor's *reported distance (RD)* to a network is less than the local router's feasible distance to the same destination network. The reported distance or advertised distance is simply an EIGRP neighbor's feasible distance to the same destination network. The reported distance is the metric that a router reports to a neighbor about its own cost to that network.

If R3 is the successor, can the neighbor R1 be a feasible successor to this same 192.161.0/24 network? In other words, if the link between R2 and R3 fails can R1 immediately be used as a backup path without a recomputation of the DUAL algorithm? R1 can only be a feasible successor if it meets the feasibility condition.

In the figure, R1 is reporting to R2 that its feasible distance to 192.168.1.0/24 is 2172416. From R2's perspective, 2172416 is R1's *reported* distance. From R1's perspective, 2172416 is its *feasible* distance.

Click Reported Distance in the figure.

R2 examines the reported distance (RD) of 2172416 from R1. Because the reported distance (RD) of R1 is less than R2's own feasible distance (FD) of 3014400, R1 meets the feasibility condition. R1 is now a feasible successor for R2 to the 192.168.1.0/24 network.

Why isn't R1 the successor if its reported distance (RD) is less than R2's feasible distance (FD) to 192.168.1.0/24? Because the total cost for R2, its feasible distance (FD), to reach 192.168.1.0/24 is greater through R1 than it is through R3.

9.4.4 Topology Table: Successor and Feasible Successor

Refer to **Figure** in online course

The successor, feasible distance, and any feasible successors with their reported distances are kept by a router in its EIGRP topology table or *topology database*. As shown in the figure, the topology table can be viewed using the `show ip eigrp topology` command. The topology table lists all successors and feasible successors that DUAL has calculated to destination networks.

Refer to **Figure** in online course

Click Play to view the animation.

A detailed description of each part of the topology table entry for destination network 192.168.1.0/24 appears below.

The first line displays:

- **P -** This route is in the *passive state*. When DUAL is not performing its diffusing computations to determine a path for a network, the route will be in a stable mode, known as the passive state. If DUAL is recalculating or searching for a new path, the route will be in an *active state*. All routes in the topology table should be in the passive state for a stable routing domain. DUAL will display an **A** if the route is "Active," which is a CCNP-level troubleshooting issue.

- **192.168.1.0/24 -** This is the destination network that is also found in the routing table.

- **1 successors -** This shows the number of successors for this network. If there are multiple equal cost paths to this network, there will be multiple successors.

- **FD is 3014400 -** This is the feasible distance, the EIGRP metric to reach the destination network.

The first entry shows the successor:

- **via 192.168.10.10 -** This is the next-hop address of the successor, R3. This address is shown in the routing table.

- **3014400 -** This is the feasible distance to 192.168.1.0/24. It is the metric shown in the routing table.

- **28160 -** This is the reported distance of the successor and is R3's cost to reach this network.

- **Serial0/0/1 -** This is the outbound interface used to reach this network, also shown in the routing table.

The second entry shows the feasible successor, R1 (if there is not a second entry, then there are no feasible successors):

- **via 172.16.3.1 -** This is the next-hop address of the feasible successor, R1.

- **41026560 -** This would be R2's new feasible distance to 192.168.1.0/24 if R1 became the new successor.

- **2172416 -** This is the reported distance of the feasible successor or R1's metric to reach this network. This value, RD, must be less than the current FD of 3014400 to meet the feasibility condition.

- **Serial0/0/0 -** This is the outbound interface used to reach feasible successor, if this router becomes the successor.

Refer to **Figure** in online course

To view detailed information about the metrics of a specific entry in the topology table, add the optional parameter [*network*] to the **show ip eigrp topology** command, as shown in the figure:

R2#**show ip eigrp topology 192.168.1.0**

Remember that EIGRP is a distance vector routing protocol. This command lists the full list of distance vector metrics available to EIGRP even though, by default, EIGRP only uses bandwidth and delay. It also displays other information included in the routing update, but not included in the composite metric: minimum MTU and hop count.

9.4.5 Topology Table: No Feasible Successor

Refer to **Figure** in online course

To continue our understanding of DUAL and its use of successors and feasible successors, let's look at the routing table for R1.

Click R1 Routing Table in the figure.

The route to 192.168.1.0/24 shows that the successor is R3 via 192.168.10.6 with a feasible distance of 2172416.

D 192.168.1.0/24 [90/
2172416] via 192.168.10.6, 00:56:13, Serial0/1

Now let's examine the topology table to see if there are any feasible successors for this route.

Click R1 Topology Table in the figure.

The topology table only shows the successor 192.168.10.6. There are no feasible successors. By looking at the actual physical topology or network diagram, it is obvious that there is a backup route to 192.168.1.0/24 through R2. Why isn't R2 listed as a feasible successor? R2 is not a feasible successor because it does not meet the feasibility condition.

Although, looking at the topology it is obvious that R2 is a backup route, EIGRP does not have a map of the network topology. EIGRP is a distance vector routing protocol and only knows about remote network information through its neighbors.

Therefore, DUAL does not store the route through R2 in the topology table. However, we can view all possible links whether they satisfy the feasible condition or not by adding the [all-links] option to the show ip eigrp topology command.

Click R1 Topology Table [all-links] in the figure.

The **show ip eigrp topology all-links** command shows all possible paths to a network including successors, feasible successors, and even those routes that are not feasible successors. R1's feasible distance to 192.168.1.0/24 is 2172416 via the successor R3. For R2 to be considered a feasible successor, it must meet the feasibility condition. R2's feasible distance to reach 192.168.1.0/24 must be less the R1's current feasible distance (FD). As we can see in the figure, R2's feasible distance is 3014400, which is higher than R1's feasible distance of 2172416.

Even though R2 looks like a viable backup path to 192.168.1.0/24, R1 has no idea that its path is not a potential loop back through itself. EIGRP is a distance vector routing protocol, without the ability to see a complete, loop-free topological map of the network. DUAL's method of guaranteeing that a neighbor has a loop-free path is that the neighbor's metric must satisfy the feasibility condition. By ensuring that the RD of the neighbor is less than its own FD, the router can assume that this neighboring router is not part of its own advertised route, thus always avoiding the potential for a loop.

Does this mean R2 cannot be used if the successor fails? No, R3 can be used, but there will be a longer delay before adding it to the routing table. Before this can happen, DUAL will need to do some further processing, which is explained in the next topic.

9.4.6 Finite State Machine

Refer to **Figure** in online course

DUAL Finite State Machine (FSM)

The centerpiece of EIGRP is DUAL and its EIGRP route-calculation engine. The actual name of this technology is DUAL Finite State Machine (FSM). This finite state machine contains all of the logic used to calculate and compare routes in an EIGRP network. The figure shows a simplified version of the DUAL FSM.

A finite state machine is an abstract machine, not a mechanical device with moving parts. FSMs define a set of possible states that something can go through, what events cause those states, and what events result from those states. Designers use FSMs to describe how a device, computer program, or routing algorithm will react to a set of input events. Finite state machines are beyond the scope of this course; however, we introduce the concept in order to examine some of the output from EIGRP's finite state machine using **debug eigrp fsm**. Let's use the command to watch what DUAL does when a route is removed from the routing table.

Refer to **Figure** in online course

Click R2 Topology Table 1 in the figure.

Remember from our previous discussions that R2 is currently using R3 as the successor to 192.168.1.0/24. In addition, R2 currently lists R1 as a feasible successor. Let's watch what happens when we simulate a failure of the link between R2 and R3.

Click R2 Debug Output in the figure.

First, we turn on DUAL debugging with the **debug eigrp fsm** command. Then, we simulate a link failure using the **shutdown** command on the Serial 0/0/1 interface on R2.

When you do this on a real router or Packet Tracer, you will see all the activity generated by DUAL when a link goes down. R2 must inform all EIGRP neighbors of the lost link as well as take care of updating its own routing and topology tables. The figure in this example only shows selected debug output. In particular, notice that the DUAL finite state machine searches for and finds a feasible successor for the route in the EIGRP topology table. The feasible successor, R1, now becomes the successor and is installed in the routing table as the new best path to 192.168.1.0/24.

Click R2 Topology Table 2 in the figure.

The topology table for R2 now shows R1 as the successor and there are no new feasible successors.

If you are following along on routers or Packet Tracer, be sure to restore the original topology by re-activating the Serial 0/0/1 interface on R2 with the **no shutdown** command.

Refer to **Figure** in online course

No Feasible Successor

What if the path to the successor fails and there are no feasible successors? Remember, just because DUAL does not have a feasible successor does not mean that there is not another path to the network. It just means that DUAL does not have a guaranteed loop-free backup path to the network, so it wasn't added to the topology table as a feasible successor. If there are no feasible successors in the topology table, DUAL will put the network into the *active* state. DUAL will actively query its neighbors for a new successor.

Click R1 Topology Table 1 in the figure.

R1 is currently using R3 as the successor to 192.168.1.0/24. However, R1 does *not* have R2 listed as a feasible successor because R2 does not satisfy the feasibility condition. Let's watch what happens when we simulate a failure of the link between R1 and R3.

Click R1 Debug Output in the figure.

First, we turn on DUAL debugging with the `debug eigrp fsm` command. Then, we simulate a link failure using the `shutdown` command on the Serial 0/0/1 interface on R1.

The selected debug output shows the 192.168.1.0/24 network put into the *active* state and EIGRP queries are sent to other neighbors. R2 replies with a path to this network, which becomes the new successor and is installed into the routing table.

When the successor is no longer available and there is no feasible successor, DUAL will put the route into active state. DUAL will send EIGRP queries asking other routers for a path to this network. Other routers will return EIGRP replies, letting the sender of the EIGRP query know whether or not they have a path to the requested network. If none of the EIGRP replies have a path to this network, the sender of the query will not have a route to this network.

If the sender of the EIGRP queries receives EIGRP replies that include a path to the requested network, the preferred path is added as the new successor and added to the routing table. This process will take longer than if DUAL had a feasible successor in its topology table and was able to quickly add the new route to the routing table.

Note: DUAL FSM and the process of queries and replies is beyond the scope of this course.

Click R1 Topology Table 2 in the figure.

The topology table for R1 now shows R2 as the successor and there are no new feasible successors.

If you are following along on routers or Packet Tracer, be sure to restore the original topology by re-activating the Serial 0/0/1 interface on R1 with the `no shutdown` command.

Refer to **Packet Tracer Activity** for this chapter

Use the Packet Tracer Activity to investigate successors and feasible successors as well as watch the DUAL FSM remove and install routes.

9.5 More EIGRP Configurations

9.5.1 The Null0 Summary Route

Refer to **Figure** in online course

Analyzing a routing table containing EIGRP routes can be confusing due to EIGRP's automatic inclusion of *Null0 summary routes*. In the figure, R1's routing table contains two routes that have an exit interface of Null0. Remember from Chapter 7, "RIPv2," that the Null0 interface is simply a route to nowhere, commonly known as "the bit bucket." So by default, EIGRP uses the Null0 interface to discard any packets that match the parent route but do not match any of the child routes.

You might think that if we configure classless routing behavior with the `ip classless` command, EIGRP would not discard that packet but would continue looking for a default or supernet route. However, the EIGRP Null0 summary route is a child route that will match any possible packets of the parent route that do not match another child route. Even with classless routing behavior, `ip classless`, where you would expect the route lookup process to check for supernets and default routes, EIGRP will use the Null0 summary route and discard the packet because this route will match any packets of the parent that do not have a child route.

Regardless of whether classful or classless routing behavior is being used, the null0 summary will be used and therefore denying the use of any supernet or default route.

In the figure, R1 will discard any packets that match the parent 172.16.0.0/16 classful network but do not match one of the child routes 172.16.1.0/24, 172.16.2.0/24 or 172.16.3.0/24. For example, a packet to 172.16.4.10 would be discarded. Even if a default route was configured, R1 would still discard the packet because it matches the Null0 summary route to 172.16.0.0/16.

```
D 172.16.0.0/16 is a summary, 00:46:10, Null0
```

Note: EIGRP automatically includes a null0 summary route as a child route whenever both of following conditions exist:

- There is at least one subnet that was learned via EIGRP.

- Automatic summarization is enabled.

Like RIP, EIGRP automatically summarizes at major network boundaries. You may have already noticed in the **show run** output that EIGRP, by default, uses the **auto-summary** command. In the next topic, you will see that disabling automatic summarization will remove the Null0 summary route and allow EIGRP to look for a supernet or default route when an EIGRP child route does not match a destination packet.

9.5.2 Disabling Automatic Summarization

Refer to
Figure
in online course

Like RIP, EIGRP automatically summarizes at major network boundaries using the default **auto-summary** command. We can see the result of this by looking at the routing table for R3.

Click R3 Routing Table in the figure.

Notice that R3 is not receiving individual routes for the 172.16.1.0/24, 172.16.2.0/24, and 172.16.3.0/24 subnets. Both R1 and R2 automatically summarized those subnets to the 172.16.0.0/16 classful boundary when sending EIGRP update packets to R3. The result is that R3 has one route to 172.16.0.0/16 through R1. R1 is the successor because of the difference in bandwidth.

```
D 172.16.0.0/16 [90/2172416] via 192.168.10.5, 01:08:30, Serial0/0/0
```

You can quickly see that this route is not optimal. R3 will route all packets destined for 172.16.2.0 through R1. R3 does not know that R1 will then have to route these packets across a very slow link to R2. The only way R3 can learn about this slow bandwidth is if R1 and R2 send individual routes for each of the 172.16.0.0/16 subnets. In other words, R1 and R2 must stop automatically summarizing 172.16.0.0/16.

Click no auto-summary in the figure.

As in RIPv2, automatic summarization can be disabled with the **no auto-summary** command. The router configuration command **eigrp log-neighbor-changes** is on by default on some IOS implementations. If on, you will see output similar to that shown for R1. DUAL takes down all neighbor adjacencies and then reestablishes them so that the effect of the **no auto-summary** command can be fully realized. All EIGRP neighbors will immediately send out a new round of updates that will not be automatically summarized.

Click R1, R2, and R3 in the figure.

We can see in the routing tables for all three routers that EIGRP is now propagating individual subnets. Notice that EIGRP no longer includes the Null0 summary route, because automatic summarization has been disabled with **no auto-summary**. As long as the default classless routing behavior (**ip classless**) is in effect, supernet and default routes will be used when there is not a match with a subnet route.

Refer to
Figure
in online course

Because routes are no longer automatically summarized at major network boundaries, the EIGRP routing and topology tables also change.

Click R1, R2, and R3 in the figure.

Without automatic summarization, R3's routing table now includes the three subnets, 172.16.1.0/24, 172.16.2.0/24, and 172.16.3.0/24. Why does R3's routing table now have two equal cost paths to 172.16.3.0/24? Shouldn't the best path only be through R1 with the 1544 Mbps link?

Remember that EIGRP only uses the link with the slowest bandwidth when calculating the composite metric. The slowest link is the 64 Kbps link that contains the 172.16.3.0/30 network. In this example, the 1544 Mbps link and the 1024 Kbps link are irrelevant in the calculation as far as the bandwidth metric is concerned. Because both paths have the same number and types of outgoing interfaces, the delay values end up being the same. As a result, the EIGRP metric for both paths is the same, even though the path through R1 would actually be the "faster" path.

9.5.3 Manual Summarization

Refer to
Figure
in online course

EIGRP can be configured to summarize routes, whether or not automatic summarization (`auto-summary`) is enabled. Because EIGRP is a classless routing protocol and includes the subnet mask in the routing updates, manual summarization can include supernet routes. Remember, a supernet is an aggregation of multiple major classful network addresses.

Click R3 New LANs in the figure.

Suppose we added two more networks to router R3 using loopback interfaces: 192.168.2.0/24 and 192.168.3.0/24. We also configure networks in R3's EIGRP routing process with `network` commands so that R3 will propagate these networks to other routers.

Click Routing Tables 1 in the figure.

To verify that R3 sent EIGRP update packets to R1 and R2, we check the routing tables. In the figure, only the pertinent routes are shown. R1 and R2 routing tables show these additional networks in their routing tables: 192.168.2.0/24 and 192.168.3.0/24. Instead of sending three separate networks, R3 can summarize the 192.168.1.0/24, 192.168.2.0/24, and 192.168.3.0/24 networks as a single route.

Click R3 Summary Route in the figure.

Determining the Summary EIGRP Route

First, let's determine what the summary of these three networks would be using the same method we used to determine summary static routes:

1. Write out the networks that you want to summarize in binary.

2. To find the subnet mask for summarization, start with the left-most bit.

3. Work your way to the right, finding all the bits that match consecutively.

4. When you find a column of bits that do not match, stop. You are at the summary boundary.

5. Now, count the number of left-most matching bits, which in our example is 22. This number becomes your subnet mask for the summarized route: /22 or 255.255.252.0

6. To find the network address for summarization, copy the matching 22 bits and add all 0 bits to the end to make 32 bits.

The result is the summary network address and mask for 192.168.0.0/22.

Configure EIGRP Manual Summarization

To establish EIGRP manual summarization on all interfaces that send EIGRP packets, use the following interface command:

```
Router(config-if)#ip summary-address eigrp as-number network-address subnet-mask
```

Because R3 has two EIGRP neighbors, the EIGRP manual summarization in configured on both Serial 0/0/0 and Serial 0/0/1.

Click Routing Tables 2 in the figure.

The routing tables of R1 and R2 now no longer include the individual 192.168.1.0/24, 192.168.2.0/24, and 192.168.3.0/24 networks. Instead, they show a single summary route of 192.168.0.0/22. As you learned in Chapter 2, "Static Routing," summary routes lessen the number of total routes in routing tables, which makes the routing table lookup process more efficient. Summary routes also require less bandwidth utilization for the routing updates because a single route can be sent instead of multiple individual routes.

9.5.4 EIGRP Default Route

Refer to **Figure** in online course

Click R2 Static Default Configuration in the figure.

Using a static route to 0.0.0.0/0 as a default route is not routing protocol dependent. The "quad zero" static default route can be used with any currently supported routing protocols. The static default route is usually configured on the router that has a connection to a network outside the EIGRP routing domain, for example, to an ISP.

EIGRP requires the use of the `redistribute static` command to include this static default route with its EIGRP routing updates. The `redistribute static` command tells EIGRP to include this static route in its EIGRP updates to other routers. The figure shows the configuration of the static default route and the `redistribute static` command on router R2.

Note: The static default route is using the exit interface of **Loopback1**. This is because the ISP router in our topology does not physically exist. By using a loopback interface we can simulate a connection to another router.

Click R1, R2, and R3 in the figure.

The routing tables now show a static default route, and a gateway of last resort is now set.

In the routing tables for R1 and R3, notice the routing source and administrative distance for the new static default route. The entry for the static default route on R1 is the following:

```
D*EX 0.0.0.0/0 [
170/3651840] via 192.168.10.6, 00:01:08, Serial0/1
```

- **D -** This static route was learned from an EIGRP routing update.
- *** -** The route is a candidate for a default route.
- **EX -** The route is an external EIGRP route, in this case a static route outside of the EIGRP routing domain.
- **170 -** This is the administrative distance of an external EIGRP route.

Default routes provide a default path to outside the routing domain and, like summary routes, minimize the number of entries in the routing table.

Note: There is another method to propagate a default route in EIGRP, using the `ip default-network` command. More information on this command can be found at:

http://www.cisco.com/en/US/tech/tk365/technologies_tech_note09186a0080094374.shtml

9.5.5 Fine-tuning EIGRP

Refer to
Figure
in online course

The last two topics of this chapter discuss two fundamental ways to fine-tune EIGRP operations. First, we will discuss EIGRP bandwidth utilization. Next, we will discuss how to change the default hello and hold time values.

EIGRP Bandwidth Utilization

By default, EIGRP will use only up to 50 percent of the bandwidth of an interface for EIGRP information. This prevents the EIGRP process from over-utilizing a link and not allowing enough bandwidth for the routing of normal traffic. The `ip bandwidth-percent eigrp` command can be used to configure the percentage of bandwidth that may be used by EIGRP on an interface.

`Router(config-if)#ip bandwidth-percent eigrp as-number percent`

In the figure, R1 and R2 share a very slow 64kbps link. The configuration to limit how much bandwidth EIGRP uses is shown, along with the bandwidth command. The `ip bandwidth-percent eigrp` command uses the amount of configured bandwidth (or the default bandwidth) when calculating the percent that EIGRP can use. In our example, we are limiting EIGRP to no more than 50 percent of the link's bandwidth. Therefore, EIGRP will never use more the 32kbps of the link's bandwidth for EIGRP packet traffic.

Refer to
Figure
in online course

Configuring Hello Intervals and Hold Times

Hello intervals and hold times are configurable on a per-interface basis and do not have to match with other EIGRP routers to establish adjacencies. The command to configure a different hello interval is:

`Router(config-if)#ip hello-interval eigrp as-number seconds`

If you change the hello interval, make sure that you also change the hold time to a value equal to or greater than the hello interval. Otherwise, neighbor adjacency will go down after the hold time expires and before the next hello interval. The command to configure a different hold time is:

`Router(config-if)#ip hold-time eigrp as-number seconds`

The *seconds* value for both hello and hold time intervals can range from 1 to 65,535. This range means that you can set the hello interval to a value of just over 18 hours, which may be appropriate for a very expensive dialup link. However, in the figure we configure both R1 and R2 to use a 60-second hello interval and 180-second hold time. The **no** form can be used on both of these commands to restore the default values.

9.6   EIGRP Configuration Labs

9.6.1   Basic EIGRP Configuration Lab

Refer to
Lab Activity
for this chapter

In this lab, you will learn how to configure the routing protocol EIGRP. A *loopback address* will be used on the R2 router to simulate a connection to an ISP, where all traffic that is not destined for the local network will be sent. Some segments of the network have been subnetted using VLSM. EIGRP is a classless routing protocol that can be used to provide subnet mask information in the routing updates. This will allow VLSM subnet information to be propagated throughout the network.

Refer to **Packet
Tracer Activity**
for this chapter

Use this Packet Tracer Activity to repeat a simulation of Lab 9.6.1. Remember, however, that Packet Tracer is not a substitute for a hands-on lab experience with real equipment.

A summary of the instructions is provided within the activity. Use the Lab PDF for more details.

9.6.2 Challenge EIGRP Configuration Lab

In this lab activity, you will be given a network address that must be subnetted using VLSM to complete the addressing of the network. A combination of EIGRP routing and static routing will be required so that hosts on networks that are not directly connected will be able to communicate with each other. EIGRP must be configured so that all IP traffic takes the shortest path to the destination address.

Use this Packet Tracer Activity to repeat a simulation of Lab 9.6.2. Remember, however, that Packet Tracer is not a substitute for a hands-on lab experience with real equipment.

A summary of the instructions is provided within the activity. Use the Lab PDF for more details.

9.6.3 Troubleshooting EIGRP Configuration Lab

In this lab, you will begin by loading corrupted configuration scripts on each of the routers. These scripts contain errors that will prevent end-to-end communication across the network. You will need to troubleshoot each router to determine the configuration errors, and then use the appropriate commands to correct the configurations. When you have corrected all of the configuration errors, all of the hosts on the network should be able to communicate with each other.

Use this Packet Tracer Activity to repeat a simulation of Lab 9.6.3. Remember, however, that Packet Tracer is not a substitute for a hands-on lab experience with real equipment.

A summary of the instructions is provided within the activity. Use the Lab PDF for more details.

Summary and Review

Summary

Refer to **Figure** in online course

EIGRP (Enhanced Interior Gateway Routing Protocol) is a *classless*, distance vector routing protocol released in 1992 by Cisco Systems. EIGRP is a Cisco proprietary routing protocol and an enhancement of another Cisco propriety protocol IGRP (Interior Gateway Routing Protocol). IGRP is a *classful*, distance vector routing protocol which is no longer supported by Cisco. EIGRP uses the source code of "D" for DUAL in the routing table. EIGRP has a default administrative distance of 90 for internal routes and 170 for routes imported from an external source, such as default routes.

EIGRP used PDMs (Protocol Dependent Modules) giving it the capability to support different Layer 3 protocols including IP, IPX and AppleTalk. EIGRP uses RTP (Reliable Transport Protocol) as the Transport layer protocol for the delivery of EIGRP packets. EIGRP uses reliable delivery for EIGRP updates, queries and replies; and uses unreliable delivery for EIGRP hellos and acknowledgments. Reliable RTP means an EIGRP acknowledgment must be returned.

Before any EIGRP updates are sent, a router must first discover their neighbors. This is done with EIGRP hello packets. On most networks EIGRP sends hello packets every 5 seconds. On multipoint nonbroadcast multiaccess networks (NBMA) such as X.25, Frame Relay, and ATM interface with access links of T1 (1.544 Mbps) or slower, Hellos are sent every 60 seconds. The hold time is three times the hello, or 15 seconds on most networks and 180 seconds on low speed NBMA networks.

The hello and hold-down values do not need to match for two routers to become neighbors. The `show ip eigrp neighbors` command is used to view the neighbor table and verify that EIGRP has established an adjacency with its neighbors.

EIGRP does not send periodic updates like RIP. EIGRP sends partial or bounded updates, which includes only the route changes and only to those routers that are affected by the change. EIGRP composite metric uses bandwidth, delay, reliability and load to determine best path. By default only bandwidth and delay are used. The default calculation is the slowest bandwidth plus the sum of the delays of the outgoing interfaces from the router to the destination network.

At the center of EIGRP is DUAL (Diffusing Update Algorithm). The DUAL finite state machine is used to determine best path and potential backup paths to every destination network. The successor is a neighboring router that is used to forward the packet using the least-cost route to the destination network. Feasible distance (FD) is the lowest calculated metric to reach the destination network through the successor. A feasible successor (FS) is a neighbor who has a loop-free backup path to the same network as the successor, and also meets the feasibility condition. The feasibility condition (FC) is met when a neighbor's reported distance (RD) to a network is less than the local router's feasible distance to the same destination network. The reported distance is simply an EIGRP neighbor's feasible distance to the destination network.

EIGRP is configured with the `router eigrp` *autonomous-system* command. The *autonomous-system* value is actually a process-id and must be the same on all routers in the EIGRP routing domain. The `network` command is similar to that used with RIP. The network is the classful network address of the directly connected interfaces on the router. A wildcard mask is an optional parameter that can be used to include only specific interfaces.

There are several ways to propagate a static default route with EIGRP. The `redistribute static` command in EIGRP router mode is a common method.

Refer to **Figure** in online course

Check Your Understanding

The Packet Tracer Skills Integration Challenge Activity integrates all the knowledge and skills you acquired in previous chapters of this course and prior courses. Skills related to this chapter's discussion of EIGRP are also included.

In this activity, you build a network from the ground up. Starting with an addressing space and network requirements, you must implement a network design that satisfies the specifications. Next, you implement an effective EIGRP routing configuration with integrated default routing. Detailed instructions are provided within the activity.

Packet Tracer Skills Integration Instructions (PDF)

Refer to **Packet Tracer Activity** for this chapter

To Learn More

Refer to **Figure** in online course

Routing TCP/IP, Volume I

There are several good sources to learn more about DUAL. *Routing TCP/IP*, Volume I by Jeff Doyle and Jennifer Carroll, includes an excellent section on the Diffusing Update Algorithm including two diffusing computation examples.

J.J. Garcia-Luna-Aceves

DUAL was first proposed by E.W. Dijkstra and C.S. Scholten, with the most prominent work done by that of J.J. Garcia-Luna-Aceves. J.J. Garcia-Luna-Aceves is the Jack Baskin Chair of Computer Engineering at the University of California, Santa Cruz (UCSC), and is a Principal Scientist at the Palo Alto Research Center (PARC). Several of J.J. Garcia-Luna-Aceves's published articles including his work done on DUAL, "Loop-Free Routing Using Diffusing Computations", IEEE/ACM Transactions on Networking, Vol. 1, No. 1, February 1993, can be found at: http://ccrg.soe.ucsc.edu/publications.html.

Go to the online course to take the quiz.

Chapter Quiz

Take the chapter quiz to test your knowledge.

Your Chapter Notes

CHAPTER 10

Link-State Routing Protocols

Chapter Introduction

Refer to
Figure
in online course

In Chapter 3, "Introduction to Dynamic Routing Protocols," we illustrated the difference between link-state and distance vector routing with an analogy. The analogy stated that distance vector routing protocols are like using road signs to guide you on your way to a destination, only giving you information about distance and direction. However, link-state routing protocols are like using a map. With a map, you can see all of the potential routes and determine your own preferred path.

Distance vector routing protocols are like road signs because routers must make preferred path decisions based on a distance or metric to a network. Just as travelers trust a road sign to accurately state the distance to the next town, a distance vector router trusts that another router is advertising the true distance to the destination network.

Link-state routing protocols take a different approach. Link-state routing protocols are more like a road map because they create a topological map of the network and each router uses this map to determine the shortest path to each network. Just as you refer to a map to find the route to another town, link-state routers use a map to determine the preferred path to reach another destination.

Routers running a link-state routing protocol send information about the state of its links to other routers in the routing domain. The state of those links refers to its directly connected networks and includes information about the type of network and any neighboring routers on those networks-hence the name link-state routing protocol.

The ultimate objective is that every router receives all of the link-state information about all other routers in the routing area. With this link-state information, each router can create its own topological map of the network and independently calculate the shortest path to every network.

This chapter introduces the concepts of link-state routing protocols. In Chapter 11, we will apply these concepts to OSPF.

10.1 Link-State Routing

10.1.1 Link-State Routing Protocols

Refer to
Figure
in online course

Link-state routing protocols are also known as *shortest path first* protocols and built around Edsger Dijkstra's *shortest path first (SPF)* algorithm. The SPF algorithm will be discussed in more detail in a later section.

The IP link-state routing protocols are shown in the figure:

- Open Shortest Path First (OSPF)

- Intermediate System-to-Intermediate System (IS-IS)

Link-state routing protocols have the reputation of being much more complex than their distance vector counterparts. However, the basic functionality and configuration of link-state routing protocols is not complex at all. Even the algorithm itself can be easily understood, as you will see in the next topic. Basic OSPF operations can be configured with a **router ospf** *process-id* command and a network statement, similar to other routing protocols like RIP and EIGRP.

Note: OSPF is discussed in Chapter 11, and IS-IS is discussed in CCNP. There are also link-state routing protocols for non-IP networks. These include DEC's DNA Phase V and Novell's NetWare Link Services Protocol (NLSP), which are not part of CCNA or CCNP curriculum.

10.1.2 Introduction to the SPF Algorithm

Dijkstra's algorithm is commonly referred to as the shortest path first (SPF) algorithm. This algorithm accumulates costs along each path, from source to destination. Although, Dijkstra's algorithm is known as the shortest path first algorithm, this is in fact the purpose of every routing algorithm.

In the figure, each path is labeled with an arbitrary value for cost. The cost of the shortest path for R2 to send packets to the LAN attached to R3 is 27. Notice that this cost is not 27 for all routers to reach the LAN attached to R3. Each router determines its own cost to each destination in the topology. In other words, each router calculates the SPF algorithm and determines the cost from its own perspective. This will become more evident later in this chapter.

Click R1 in the figure.

For R1, the shortest path to each LAN - along with the cost - is shown in the table. The shortest path is not necessarily the path with the least number of hops. For example, look at the path to the R5 LAN. You might think that R1 would send directly to R4 instead of to R3. However, the cost to reach R4 directly (22) is higher than the cost to reach R4 through R3 (17).

Continue to click R2 through R5 in the figure.

Observe the shortest path for each router to reach each of the LANs, as shown in the tables.

10.1.3 Link-State Routing Process

So exactly how does a link-state routing protocol work? All routers in our topology will complete the following generic link-state routing process to reach a state of convergence:

1. **Each router learns about its own links, its own directly connected networks.** This is done by detecting that an interface is in the **up** state.

2. **Each router is responsible for meeting its neighbors on directly connected networks.** Similar to EIGRP, link state routers do this by exchanging Hello packets with other link-state routers on directly connected networks.

3. **Each router builds a** *Link-State Packet (LSP)* **containing the state of each directly connected link. This is done by recording all the pertinent information about each neighbor, including neighbor ID, link type, and bandwidth.**

4. **Each router floods the LSP to all neighbors, who then store all LSPs received in a database.** Neighbors then flood the LSPs to their neighbors until all routers in the area have received the LSPs. Each router stores a copy of each LSP received from its neighbors in a local database.

5. **Each router uses the database to construct a complete map of the topology and computes the best path to each destination network.** Like having a road map, the router now has a complete map of all destinations in the topology and the routes to reach them. The SPF algorithm is used to construct the map of the topology and to determine the best path to each network.

We will discuss this process in more detail in the following topics.

10.1.4 Learning about Directly Connected Networks

Refer to
Figure
in online course

Click Link-State Routing Process in the figure.

The topology now shows the network addresses for each link. **Each router learns about its own links, its own directly connected networks** in the same way as was discussed in Chapter 1, "Introduction to Routing and Packet Forwarding." When a router interface is configured with an IP address and subnet mask, the interface becomes part of that network.

Click R1 in the figure.

When you correctly configure and activate the interfaces, the router learns about its own directly connected networks. Regardless of the routing protocols used, these directly connected networks are now part of the routing table. For purposes of our discussion, we will focus on the link-state routing process from the perspective of R1.

Refer to
Figure
in online course

Link

With link-state routing protocols, a *link* is an interface on a router. As with distance vector protocols and static routes, the interface must be properly configured with an IP address and subnet mask and the link must be in the **up** state before the link-state routing protocol can learn about a link. Also like distance vector protocols, the interface must be included in one of the `network` statements before it can participate in the link-state routing process.

The figure shows R1 linked to four directly connected networks:

- FastEthernet 0/0 interface on the 10.1.0.0/16 network

- Serial 0/0/0 network on the 10.2.0.0/16 network

- Serial 0/0/1 network on the 10.3.0.0/16 network

- Serial 0/0/2 network on the 10.4.0.0/16 network

Link-State

Information about the state of those links is known as *link-states*. As you can see in the figure, this information includes:

- The interface's IP address and subnet mask.

- The type of network, such as Ethernet (broadcast) or Serial point-to-point link.

- The cost of that link.

- Any neighbor routers on that link.

Note: We will see that Cisco's implementation of OSPF specifies the cost of the link, the OSPF routing metric, as the bandwidth of the outgoing interface. But for the purposes of this chapter, we are using arbitrary cost values to simplify our demonstration.

10.1.5 Sending Hello Packets to Neighbors

Refer to
Figure
in online course

The second step in the link-state routing process is:

Each router is responsible for meeting its neighbors on directly connected networks.

Routers with link-state routing protocols use a Hello protocol to discover any neighbors on its links. A *neighbor* is any other router that is enabled with the same link-state routing protocol.

Refer to
Figure
in online course

Click Play to view the animation.

R1 sends Hello packets out its links (interfaces) to discover if there are any neighbors. R2, R3, and R4 reply to the Hello packet with their own Hello packets because these routers are configured with the same link-state routing protocol. There are no neighbors out the FastEthernet 0/0 interface. Because R1 does not receive a Hello on this interface, it will not continue with the link-state routing process steps for the FastEthernet 0/0 link.

Similar to EIGRP's Hello packets, when two link-state routers learn that they are neighbors, they form an *adjacency*. These small Hello packets continue to be exchanged between two adjacent neighbors which serve as a "keepalive" function to monitor the state of the neighbor. If a router stops receiving Hello packets from a neighbor, that neighbor is considered unreachable and the adjacency is broken. In the figure, R1 forms an adjacency with all three routers.

10.1.6 Building the Link-State Packet

Refer to **Figure** in online course

Click Link-State Routing Process in the figure.

We are now at the third step in the link-state routing process:

Each router builds a Link-State Packet (LSP) containing the state of each directly connected link.

Click R1 in the figure.

Once a router has established its adjacencies, it can build its link-state packets (LSPs) that contain the link-state information about its links. A simplified version of the LSPs from R1 is:

1. R1; Ethernet network 10.1.0.0/16; Cost 2

2. R1 -> R2; Serial point-to-point network; 10.2.0.0/16; Cost 20

3. R1 -> R3; Serial point-to-point network; 10.3.0.0/16; Cost 5

4. R1 -> R4; Serial point-to-point network; 10.4.0.0/16; Cost 20

10.1.7 Flooding Link-State Packets to Neighbors

Refer to **Figure** in online course

As shown in the figure, the fourth step in the link-state routing process is:

Each router floods the LSP to all neighbors, who then store all LSPs received in a database.

Each router floods its link-state information to all other link-state routers in the routing area. Whenever a router receives an LSP from a neighboring router, it immediately sends that LSP out all other interfaces except the interface that received the LSP. This process creates a flooding effect of LSPs from all routers throughout the routing area.

Refer to **Figure** in online course

Click Play to view the animation.

As you can see in the animation, LSPs are flooded almost immediately after being received, without any intermediate calculations. Unlike distance vector routing protocols that must first run the Bellman-Ford algorithm to process routing updates *before* sending them to other routers, link-state routing protocols calculate the SPF algorithm *after* the flooding is complete. As a result, link-state routing protocols reach convergence much faster than distance vector routing protocols.

Remember that LSPs do not need to be sent periodically. An LSP only needs to be sent:

- During initial startup of the router or of the routing protocol process on that router

- Whenever there is a change in the topology, including a link going down or coming up, or a neighbor adjacency being established or broken

In addition to the link-state information, other information is included in the LSP - such as sequence numbers and aging information - to help manage the flooding process. This information is used by each router to determine if it has already received the LSP from another router or if the LSP has newer information than what is already contained in the *link-state database*. This process allows a router to keep only the most current information in its link-state database.

Note: How these sequence numbers and aging information is used is beyond the scope of this curriculum. Additional information can be found in *Routing TCP/IP* by Jeff Doyle.

10.1.8 Constructing a Link-State Database

Refer to
Figure
in online course

The final step in the link-state routing process is:

Each router uses the database to construct a complete map of the topology and computes the best path to each destination network.

After each router has propagated its own LSPs using the link-state flooding process, each router will then have an LSP from every *link-state router* in the routing area. These LSPs are stored in the link-state database. Each router in the routing area can now use the SPF algorithm to construct the SPF trees that you saw earlier.

Refer to
Figure
in online course

Let's take a look at the link-state database for R1 as well as the SPF tree that results from the calculation of the SPF algorithm.

Click R1 Link-State Database in the figure.

As a result of the flooding process, router R1 has learned the link-state information for each router in its routing area. The figure shows the link-state information that R1 has received and stored in its link-state database. Notice that R1 also includes its own link-state information in the link-state database.

Click R1 SPF Tree in the figure.

With a complete link-state database, R1 can now use the database and the shortest path first (SPF) algorithm to calculate the preferred path or shortest path to each network. In the figure, notice that R1 does not use the path between itself and R4 to reach any LAN in the topology, including the LAN attached to R4. The path through R3 has a lower cost. Also, R1 does not use the path between R2 and R5 to reach R5. The path through R3 has a lower cost. Each router in the topology determines the shortest path from its own perspective.

Note: The link-state database and the SPF tree would still include those directly connected networks, those links which have been shaded in the graphic.

10.1.9 Shortest Path First (SPF) Tree

Refer to
Figure
in online course

Building the SPF Tree

Let's examine in more detail how R1 constructs its SPF tree. R1's current topology only includes its neighbors. However, using the link-state information from all other routers, R1 can now begin to construct an SPF tree of the network with itself at the root of the tree.

Note: The process described in this section is only a conceptual form of the SPF algorithm and SPF tree to help make it more understandable.

Click R2 LSPs in the figure.

The SPF algorithm begins by processing the following LSP information from R2:

1. Connected to neighbor R1 on network 10.2.0.0/16, cost of 20

Refer to
Figure
in online course

2. Connected to neighbor R5 on network 10.9.0.0/16, cost of 10

3. Has a network 10.5.0.0/16, cost of 2

R1 can ignore the first LSP, because R1 already knows that it is connected to R2 on network 10.2.0.0/16 with a cost of 20. R1 can use the second LSP and create a link from R2 to another router, R5, with the network 10.9.0.0/16 and a cost of 10. This information is added to the SPF tree. Using the third LSP, R1 has learned that R2 has a network 10.5.0.0/16 with a cost of 2 and with no neighbors. This link is added to R1's SPF tree.

Click R3 LSPs in the figure.

The SPF algorithm now processes the LSPs from R3:

1. Connected to neighbor R1 on network 10.3.0.0/16, cost of 5

2. Connected to neighbor R4 on network 10.7.0.0/16, cost of 10

3. Has a network 10.6.0.0/16, cost of 2

R1 can ignore the first LSP, because R1 already knows that it is connected to R3 on network 10.3.0.0/16 with a cost of 5. R1 can use the second LSP and create a link from R3 to the router R4, with the network 10.7.0.0/16 and a cost of 10. This information is added to the SPF tree. Using the third LSP, R1 has learned that R3 has a network 10.6.0.0/16 with a cost of 2 and with no neighbors. This link is added to R1's SPF tree.

Click R4 LSPs in the figure.

The SPF algorithm now processes the LSPs from R4:

1. Connected to neighbor R1 on network 10.4.0.0/16, cost of 20

2. Connected to neighbor R3 on network 10.7.0.0/16, cost of 10

3. Connected to neighbor R5 on network 10.10.0.0/16, cost of 10

4. Has a network 10.8.0.0/16, cost of 2

R1 can ignore the first LSP because R1 already knows that it is connected to R4 on network 10.4.0.0/16 with a cost of 20. R1 can also ignore the second LSP because SPF has already learned about the network 10.6.0.0/16 with a cost of 10 from R3.

However, R1 can use the third LSP to create a link from R4 to the router R5, with the network 10.10.0.0/16 and a cost of 10. This information is added to the SPF tree. Using the fourth LSP, R1 learns that R4 has a network 10.8.0.0/16 with a cost of 2 and with no neighbors. This link is added to R1's SPF tree.

Click R5 LSPs in the figure.

The SPF algorithm now processes the final LSPs from R5:

1. Connected to neighbor R2 on network 10.9.0.0/16, cost of 10

2. Connected to neighbor R4 on network 10.10.0.0/16, cost of 10

3. Has a network 10.11.0.0/16, cost of 2

R1 can ignore the first two LSPs (for the networks 10.9.0.0/16 and 10.10.0.0/16), because SPF has already learned about these links and added them to the SPF tree. R1 can process the third LSP learning that R5 has a network 10.11.0.0/16 with a cost of 2 and with no neighbors. This link is added to the SPF tree for R1.

Determining the Shortest Path

Because all LSPs have been processed using the SPF algorithm, R1 has now constructed the complete SPF tree. The 10.4.0.0/16 and 10.9.0.0/16 links are not used to reach other networks, because lower-cost or shorter paths exist. However these networks still exist as part of the SPF tree and are used to reach devices on those networks.

Note: The actual SPF algorithm determines the shortest path as it is building the SPF tree. We have done it in two steps to simplify the understanding of the algorithm.

The figure shows the SPF tree for R1. Using this tree, the SPF algorithm results indicate the shortest path to each network. Only the LANs are shown in the table, but SPF can also be used to determine the shortest path to each WAN link network. In this case, R1 determines that the shortest path for each network is:

Network 10.5.0.0/16 via R2 serial 0/0/0 at a cost of 22

Network 10.6.0.0/16 via R3 serial 0/0/1 at a cost of 7

Network 10.7.0.0/16 via R3 serial 0/0/1 at a cost of 15

Network 10.8.0.0/16 via R3 serial 0/0/1 at a cost of 17

Network 10.9.0.0/16 via R2 serial 0/0/0 at a cost of 30

Network 10.10.0.0/16 via R3 serial 0/0/1 at a cost of 25

Network 10.11.0.0/16 via R3 serial 0/0/1 at a cost of 27

Each router constructs its own SPF tree independently from all other routers. To ensure proper routing, the link-state databases used to construct those trees must be identical on all routers. In Chapter 11, "OSFP," we will examine this in more detail.

Generating a Routing Table from the SPF Tree

Using the shortest path information determined by the SPF algorithm, these paths can now be added to the routing table. You can see in the figure how the following routes have now been added to R1's routing table:

- 10.5.0.0/16 via R2 Serial 0/0/0, cost = 22
- 10.6.0.0/16 via R3 Serial 0/0/1, cost = 7
- 10.7.0.0/16 via R3 Serial 0/0/1, cost = 15
- 10.8.0.0/16 via R3 Serial 0/0/1, cost = 17
- 10.9.0.0/16 via R2 Serial 0/0/0, cost = 30
- 10.10.0.0/16 via R3 Serial 0/0/1, cost = 25
- 10.11.0.0/16 via R3 Serial 0/0/1, cost = 27

The routing table will also include all directly connected networks and routes from any other sources, such as static routes. Packets will now be forwarded according to these entries in the routing table.

10.2 Implementing Link-State Routing Protocols

Refer to **Figure** in online course

Refer to
Figure
in online course

10.2.1 Advantages of a Link-State Routing Protocol

There are several advantages of link-state routing protocols compared to distance vector routing protocols.

Builds a Topological Map

Link-state routing protocols create a topological map, or SPF tree of the network topology. Distance vector routing protocols do not have a topological map of the network. Routers implementing a distance vector routing protocol only have a list of networks, which includes the cost (distance) and next-hop routers (direction) to those networks. Because link-state routing protocols exchange link-states, the SPF algorithm can build an SPF tree of the network. Using the SPF tree, each router can independently determine the shortest path to every network.

Fast Convergence

When receiving a Link-state Packet (LSP), link-state routing protocols immediately flood the LSP out all interfaces except for the interface from which the LSP was received. A router using a distance vector routing protocol needs to process each routing update and update its routing table before flooding them out other interfaces, even with triggered updates. Faster convergence is achieved for link-state routing protocols. A notable exception is EIGRP.

Event-driven Updates

After the initial flooding of LSPs, link-state routing protocols only send out an LSP when there is a change in the topology. The LSP contains only the information regarding the affected link. Unlike some distance vector routing protocols, link-state routing protocols do not send periodic updates.

Refer to
Figure
in online course

Note: OSPF routers *do* flood their own link-states every 30 minutes. This is known as a paranoid update and is discussed in the following chapter. Also, not all distance vector routing protocols send periodic updates. RIP and IGRP send periodic updates; however, EIGRP does not.

Hierarchical Design

Link-state routing protocols such as OSPF and IS-IS use the concept of *areas*. Multiple areas create a hierarchical design to networks, allowing for better route aggregation (summarization) and the isolation of routing issues within an area. Multi-area OSPF and IS-IS are discussed further in CCNP.

10.2.2 Requirements of a Link-State Routing Protocol

Modern link-state routing protocols are designed to minimize the effects on memory, CPU, and bandwidth. The use and configuration of multiple areas can reduce the size of the link-state databases. Multiple areas can also limit the amount of link-state information flooding in a routing domain and send LSPs only to those routers that need them.

For example, when there is a change in the topology, only those routers in the affected area receive the LSP and run the SPF algorithm. This can help isolate an unstable link to a specific area in the routing domain. In the figure, there are three separate routing domains: Area 1, Area 0, and Area 51. If a network in Area 51 goes down, the LSP with the information about this downed link is only flooded to other routers in that area. Only routers in Area 51 will need to update their link-state databases, rerun the SPF algorithm, create a new SPF tree, and update their routing tables. Routers in other areas will learn that this route is down, but this will be done with a type of link-state packet that does not cause them to rerun their SPF algorithm. Routers in other areas can update their routing tables directly.

Refer to
Figure
in online course

Note: Multiple areas with OSPF and IS-IS are discussed in CCNP.

Memory Requirements

Link-state routing protocols typically require more memory, more CPU processing, and at times more bandwidth than distance vector routing protocols. The memory requirements are due to the use of link-state databases and the creation of the SPF tree.

Processing Requirements

Link-state protocols can also require more CPU processing than distance vector routing protocols. The SPF algorithm requires more CPU time than distance vector algorithms such as Bellman-Ford because link-state protocols build a complete map of the topology.

Bandwidth Requirements

The flooding of link-state packets can adversely affect the available bandwidth on a network. This should only occur during initial startup of routers, but can also be an issue on unstable networks.

10.2.3 Comparison of Link-State Routing Protocols

Refer to
Figure
in online course

There are two link-state routing protocols used for routing IP today:

- Open Shortest Path First (OSPF)

- Intermediate System-to-Intermediate System (IS-IS)

OSPF

OSPF was designed by the IETF (Internet Engineering Task Force) OSPF Working Group, which still exists today. The development of OSPF began in 1987 and there are two current versions in use:

- OSPFv2: OSPF for IPv4 networks (RFC 1247 and RFC 2328)

- OSPFv3: OSPF for IPv6 networks (RFC 2740)

Most of the work on OSPF was done by John Moy, author of most of the RFCs regarding OSPF. His book, *OSPF, Anatomy of an Internet Routing Protocol,* provides interesting insight to the development of OSPF.

Note: OSPF is discussed in the following chapter. Multiple Area OSPF and OSPFv3 are discussed in CCNP.

IS-IS

IS-IS was designed by ISO (International Organization for Standardization) and is described in ISO 10589. The first incarnation of this routing protocol was developed at DEC (Digital Equipment Corporation) and is known as DECnet Phase V. Radia Perlman was the chief designer of the IS-IS routing protocol.

IS-IS was originally designed for the OSI protocol suite and not the TCP/IP protocol suite. Later, Integrated IS-IS, or Dual IS-IS, included support for IP networks. Although IS-IS has been known as the routing protocol used mainly by ISPs and carriers, more enterprise networks are beginning to use IS-IS.

OSPF and IS-IS share many similarities and also have many differences. There are many pro-OSPF and pro-IS-IS factions who discuss and debate the advantages of one routing protocol over the other. Both routing protocols provide the necessary routing functionality needed. You can learn more about IS-IS and OSPF in CCNP and begin to make your own determination if one protocol is more advantageous than the other.

Summary and Review

Refer to **Figure** in online course

Summary

Link-state routing protocols are also known as shortest path first protocols and are built around Edsger Dijkstra's shortest path first (SPF) algorithm. There are two link-state routing protocols for IP: OSPF (Open Shortest Path First) and IS-IS (Intermediate-System-to-Intermediate-System).

The link-state process can be summarized as follows:

1. Each router learns about its own directly connected networks.

2. Each router is responsible for "saying hello" to its neighbors on directly connected networks.

3. Each router builds a Link-State Packet (LSP) containing the state of each directly connected link.

4. Each router floods the LSP to all neighbors, who then store all LSPs received in a database.

5. Each router uses the database to construct a complete map of the topology and computes the best path to each destination network.

A link is an interface on the router. A link-state is the information about that interface including its IP address and subnet mask, the type of network, the cost associated with the link, and any neighbor routers on that link.

Each router determines its own link-states and floods the information to all other routers in the area. As a result, each router builds a link-state database (LSDB) containing the link-state information from all other routers. Each router will have identical LSDBs. Using the information in the LSDB, each router will run the SPF algorithm. The SPF algorithm will create an SPF tree, with the router at the root of the tree. As each link is connected to other links, the SPF tree is created. Once the SPF tree is completed, the router can determine on its own the best path to each network in the tree. This best path information is then stored in the router's routing table.

Link-state routing protocols build a local topology map of the network that allows each router to determine the best path to a given network. A new LSP is sent only when there is a change in the topology. When a link is added, removed or modified, the router will flood the new LSP to all other routers. When a router receives the new LSP, it will update is LSDB, rerun the SPF algorithm, create a new SPF tree, and update its routing table.

Link-state routing protocols tend to have a faster convergence time than distance vector routing protocols. A notable exception is EIGRP. However, link-state routing protocols do require more memory and processing requirements. This is usually not an issue with today's newer routers.

In the next and final chapter of this course, you will learn about the link-state routing protocol, OSPF.

Refer to **Figure** in online course

Refer to **Packet Tracer Activity** for this chapter

The Packet Tracer Skills Integration Challenge Activity for this chapter is very similar to the activity you completed at the end of Chapter 9. The scenario is slightly different, allowing you to better practice your skills.

Packet Tracer Skills Integration Instructions (PDF)

To Learn More

Refer to **Figure** in online course

Suggested Books

Understanding the SPF algorithm is not difficult. There are several good books and online resources that explain Dijkstra's algorithm and how it is used in networking. There are several web sites devoted to explaining how these algorithms work. Seek out some of the resources and familiarize yourself with how this algorithm works.

Here are some suggested resources:

- *Interconnections, Bridges, Routers, Switches, and Internetworking Protocols*, by Radia Perlman

- *Cisco IP Routing*, by Alex Zinin

- *Routing the Internet*, by Christian Huitema

Classroom Analogy

An exercise to help you understand the SPF algorithm can be done with a classroom of students and a set of index cards. Each student gets a set four index cards. On the first index card the student will write down their name along with the name of the student sitting to their left. If there is not a student there, have them write the word "none". On the next card the student will do the same thing but for the student on their right. The next two cards are for the students sitting in front, and sitting in back. These index cards are representative of link-state information.

For example, Teri has a set of four cards with the following information:

- Teri —-> Jen

- Teri —-> Pat

- Teri —-> Rick

- Teri —-> Allan

Once all of the students in the classroom have filled out the index cards, the instructor collects all of the index cards. This is similar to the link-state flooding process. The stack of index cards is similar to the link-state database. In a network, all routers would have this identical link-state database.

The instructor takes each card and lists the name and the neighbor student on the board with a line between them. After all of the index cards are transcribed to the board, the end result will be a map of the students in the classroom. To make it easier, the instructor should map the names similar to how students are sitting in the classroom, for example, Jen is sitting to the left of Teri. This is similar to the SPF tree that a link-state routing protocol creates.

Using this topology map on the board the instructor can see all of the paths to the various students in the class.

Chapter Quiz

Go to the online course to take the quiz.

Take the chapter quiz to test your knowledge.

Your Chapter Notes

CHAPTER 11

OSPF

Chapter Introduction

Refer to
Figure
in online course

Open Shortest Path First (OSPF) is a link-state routing protocol that was developed as a replacement for the distance vector routing protocol RIP. RIP was an acceptable routing protocol in the early days of networking and the Internet, but its reliance on hop count as the only measure for choosing the best route quickly became unacceptable in larger networks that needed a more robust routing solution. OSPF is a classless routing protocol that uses the concept of *areas* for scalability. RFC 2328 defines the OSPF metric as an arbitrary value called *cost*. The Cisco IOS uses bandwidth as the OSPF cost metric.

OSPF's major advantages over RIP are its fast convergence and its scalability to much larger network implementations. In this final chapter of the *Routing Protocols and Concepts* course, you will learn basic, single-area OSPF implementations and configurations. More complex OSPF configurations and concepts are reserved for CCNP-level courses.

11.1 Introduction to OSPF

11.1.1 Background of OSPF

Refer to
Figure
in online course

The initial development of OSPF began in 1987 by the Internet Engineering Task Force (IETF) OSPF Working Group. At that time the Internet was largely an academic and research network funded by the U.S. government.

Roll over the dates in the OSPF Development Timeline figure to see related events.

In 1989, the specification for OSPFv1 was published in RFC 1131. There were two implementations written: one to run on routers and the other to run on UNIX workstations. The latter implementation later became a widespread UNIX process known as GATED. OSPFv1 was an experimental routing protocol and never deployed.

In 1991, OSPFv2 was introduced in RFC 1247 by John Moy. OSPFv2 offered significant technical improvements over OSPFv1. At the same time, ISO was working on a link-state routing protocol of their own, Intermediate System-to-Intermediate System (IS-IS). Not surprisingly, IETF chose OSPF as their recommended IGP (Interior Gateway Protocol).

In 1998, the OSPFv2 specification was updated in RFC 2328 and is the current RFC for OSPF.

Note: In 1999 OSPFv3 for IPv6 was published in RFC 2740. RFC 2740 was written by John Moy, Rob Coltun, and Dennis Ferguson. OSPFv3 is discussed in CCNP.

Links

"OSPF Version 2," http://www.ietf.org/rfc/rfc2328.txt

11.1.2 OSPF Message Encapsulation

Refer to
Figure
in online course

The data portion of an OSPF message is encapsulated in a packet. This data field can include one of five OSPF packet types. Each packet type is briefly discussed in the next topic.

Roll over the fields in the Encapsulated OSPF Message figure to see the encapsulation process.

The OSPF packet header is included with every OSPF packet, regardless of its type. The OSPF packet header and packet type-specific data are then encapsulated in an IP packet. In the IP packet header, the protocol field is set to 89 to indicate OSPF, and the destination address is set to one of two multicast addresses: 224.0.0.5 or 224.0.0.6. If the OSPF packet is encapsulated in an Ethernet frame, the destination MAC address is also a multicast address: 01-00-5E-00-00-05 or 01-00-5E-00-00-06.

11.1.3 OSPF Packet Types

Refer to
Figure
in online course

In the previous chapter, we introduced Link-State Packets (LSPs). The figure shows the five different types of OSPF LSPs. Each packet serves a specific purpose in the OSPF routing process:

1. **Hello** - Hello packets are used to establish and maintain adjacency with other OSPF routers. The hello protocol is discussed in detail in the next topic.

2. **DBD** - The *Database Description (DBD)* packet contains an abbreviated list of the sending router's link-state database and is used by receiving routers to check against the local link-state database.

3. **LSR** - Receiving routers can then request more information about any entry in the DBD by sending a *Link-State Request (LSR)*.

4. **LSU** - *Link-State Update (LSU)* packets are used to reply to LSRs as well as to announce new information. LSUs contain seven different types of Link-State Advertisements (LSAs). LSUs and LSAs are briefly discussed in a later topic.

5. **LSAck** - When an LSU is received, the router sends a *Link-State Acknowledgement (LSAck)* to confirm receipt of the LSU.

11.1.4 Hello Protocol

Refer to
Figure
in online course

The figure shows the OSPF packet header and Hello packet. The blue-shaded fields will be discussed in more detail later in the chapter. For now, let's focus on the uses of the Hello packet.

OSPF packet Type 1 is the OSPF Hello packet. Hello packets are used to:

- Discover OSPF neighbors and establish neighbor adjacencies.
- Advertise parameters on which two routers must agree to become neighbors.
- Elect the *Designated Router (DR)* and *Backup Designated Router (BDR)* on multiaccess networks like Ethernet and Frame Relay.

Important fields shown in the figure include:

- *Type:* OSPF Packet Type: Hello (1), DD (2), LS Request (3), LS Update (4), LS ACK (5)
- *Router ID:* ID of the originating router
- *Area ID:* area from which the packet originated
- *Network Mask:* Subnet mask associated with the sending interface
- *Hello Interval:* number of seconds between the sending router's hellos

- *Router Priority:* Used in DR/BDR election (discussed later)

- *Designated Router (DR):* Router ID of the DR, if any

- *Backup Designated Router (BDR):* Router ID of the BDR, if any

- *List of Neighbors:* lists the OSPF Router ID of the neighboring router(s)

Neighbor Establishment

Refer to **Figure** in online course

Before an OSPF router can flood its link-states to other routers, it must first determine if there are any other OSPF neighbors on any of its links. In the figure, the OSPF routers are sending Hello packets on all OSPF-enabled interfaces to determine if there are any neighbors on those links. The information in the OSPF Hello includes the OSPF Router ID of the router sending the Hello packet (Router ID is discussed later in the chapter). Receiving an OSPF Hello packet on an interface confirms for a router that there is another OSPF router on this link. OSPF then establishes adjacency with the neighbor. For example, in the figure, R1 will establish adjacencies with R2 and R3.

OSPF Hello and Dead Intervals

Before two routers can form an OSPF neighbor adjacency, they must agree on three values: Hello interval, Dead interval, and network type. The OSPF Hello interval indicates how often an OSPF router transmits its Hello packets. By default, OSPF Hello packets are sent every 10 seconds on multiaccess and point-to-point segments and every 30 seconds on *non-broadcast multiaccess (NBMA)* segments (Frame Relay, X.25, ATM).

In most cases, OSPF Hello packets are sent as multicast to an address reserved for *ALLSPFRouters at 224.0.0.5. Using a multicast address allows a device to ignore the packet if its interface is not enabled to accept OSPF packets. This saves CPU processing time on non-OSPF devices.*

The Dead interval is the period, expressed in seconds, that the router will wait to receive a Hello packet before declaring the neighbor "down." Cisco uses a default of four times the Hello interval. For multiaccess and point-to-point segments, this period is 40 seconds. For NBMA networks, the Dead interval is 120 seconds.

If the Dead interval expires before the routers receive a Hello packet, OSPF will remove that neighbor from its link-state database. The router floods the link-state information about the "down" neighbor out all OSPF enabled interfaces.

Network types are discussed later in the chapter.

Electing a DR and BDR

To reduce the amount of OSPF traffic on multiaccess networks, OSPF elects a Designated Router (DR) and Backup Designated Router (BDR). The DR is responsible for updating all other OSPF routers (called *DROthers*) when a change occurs in the multiaccess network. The BDR monitors the DR and takes over as DR if the current DR fails.

In the figure, R1, R2, and R3 are connected through point-to-point links. Therefore, no DR/BDR election occurs. The DR/BDR election and processes will be discussed in a later topic and the topology will be changed to a multiaccess network.

Note: The Hello packet is discussed in more detail in CCNP along with the other types of OSPF packets.

11.1.5 OSPF Link-state Updates

Refer to **Figure** in online course

Link-state updates (LSUs) are the packets used for OSPF routing updates. An LSU packet can contain 11 different types of Link-State Advertisements (LSAs), as shown in the figure. The difference between the terms Link-State Update (LSU) and *Link-State Advertisement (LSA)* can sometimes be confusing. At times, these terms are used interchangeably. An LSU contains one or more LSAs and either term can be used to refer to link-state information propagated by OSPF routers.

Note: The different types of LSAs are discussed in CCNP.

11.1.6 OSPF Algorithm

Each OSPF router maintains a link-state database containing the LSAs received from all other routers. Once a router has received all of LSAs and built its local link-state database, OSPF uses Dijkstra's shortest path first (SPF) algorithm to create an SPF tree. The SPF tree is then used to populate the IP routing table with the best paths to each network.

11.1.7 Administrative Distance

Refer to
Figure
in online course

As you know from Chapter 3, "Introduction to Dynamic Routing," administrative distance (AD) is the trustworthiness (or preference) of the route source. OSPF has a default administrative distance of 110. As you can see from the figure, when compared to other interior gateway protocols (IGPs), OSPF is preferred over IS-IS and RIP.

11.1.8 Authentication

Refer to
Figure
in online course

As stated in previous chapters, configuring routing protocols to use authentication will be discussed in a later course. Like other routing protocols, OSPF can be configured for authentication.

It is good practice to authenticate transmitted routing information. RIPv2, EIGRP, OSPF, IS-IS, and BGP can all be configured to encrypt and authenticate their routing information. This practice ensures that routers will only accept routing information from other routers that have been configured with the same password or authentication information.

Note: Authentication does not encrypt the router's routing table.

11.2 Basic OSPF Configuration

11.2.1 Lab Topology

The figure shows the topology for this chapter. Notice that the addressing scheme is discontiguous. OSPF is a classless routing protocol. Therefore, we will configure the mask as part of our OSPF configuration. As you know, doing this overcomes the problem with discontiguous addressing. Also notice in this topology that there are three serial links that can have various bandwidths and that each router has multiple paths to each remote network. Currently, all serial links are set to default bandwidth 1544kbps.

Click Addressing to review the IP addresses.

Click R1, R2, and R3 to review each router's starting configuration.

11.2.2 The router ospf Command

OSPF is enabled with the **router ospf** *process-id* global configuration command. The *process-id* is a number between 1 and 65535 and is chosen by the network administrator. The *process-id* is locally significant, which means that it does not have to match other OSPF routers in order to establish adjacencies with those neighbors. This differs from EIGRP. The EIGRP process ID or autonomous system number *does* need to match for two EIGRP neighbors to become adjacent.

In our topology, we will enable OSPF on all three routers using the same process ID of 1. We are using the same process ID simply for consistency.

```
R1(config)#router ospf 1
R1(config-router)#
```

11.2.3 The network Command

Refer to
Figure
in online course

The **network** command used with OSPF has the same function as when used with other IGP routing protocols:

- Any interfaces on a router that match the network address in the **network** command will be enabled to send and receive OSPF packets.

- This network (or subnet) will be included in OSPF routing updates.

The **network** command is used in router configuration mode.

```
Router(config-router)#network network-address wildcard-mask area area-id
```

The OSPF **network** command uses a combination of *network-address* and *wildcard-mask* similar to that which can be used by EIGRP. Unlike EIGRP, however, OSPF requires the wildcard mask. The network address along with the wildcard mask is used to specify the interface or range of interfaces that will be enabled for OSPF using this **network** command.

As with EIGRP, the wildcard mask can be configured as the inverse of a subnet mask. For example, R1's FastEthernet 0/0 interface is on the 172.16.1.16/28 network. The subnet mask for this interface is /28 or 255.255.255.240. The inverse of the subnet mask results in the wildcard mask.

Note: Like EIGRP, some IOS versions allow you to simply enter the subnet mask instead of the wildcard mask. The IOS then converts the subnet mask to the wildcard mask format.

```
  255.255.255.255
- 255.255.255.240 Subtract the subnet mask
  _ _ _ _ _ _ _ _ _ _
  0. 0. 0. 15 Wildcard mask
```

The **area** *area-id* refers to the *OSPF area*. An OSPF area is a group of routers that share link-state information. All OSPF routers in the same area must have the same link-state information in their link-state databases. This is accomplished by routers flooding their individual link-states to all other routers in the area. In this chapter, we will configure all of the OSPF routers within a single area. This is known as single-area OSPF.

An OSPF network can also be configured as multiple areas. There are several advantages to configuring large OSPF networks as multiple areas, including smaller link-state databases and the ability to isolate unstable network problems within an area. Multi-area OSPF is covered in CCNP.

When all of the routers are within the same OSPF area, the network commands must be configured with the same *area-id* on all routers. Although any *area-id* can be used, it is good practice to use an *area-id* of 0 with single-area OSPF. This convention makes it easier if the network is later configured as multiple OSPF areas where area 0 becomes the backbone area.

The figure shows the **network** commands for all three routers, enabling OSPF on all interfaces. At this point all routers should be able to ping all networks.

11.2.4 OSPF Router ID

Refer to
Figure
in online course

Determining the Router ID

The OSPF router ID is used to uniquely identify each router in the OSPF routing domain. A router ID is simply an IP address. Cisco routers derive the router ID based on three criteria and with the following precedence:

1. Use the IP address configured with the OSPF **router-id** command.

2. If the **router-id** is not configured, the router chooses highest IP address of any of its loopback interfaces.

3. If no loopback interfaces are configured, the router chooses highest active IP address of any of its physical interfaces.

Highest Active IP Address

If an OSPF router is not configured with an OSPF **router-id** command and there are no loopback interfaces configured, the OSPF router ID will be the highest active IP address on any of its interfaces. The interface does not need to be enabled for OSPF, meaning that it does not need to be included in one of the OSPF **network** commands. However, the interface must be active - it must be in the **up** state.

Click the Topology button in the figure.

Using the criteria described above, can you determine the router IDs for R1, R2, and R3? The answer is on the next page.

Refer to
Figure
in online course

Verifying the Router ID

Because we have not configured router IDs or loopback interfaces on our three routers, the router ID for each router is determined by the number three criterion in the list: the highest active IP address on any of the router's physical interfaces. As shown in the figure, the router ID for each router is:

R1: 192.168.10.5, which is higher than either 172.16.1.17 or 192.168.10.1

R2: 192.168.10.9, which is higher than either 10.10.10.1 or 192.168.10.2

R3: 192.168.10.10, which is higher than either 172.16.1.33 or 192.168.10.6

One command you can use to verify the current router ID is **show ip protocols**. Some IOS versions do not display the router ID as shown in the figure. In those cases, use the **show ip ospf** or **show ip ospf interface** commands to verify the router ID.

Refer to
Figure
in online course

Loopback Address

If the OSPF **router-id** command is not used and loopback interfaces are configured, OSPF will choose highest IP address of any of its loopback interfaces. A loopback address is a virtual interface and is automatically in the **up** state when configured. You already know the commands to configure a loopback interface:

```
Router(config)#interface loopback number
Router(config-if)#ip address ip-address subnet-mask
```

Click the Topology button in the figure.

In this topology, all three routers have been configured with loopback addresses to represent the OSPF router IDs. The advantage of using a loopback interface is that - unlike physical interfaces - it cannot fail. There are no actual cables or adjacent devices on which the loopback interface depends for being in the **up** state. Therefore, using a loopback address for the router ID provides stability to the OSPF process. Because the OSPF **router-id** command, which is discussed next, is a fairly recent addition to IOS, it is more common to find loopback addresses used for configuring OSPF router IDs.

The OSPF **router-id** command

The OSPF **router-id** command was introduced in IOS 12.0(T) and takes precedence over loopback and physical interface IP addresses for determining the router ID. The command syntax is:

```
Router(config)#router ospf process-id
Router(config-router)#router-id ip-address
```

Modifying the Router ID

The router ID is selected when OSPF is configured with its first OSPF **network** command. If the OSPF **router-id** command or the loopback address is configured *after* the OSPF **network** command, the router ID will be derived from the interface with the highest active IP address.

The router ID can be modified with the IP address from a subsequent OSPF **router-id** command by reloading the router or by using the following command:

```
Router#clear ip ospf process
```
Note: Modifying a router ID with a new loopback or physical interface IP address may require reloading the router.

Duplicate Router IDs

When two routers have the same router ID in an OSPF domain, routing may not function properly. If the router ID is the same on two neighboring routers, the neighbor establishment may not occur. When duplicate OSPF router IDs occur, IOS will display a message similar to:

```
%OSPF-4-DUP_RTRID1: Detected router with duplicate router ID
```
To correct this problem, configure all routers so that they have unique OSPF router IDs.

Click New Router IDs in the figure.

Because some IOS versions do not support the **router-id** command, we will use the loopback address method for assigning router IDs. An IP address from a loopback interface will usually only replace a current OSPF router ID by reloading the router. In the figure, the routers have been reloaded. The **show ip protocols** command is used to verify that each router is now using the loopback address for the router ID.

11.2.5 Verifying OSPF

Refer to **Figure** in online course

The **show ip ospf neighbor** command can be used to verify and troubleshoot OSPF neighbor relationships. For each neighbor, this command displays the following output:

- **Neighbor ID** - The router ID of the neighboring router.

- **Pri** - The OSPF priority of the interface. This is discussed in a later section.

- **State** - The OSPF state of the interface. **FULL** state means that the router and its neighbor have identical OSPF link-state databases. OSPF states are discussed in CCNP.

- **Dead Time** - The amount of time remaining that the router will wait to receive an OSPF Hello packet from the neighbor before declaring the neighbor down. This value is reset when the interface receives a Hello packet.

- **Address** - The IP address of the neighbor's interface to which this router is directly connected.

■ **Interface** - The interface on which this router has formed adjacency with the neighbor.

When troubleshooting OSPF networks, the **show ip ospf** neighbor command can be used to verify that the router has formed an adjacency with its neighboring routers. If the router ID of the neighboring router is not displayed, or if it does not show as a state of **FULL**, the two routers have not formed an OSPF adjacency. If two routers do not establish adjacency, link-state information will not be exchanged. Incomplete link-state databases can cause inaccurate SPF trees and routing tables. Routes to destination networks may either not exist or may not be the most optimum path.

Note: On multiaccess networks such as Ethernet, two routers that are adjacent may have their states displayed as 2WAY. This will be discussed in a later section.

Two routers may not form an OSPF adjacency if:

■ The subnet masks do not match, causing the routers to be on separate networks.

■ OSPF Hello or Dead Timers do not match.

■ OSPF Network Types do not match.

■ There is a missing or incorrect OSPF **network** command.

Other powerful OSPF troubleshooting commands include:

```
show ip protocols
 show ip ospf
show ip ospf interface
```

Refer to
Figure
in online course

As shown in the figure, the **show ip protocols** command is a quick way to verify vital OSPF configuration information, including the OSPF process ID, the router ID, networks the router is advertising, the neighbors the router is receiving updates from, and the default administrative distance, which is 110 for OSPF.

Click show ip ospf in the figure.

The **show ip ospf** command can also be used to examine the OSPF process ID and router ID. Additionally, this command displays the OSPF area information as well as the last time the SPF algorithm was calculated. As you can see from the sample output, OSPF is a very stable routing protocol. The only OSPF-related event that R1 has participated in during the past 11 and a half hours is to send small Hello packets to its neighbors.

Note: Additional information displayed by the **show ip ospf** command is discussed in CCNP courses.

The command output includes important SPF algorithm information which includes the *SPF schedule delay*:

```
Initial SPF schedule delay 5000 msecs
 Minimum hold time between two consecutive SPFs 10000 msecs
Maximum wait time between two consecutive SPFs 10000 msecs
```

Any time a router receives new information about the topology (addition, deletion, or modification of a link), the router must rerun the SPF algorithm, create a new SPF tree, and update the routing table. The SPF algorithm is CPU-intensive and the time it takes for calculation depends on the size of the area. The size of an area is measured by the number of routers and the size of the link-state database.

A network that cycles between an **up** state and a **down** state is referred to as a *flapping link*. A flapping link can cause OSPF routers in an area to constantly recalculate the SPF algorithm, preventing proper convergence. To minimize this problem, the router waits 5 seconds (5000 msecs) after receiving an LSU before running the SPF algorithm. This is known as the SPF schedule delay. In order to prevent a router from constantly running the SPF algorithm, there is an additional Hold Time of 10 seconds (10000 msecs). The router waits 10 seconds after running the SPF algorithm before rerunning the algorithm again.

Click `show ip ospf interface` in the figure.

The quickest way to verify Hello and Dead intervals is to use the `show ip ospf interface` command. As shown in the figure, adding the interface name and number to the command displays output for a specific interface. These intervals are included in the OSPF Hello packets sent between neighbors. OSPF may have different Hello and Dead intervals on various interfaces, but for OSPF routers to become neighbors, their OSPF Hello and Dead intervals must be identical. For example, in the figure, R1 is using a Hello interval of 10 and a Dead interval of 40 on the Serial 0/0/0 interface. R2 must also use the same intervals on its Serial 0/0/0 interface or the two routers will not form an adjacency.

11.2.6 Examining the Routing Table

Refer to **Figure** in online course

As you know, the quickest way to verify OSPF convergence is to look at the routing table for each router in the topology.

Click R1, R2, and R3 in the figure to see `show ip route` output.

The `show ip route` command can be used to verify that OSPF is sending and receiving routes via OSPF. The **O** at the beginning of each route indicates that the route source is OSPF. The routing table and OSPF will be examined more closely in the following section. However, you should immediately notice two distinct differences in the OSPF routing table compared to routing tables you have seen in previous chapters. First, notice that each router has four directly connected networks because the loopback interface counts as the fourth network. These loopback interfaces are not advertised in OSPF. Therefore, each router lists seven known networks. Second, unlike RIPv2 and EIGRP, OSPF does not automatically summarize at major network boundaries. OSPF is inherently classless.

Refer to **Packet Tracer Activity** for this chapter

Use the Packet Tracer Activity to configure and verify basic OSPF routing.

11.3 The OSPF Metric

11.3.1 OSPF Metric

Refer to **Figure** in online course

The OSPF metric is called cost. From RFC 2328: *"A cost is associated with the output side of each router interface. This cost is configurable by the system administrator. The lower the cost, the more likely the interface is to be used to forward data traffic."*

Notice that RFC 2328 does not specify which values should be used to determine the cost.

The Cisco IOS uses the cumulative bandwidths of the outgoing interfaces from the router to the destination network as the cost value. At each router, the cost for an interface is calculated as 10 to the 8th power divided by bandwidth in bps. This is known as the *reference bandwidth*. Dividing 10 to the 8th power by the interface bandwidth is done so that interfaces with the higher bandwidth values will have a lower calculated cost. Remember, in routing metrics, the lowest cost route is the preferred route (for example, with RIP, 3 hops is better than 10 hops). The figure shows the default OSPF costs for several types of interfaces.

Reference Bandwidth

The reference bandwidth defaults to 10 to the 8th power, 100,000,000 bps or 100 Mbps. This results in interfaces with a bandwidth of 100 Mbps and higher having the same OSPF cost of 1. The reference bandwidth can be modified to accommodate networks with links faster than 100,000,000 bps (100 Mbps) using the OSPF command `auto-cost reference-bandwidth`. When this command is necessary, it is recommended that it is used on all routers so the OSPF routing metric remains consistent.

Refer to
Figure
in online course

OSPF Accumulates Costs

The cost of an OSPF route is the accumulated value from one router to the destination network. For example, in the figure, the routing table on R1 shows a cost of 65 to reach the 10.10.10.0/24 network on R2. Because 10.10.10.0/24 is attached to a FastEthernet interface, R2 assigns the value 1 as the cost for 10.10.10.0/24. R1 then adds the additional cost value of 64 to send data across the default T1 link between R1 and R2.

Refer to
Figure
in online course

Default Bandwidth on Serial Interfaces

You may recall from Chapter 9, "EIGRP," that you can use the `show interface` command to view the bandwidth value used for an interface. On Cisco routers, the bandwidth value on many serial interfaces defaults to T1 (1.544 Mbps). However, some serial interfaces may default to 128 kbps. Therefore, never assume that OSPF is using any particular bandwidth value. Always check the default value with the `show interface` command.

Remember, this bandwidth value does not actually affect the speed of the link; it is used by some routing protocols to compute the routing metric. Most likely, on serial interfaces the actual speed of the link is different than the default bandwidth. It is important that the bandwidth value reflect the actual speed of the link so that the routing table has accurate best path information. For example, you may only be paying for a fractional T1 connection from your service provider, one fourth of a full T1 connection (384 kbps). However, for routing protocol purposes, the IOS assumes a T1 bandwidth value even though the interface is actually only sending and receiving one fourth of a full T1 connection (384 kbps).

The figure shows the output for the Serial 0/0/0 interface on R1. The topology also now reflects the actual bandwidth of the link between the routers. Notice that the default bandwidth value in the command output for R1 is 1544 kbps. However, the actual bandwidth of this link is 64 kbps. This means that the router has routing information that does not accurately reflect the network topology.

Click `show ip route` in the figure.

The figure displays the routing table for R1. R1 believes that both of its serial interfaces are connected to T1 links, although one of the links is a 64 kbps link and the other one is a 256 kbps link. This results in R1's routing table having two equal-cost paths to the 192.168.8.0/30 network, when Serial 0/0/1 is actually the better path.

```
O 192.168.10.8 [110/
128] via 192.168.10.6, 00:03:41, Serial0/0/1
   [110/
128] via 192.168.10.2, 00:03:41, Serial0/0/0
```
Click `show ip ospf interface` in the figure.

The calculated OSPF cost of an interface can be verified with the `show ip ospf interface` command. In the figure, we can verify that R1 is indeed assigning a cost of 64 to the Serial 0/0/0 interface. Although you might think that this is the correct cost because this interface is attached to a 64 kbps link, remember that cost is derived from the cost formula. The cost of a 64 kbps link is 1562 (100,000,000/64,000). The value of 64 displayed corresponds to the cost of a T1 link. In the next topic, you will learn how to modify the cost of all the links in the topology.

11.3.2 Modifying the Cost of the Link

Refer to
Figure
in online course

When the serial interface is not actually operating at the default T1 speed, the interface requires manual modification. Both sides of the link should be configured to have the same value. Both the

bandwidth interface command or the **ip ospf cost** interface command achieve this purpose - an accurate value for use by OSPF in determining the best route.

The **bandwidth** Command

The **bandwidth** command is used to modify the bandwidth value used by the IOS in calculating the OSPF cost metric. The interface command syntax is the same syntax that you learned in Chapter 9, "EIGRP":

`Router(config-if)#`**bandwidth** `bandwidth-kbps`

The figure shows the **bandwidth** commands used to modify the costs of all the serial interfaces in the topology. For R1, the **show ip ospf interface** command shows that the cost of the Serial 0/0/0 link is now 1562, the result of the Cisco OSPF cost calculation 100,000,000/64,000.

Refer to **Figure** in online course

The **ip ospf cost** Command

An alternative method to using the **bandwidth** command is to use the **ip ospf cost** command, which allows you to directly specify the cost of an interface. For example, on R1 we could configure Serial 0/0/0 with the following command:

`R1(config)#`**interface serial 0/0/0**
`R1(config-if)#`**ip ospf cost 1562**

Obviously, this would not change the output of the **show ip ospf interface** command, which still shows the cost as 1562. This is the same cost calculated by the IOS when we configured the bandwidth as 64.

Refer to **Figure** in online course

The **bandwidth** Command vs. the **ip ospf cost** Command

The **ip ospf cost** command is useful in multi-vendor environments where non-Cisco routers use a metric other than bandwidth to calculate the OSPF costs. The main difference between the two commands is that the **bandwidth** command uses the result of the cost calculation to determine the cost of the link. The **ip ospf cost** command bypasses this calculation by directly setting the cost of the link to a specific value.

The figure shows the two alternatives that can be used in modifying the costs of the serial links in the topology. The right side of the figure shows the **ip ospf cost** command equivalents of the **bandwidth** commands on the left.

Refer to **Packet Tracer Activity** for this chapter

Use the Packet Tracer Activity to modify the cost values for OSPF.

11.4 OSPF and Multiaccess Networks

11.4.1 Challenges in Multiaccess Networks

Refer to **Figure** in online course

A *multiaccess network* is a network with more than two devices on the same shared media. In the top portion of the figure, the Ethernet LAN attached to R1 is extended to show possible devices that might be attached to the 172.16.1.16/28 network. Ethernet LANs are an example of a broadcast multiaccess network. They are broadcast networks because all devices on the network see all broadcast frames. They are multiaccess networks because there may be numerous hosts, printers, routers, and other devices that are all members of the same network.

In contrast, on a point-to-point network there are only two devices on the network, one at each end. The WAN link between R1 and R3 is an example of a point-to-point link. The bottom portion of the figure shows the point-to-point link between R1 and R3.

Refer to **Figure** in online course

OSPF defines five network types:

- Point-to-point

- ▪ Broadcast Multiaccess

- ▪ Nonbroadcast Multiaccess (NBMA)

- ▪ Point-to-multipoint

- ▪ Virtual links

NBMA and point-to-multi-point networks include Frame Relay, ATM, and X.25 networks. NBMA networks are discussed in another CCNA course. Point-to-multipoint networks are discussed in CCNP. Virtual links are a special type of link that can be used in multi-area OSPF. OSPF virtual links are discussed in CCNP.

Click Play to view the animation.

The animation shows that the topology uses both point-to-point and broadcast networks.

Refer to **Figure** in online course

Multiaccess networks can create two challenges for OSPF regarding the flooding of LSAs:

1. Creation of multiple adjacencies, one adjacency for every pair of routers.

2. Extensive flooding of LSAs (Link-State Advertisements).

Multiple Adjacencies

The creation of an adjacency between every pair of routers in a network would create an unnecessary number of adjacencies. This would lead to an excessive number of LSAs passing between routers on the same network.

To understand the problem with multiple adjacencies, we need to study a formula. For any number of routers (designated as **n**) on a multiaccess network, there will be **n (n - 1) / 2** adjacencies. The figure shows a simple topology of five routers, all of which are attached to the same multiaccess Ethernet network. Without some type of mechanism to reduce the number of adjacencies, collectively these routers would form 10 adjacencies: **5 (5 - 1) / 2 = 10.** This may not seem like much, but as routers are added to the network, the number of adjacencies increases dramatically. Although the 5 routers in the figure will only need 10 adjacencies, you can see that 10 routers would require 45 adjacencies. Twenty routers would require 190 adjacencies!

Refer to **Figure** in online course

Flooding of LSAs

Remember from Chapter 10, "Link-State Routing Protocols," that link-state routers flood their link-state packets when OSPF is initialized or when there is a change in the topology.

Click Play to see the animation of a scenario of LSA flooding.

In a multiaccess network this flooding can become excessive. In the animation, R2 sends out an LSA. This event triggers every other router to also send out an LSA. Not shown in the animation are the required acknowledgements sent for every LSA received. If every router in a multiaccess network had to flood and acknowledge all received LSAs to all other routers on that same multiaccess network, the network traffic would become quite chaotic.

To illustrate this point, imagine that you are in a room with a large number of people. What if everyone had to introduce themselves individually to everyone else? Not only would each person have to tell everyone their name, but whenever one person learned another person's name, that person would then have to tell everyone else in the room, one person at a time. As you can see, this process leads to chaos!

Refer to **Figure** in online course

Solution: Designated Router

The solution to managing the number of adjacencies and the flooding of LSAs on a multiaccess network is the Designated Router (DR). Continuing our previous example, this solution is analogous to electing someone in the room to go around and learn everyone's names and then announce these names to everyone in the room at once.

On multiaccess networks, OSPF elects a Designated Router (DR) to be the collection and distribution point for LSAs sent and received. A Backup Designated Router (BDR) is also elected in case the Designated Router fails. All other routers become DROthers (this indicates a router that is neither the DR or the BDR).

Click Play to see the animation of the role of DR.

Routers on a multiaccess network elect a DR and BDR. DROthers only form full adjacencies with the DR and BDR in the network. This means that instead of flooding LSAs to all routers in the network, DROthers only send their LSAs to the DR and BDR using the multicast address 224.0.0.6 (ALLDRouters - All DR routers). In the animation, R1 sends LSAs to the DR. The BDR listens as well. The DR is responsible for forwarding the LSAs from R1 to all other routers. The DR uses the multicast address 224.0.0.5 (AllSPFRouters - All OSPF routers). The end result is that there is only one router doing all of the flooding of all LSAs in the multiaccess network.

11.4.2 DR/BDR Election Process

Refer to **Figure** in online course

Topology Change

DR/BDR elections do not occur in point-to-point networks. Therefore, in a standard three-router topology, R1, R2, and R3 do not need to elect a DR and BDR, because the links between these routers are not multiaccess networks.

Click Multiaccess Topology in the figure.

For the rest of the discussion on DR and BDR, we will use the multiaccess topology shown in the figure. The names of the routers are different, solely to emphasize that this topology is not the same three-router topology we have been using up to this point. We will return to our chapter topology after the discussion of the DR/BDR election process. In this new topology, we have three routers sharing a common Ethernet multiaccess network, 192.168.1.0/24. Each router is configured with an IP address on the Fast Ethernet interface and a loopback address for the router ID.

Refer to **Figure** in online course

DR/BDR Election

How do the DR and BDR get elected? The following criteria are applied:

1. DR: Router with the highest OSPF interface priority.

2. BDR: Router with the second highest OSPF interface priority.

3. If OSPF interface priorities are equal, the highest router ID is used to break the tie.

In this example, the default OSPF interface priority is 1. As a result, based on the selection criteria listed above, the OSPF router ID is used to elect the DR and BDR. As you can see, RouterC becomes the DR and RouterB, with the second highest router ID, becomes the BDR. Because RouterA is not elected as either the DR or BDR, it becomes the DROther.

DROthers only form **FULL** adjacencies with the DR and BDR, but will still form a neighbor adjacency with any DROthers that join the network. This means that all DROther routers in the multiaccess network still receive Hello packets from all other DROther routers. In this way, they are aware of all routers in the network. When two DROther routers form a neighbor adjacency, the neighbor state is displayed as **2WAY**. The different neighbor states are discussed in CCNP.

Click `show ip ospf neighbor` in the figure.

The command output in the figure displays the neighbor adjacency of each router on the multiaccess network. Notice for RouterA that it shows that the DR is RouterC with the router ID of 192.168.31.33 and that the BDR is RouterB with the router ID of 192.168.31.22.

Click `show ip ospf interface` in the figure.

Because RouterA shows both its neighbors as the DR and BDR, RouterA is a DROther. This can be verified using the `show ip ospf interface fastethernet 0/0` command on RouterA, as shown in the figure. This command will show the DR, BDR, or DROTHER state of this router, along with the router ID of the DR and BDR on this multiaccess network.

Refer to
Figure
in online course

Timing of DR/BDR Election

The DR and BDR election process takes place as soon as the first router with an OSPF enabled interface is active on the multiaccess network. This can happen when the routers are powered-on or when the OSPF `network` command for that interface is configured. The election process only takes a few seconds. If all of the routers on the multiaccess network have not finished booting, it is possible that a router with a lower router ID will become the DR. This could be a lower-end router that took less time to boot.

When the DR is elected, it remains the DR until one of the following conditions occurs:

■ The DR fails.

■ The OSPF process on the DR fails.

■ The multiaccess interface on the DR fails.

In the figure, a red **X** indicates one or more of these failures.

Click DR Fails in the figure.

If the DR fails, the BDR assumes the role of DR and an election is held to choose a new BDR. In the figure, RouterC fails and the former BDR, RouterB, becomes DR. The only other router available to be BDR is RouterA.

Click New Router in the figure.

RouterD joins the network. If a new router enters the network after the DR and BDR have been elected, it will not become the DR or the BDR even if it has a higher OSPF interface priority or router ID than the current DR or BDR. The new router can be elected the BDR if the current DR or BDR fails. If the current DR fails, the BDR will become the DR, and the new router can be elected the new BDR. After the new router becomes the BDR, if the DR fails, then the new router will become the DR. The current DR and BDR must both fail before the new router can be elected DR or BDR.

Click Old DR Returns in the figure.

A previous DR does not regain DR status if it returns to the network. In the figure, RouterC has finished a reboot and becomes a DROther even though its router ID, 192.168.31.33, is higher than the current DR and BDR.

Click BDR Fails in the figure.

If the BDR fails, an election is held among the DRothers to see which router will be the new BDR. In the figure, the BDR router fails. An election is held between RouterC and RouterD. RouterD wins the election with the higher router ID.

Click New DR Fails in the figure.

In the figure, RouterB fails. Because RouterD is the current BDR, it is promoted to DR. RouterC becomes the BDR.

So, how do you make sure that the routers you want to be DR and BDR win the election? Without further configurations, the solution is to either:

- Boot up the DR first, followed by the BDR, and then boot all other routers, or

- Shut down the interface on all routers, followed by a **no shutdown** on the DR, then the BDR, and then all other routers.

However, as you may have already guessed, we can change the OSPF interface priority to better control our DR/BDR elections.

11.4.3 OSPF Interface Priority

Refer to
Figure
in online course

Because the DR becomes the focal point for the collection and distribution of LSAs, it is important for this router to have sufficient CPU and memory capacity to handle the responsibility. Instead of relying on the router ID to decide which routers are elected the DR and BDR, it is better to control the election of these routers with the **ip ospf priority** interface command.

```
Router(config-if)#ip ospf priority {0 - 255}
```

In our previous discussion, the OSPF priority was equal. This is because the priority value defaults to 1 for all router interfaces. Therefore, router ID determined the DR and BDR. But if you change the default value from 1 to a higher value, the router with the highest priority will become the DR and the router with the next highest priority will become the BDR. A value of 0 makes the router ineligible to become a DR or BDR.

Because priorities are an interface-specific value, they provide better control of the OSPF multiaccess networks. They also allow a router to be the DR in one network and a DROther in another.

Click show ip ospf interface in the figure.

To simplify our discussion, we removed RouterD from the topology. The OSPF interface priority can be viewed using **show ip ospf interface** command. In the figure, we can verify that the priority on RouterA is at the default value of 1.

Click Modify Priority in the figure.

The figure shows the OSPF interface priorities of RouterA and RouterB modified so that RouterA with the highest priority becomes the DR and RouterB becomes the BDR. The OSPF interface priority of RouterC remains at the default value of 1.

Click Force Election in the figure.

After doing a **shutdown** and a **no shutdown** on the FastEthernet 0/0 interfaces of all three routers, we see the result of the change of OSPF interface priorities. The **show ip ospf neighbor** command on RouterC now shows that RouterA (Router ID 192.168.31.11) is the DR with the highest OSPF interface priority of 200 and that RouterB (Router ID 192.168.31.22) is still the BDR with the next highest OSPF interface priority of 100. Notice from RouterA's output of **show ip ospf neighbor** that it does not show a DR, because RouterA is the actual DR on this network.

Refer to **Packet Tracer Activity** for this chapter

Use this Packet Tracer Activity to examine current DR and BDR roles, watch the roles change, and then force new roles by changing priority.

11.5 More OSPF Configuration

11.5.1 Redistributing an OSPF Default Route

Refer to
Figure
in online course

Topology

Let's return to the earlier topology, which now includes a new link to ISP. As with RIP and EIGRP, the router connected to the Internet is used to propagate a default route to other routers in the OSPF routing domain. This router is sometimes called the edge, entrance or gateway router. However, in OSPF terminology, the router located between an OSPF routing domain and a non-OSPF network is called the *Autonomous System Boundary Router (ASBR)*. In this topology, the Loopback1 (Lo1) represents a link to a non-OSPF network. We will not configure the 172.30.1.1/30 network as part of the OSPF routing process.

Click R1 Static Default Configuration in the figure.

The figure shows the ASBR (R1) configured with the Loopback1 IP address and static default route forwarding traffic toward the ISP router:

```
R1(config)#ip route 0.0.0.0 0.0.0.0 loopback 1
```
Note: The static default route is using the loopback as an exit interface because the ISP router in this topology does not physically exist. By using a loopback interface, we can simulate the connection to another router.

Like RIP, OSPF requires the use of the `default-information originate` command to advertise the 0.0.0.0/0 static default route to the other routers in the area. If the `default-information originate` command is not used, the default "quad-zero" route will not be propagated to other routers in the OSPF area.

The command syntax is:

```
R1(config-router)#default-information originate
```
Click R1, R2, and R3 in the figure.

R1, R2, and R3 now have a "gateway of last resort" set in the routing table. Notice the default route in R2 and R3 with the routing source OSPF, but with the additional code, **E2**. For R2, the route is:

```
O*
E2 0.0.0.0/0 [110/1] via 192.168.10.10, 00:05:34, Serial0/0/1
```
E2 denotes that this route is an OSPF External Type 2 route.

OSPF external routes fall in one of two categories: External Type 1 (E1) or External Type 2 (E2). The difference between the two is in the way the OSPF cost of the route is calculated at each router. OSPF accumulates cost for an E1 route as the route is being propagated throughout the OSPF area. This process is identical to cost calculations for normal OSPF internal routes. However, the cost of an E2 route is always the external cost, irrespective of the interior cost to reach that route. In this topology, because the default route has an external cost of 1 on the R1 router, R2 and R3 also show a cost of 1 for the default **E2** route. E2 routes at a cost of 1 are the default OSPF configuration. Changing these defaults, as well as more external route information, is discussed in CCNP.

11.5.2 Fine-tuning OSPF

Refer to
Figure
in online course

Reference Bandwidth

As you remember, Cisco OSPF cost uses accumulated bandwidth. The bandwidth value of each interface is calculated using 100,000,000/bandwidth. 100,000,000 or 10 to the 8th is known as the reference bandwidth.

Therefore, 100,000,000 is the default bandwidth referenced when the actual bandwidth is converted into a cost metric. As you know from previous studies, we now have link speeds that are much faster than Fast Ethernet speeds, including Gigabit Ethernet and 10GigE. Using a reference bandwidth of 100,000,000 results in interfaces with bandwidth values of 100 Mbps and higher having the same OSPF cost of 1.

In order to obtain more accurate cost calculations, it may be necessary to adjust the reference bandwidth value. The reference bandwidth can be modified to accommodate these faster links by using the OSPF command **auto-cost reference-bandwidth**. When this command is necessary, use it on all routers so that the OSPF routing metric remains consistent.

```
R1(config-router)#auto-cost reference-bandwidth ?
 1-4294967 The reference bandwidth in terms of Mbits per second
```

Notice that the value is expressed in Mbps. Therefore, the default value is equivalent to 100. To increase it to 10GigE speeds, you would need to change the reference bandwidth to 10000.

```
R1(config-router)#auto-cost reference-bandwidth 10000
```

Again, make sure you configure this command on all routers in the OSPF routing domain. The IOS may also remind you, as shown in the figure.

Click R1 Before and R1 After in the figure.

The routing table for R1 shows the change in the OSPF cost metric. Notice that the values are much larger cost values for OSPF routes. For example, in **R1 Before**, the cost to 10.10.10.0/24 is **1172**. After configuring a new reference bandwidth, the cost for the same route is now **117287**.

Refer to
Figure
in online course

Modifying OSPF Intervals

Click R1 Neighbors 1 in the figure.

The **show ip ospf neighbor** command on R1 verifies that R1 is adjacent to R2 and R3. Notice in the output that the Dead Time is counting down from 40 seconds. By default, this value is refreshed every 10 seconds when R1 receives a Hello from the neighbor.

It may be desirable to change the OSPF timers so that routers will detect network failures in less time. Doing this will increase traffic, but sometimes there is a need for quick convergence that outweighs the extra traffic.

OSPF Hello and Dead intervals can be modified manually using the following interface commands:

```
Router(config-if)#ip ospf hello-interval seconds
Router(config-if)#ip ospf dead-interval seconds
```

Click Modify R1 Timers in the figure.

The figure shows the Hello and Dead intervals modified to 5 seconds and 20 seconds, respectively, on the Serial 0/0/0 interface for R1. Immediately after changing the Hello interval, Cisco IOS automatically modifies the Dead interval to four times the Hello interval. However, it is always good practice to explicitly modify the timer instead of relying on an automatic IOS feature so that modifications are documented in the configuration.

After 20 seconds, the Dead Timer on R1 expires. R1 and R2 lose adjacency. We only modified the values on one side of the serial link between R1 and R2.

```
%OSPF-5-ADJCHG: Process 1, Nbr 10.2.2.2 on Serial0/0/0 from FULL to DOWN, Neighbor
Down: Dead timer expired
```

Click R1 Neighbors 2 in the figure.

Remember, OSPF Hello and Dead intervals must be equivalent between neighbors. You can verify the loss of adjacency with the **show ip ospf neighbor** command on R1. Notice that the 10.2.2.2 neighbor is no longer present. However, 10.3.3.3 or R3 is still a neighbor. The timers set on Serial 0/0/0 do not affect the neighbor adjacency with R3.

Click R2 Timers in the figure.

The mismatching Hello and Dead intervals can be verified on R2 using **`show ip ospf interface serial 0/0/0`** command. The interval values on R2, Router ID 10.2.2.2, are still set with a Hello interval of 10 seconds and Dead interval of 40 seconds.

Click Modify R2 Timers in the figure.

To restore adjacency between R1 and R2, modify the Hello and Dead intervals on the Serial 0/0/0 interface on R2 to match the intervals on the Serial 0/0/0 interface on R1. The IOS displays a message that adjacency has been established with a state of **FULL**.

```
14:22:27: %OSPF-5-ADJCHG: Process 1, Nbr 10.1.1.1 on Serial0/0 from LOADING to
FULL, Loading Done
```

Click R1 Neighbors 3 in the figure.

Verify that neighbor adjacency is restored with the show ip ospf neighbor command on R1. Notice that the Dead Time for Serial 0/0/0 is now much lower because it is counting down from 20 seconds instead of the default 40 seconds. Serial 0/0/1 is still operating with default timers.

Note: OSPF requires that the Hello and Dead intervals match between two routers for them to become adjacent. This differs from EIGRP where the Hello and Holddown timers do not need to match for two routers to form an EIGRP adjacency.

> **Refer to Packet Tracer Activity** for this chapter

Use the Packet Tracer Activity to configure a default route and propagate it within the OSPF routing process. Also, practice changing the reference bandwidth as well as the Hello and Dead intervals.

11.6   OSPF Configuration Labs

11.6.1   Basic OSPF Configuration Lab

> **Refer to Lab Activity** for this chapter

In this lab activity, there are two separate scenarios. In the first scenario, you will learn how to configure the routing protocol OSPF using the network shown in the Topology Diagram in Scenario A. The segments of the network have been subnetted using VLSM. OSPF is a classless routing protocol that can be used to provide subnet mask information in the routing updates. This will allow VLSM subnet information to be propagated throughout the network.

In the second scenario, you will learn to configure OSPF on a multi-access network. You will also learn to use the OSPF election process to determine the designated router (DR), backup designated router (BDR), and DRother states.

> **Refer to Packet Tracer Activity** for this chapter

Use this Packet Tracer Activity to repeat a simulation of Lab 11.6.1. Remember, however, that Packet Tracer is not a substitute for a hands-on lab experience with real equipment.

A summary of the instructions is provided within the activity. Use the Lab PDF for more details.

Clicking the Packet Tracer icon will launch Scenario A. All scenarios for this simulation of the hands-on lab can be launched from the links below.

Scenario A

Scenario B

11.6.2   Challenge OSPF Configuration Lab

> **Refer to Lab Activity** for this chapter

In this lab activity, you will be given a network address that must be subnetted using VLSM to complete the addressing of the network shown in the Topology Diagram. A combination OSPF routing and static routing will be required so that hosts on networks that are not directly connected will be able to communicate with each other. OSPF area ID of 0 and process ID of 1 will be used in all OSPF configurations.

Use this Packet Tracer Activity to repeat a simulation of Lab 11.6.2. Remember, however, that Packet Tracer is not a substitute for a hands-on lab experience with real equipment.

A summary of the instructions is provided within the activity. Use the Lab PDF for more details.

11.6.3 Troubleshooting OSPF Configuration Lab

In this lab, you will begin by loading configuration scripts on each of the routers. These scripts contain errors that will prevent end-to-end communication across the network.

You will need to troubleshoot each router to determine the configuration errors, and then use the appropriate commands to correct the configurations.

When you have corrected all of the configuration errors, all of the hosts on the network should be able to communicate with each other.

Use this Packet Tracer Activity to repeat a simulation of Lab 11.6.3. Remember, however, that Packet Tracer is not a substitute for a hands-on lab experience with real equipment.

A summary of the instructions is provided within the activity. Use the Lab PDF for more details.

Summary and Review

Refer to
Figure
in online course

Summary

OSPF (Open Shortest Path First) is a classless, link-state routing protocol. The current version of OSPF for IPv4 is OSPFv2 introduced in RFC 1247 and updated in RFC 2328 by John Moy. In 1999, OSPFv3 for IPv6 was published in RFC 2740.

OSPF has a default administrative distance of 110, and is denoted in the routing table with a route source code of **O**. OSPF is enabled with the **router ospf** *process-id* global configuration command. The *process-id* is locally significant, which means that it does not have to match other OSPF routers in order to establish adjacencies with those neighbors.

The network command used with OSPF has the same function as when used with other IGP routing protocols, but with slightly different syntax.

```
Router(config-router)#network network-address wildcard-mask area area-id
```
The *wildcard-mask* is the inverse of the subnet mask, and the *area-id* should be set to 0.

OSPF does not use a Transport layer protocol, as OSPF packets are sent directly over IP. The OSPF Hello packet is used by OSPF to establish neighbor adjacencies. By default, OSPF Hello packets are sent every 10 seconds on multiaccess and point-to-point segments and every 30 seconds on non-broadcast multiaccess (NBMA) segments (Frame Relay, X.25, ATM). The Dead interval is the period of time an OSPF router will wait before terminating adjacency with a neighbor. The Dead interval is four times the Hello interval, by default. For multiaccess and point-to-point segments, this period is 40 seconds. For NBMA networks, the Dead interval is 120 seconds.

For routers to become adjacent, their Hello interval, Dead interval, network types and subnet masks must match. The **show ip ospf neighbors** command can be used to verify OSPF adjacencies.

The OSPF router ID is used to uniquely identify each router in the OSPF routing domain. Cisco routers derive the router ID based on three criteria and with the following precedence:

1. Use the IP address configured with the OSPF **router-id** command.

2. If the **router-id** is not configured, the router chooses highest IP address of any of its loopback interfaces.

3. If no loopback interfaces are configured, the router chooses highest active IP address of any of its physical interfaces.

RFC 2328 does not specify which values should be used to determine the cost. Cisco IOS uses the cumulative bandwidths of the outgoing interfaces from the router to the destination network as the cost value.

Multiaccess networks can create two challenges for OSPF regarding the flooding of LSAs, including the creation of multiple adjacencies - one adjacency for every pair of routers, and extensive flooding of LSAs (Link-State Advertisements). OSPF elects a DR (Designated Router) to act as collection and distribution point for LSAs sent and received in the multiaccess network. A BDR (Backup Designated Router) is elected to take over the role of the DR should the DR fail. All other routers are known as DROthers. All routers send their LSAs to the DR, which then floods the LSA to all other routers in the multiaccess network.

The router with the highest router ID is the DR, and the router with the second highest router ID is the BDR. This can be superseded by the **ip ospf priority** command on that interface. By default, the **ip ospf priority** is "1" on all multiaccess interfaces. If a router is configured with a new priority value, the router with the highest priority value is the DR, and next-highest the BDR. A priority value of "0" means the router is ineligible to become the DR or BDR.

A default route is propagated in OSPF similar to that of RIP. The OSPF router mode command, `default-information originate` is used to propagate a static default route.

The `show ip protocols` command is used to verify important OSPF configuration information, including the OSPF process ID, the router ID and the networks the router is advertising.

Refer to **Figure** in online course

 Refer to **Packet Tracer Activity** for this chapter

The Packet Tracer Skills Integration Challenge Activity integrates all the knowledge and skills you acquired in previous chapters of this course and prior courses. Skills related to this chapter's discussion of OSPF are also included.

In this activity, you build a network from the ground up. Starting with an addressing space and network requirements, you must implement a network design that satisfies the specifications. Next, you implement an effective OSPF routing configuration with integrated default routing. Detailed instructions are provided within the activity.

Packet Tracer Skills Integration Instructions (PDF)

Refer to **Figure** in online course

To Learn More

RFC 2328 OSPF version 2

RFCs (Request for Comments) are a series of documents submitted to the IETF (Internet Engineering Task Force) to propose an Internet standard or convey new concepts, information or even occasionally even humor. RFC 2328 is the current RFC for OSPFv2.

RFCs can be accessed from several web sites including www.ietf.org. Read all or parts of RFC OSPF to learn more about this classless, link-state routing protocol.

Multi-area OSPF

Some of the real advantages of OSPF especially in large networks can be seen with multi-area OSPF. Multi-area OSPF is discussed in CCNP, but you may be interested in looking at some of these new concepts now.

Here are some suggested resources:

- *Routing TCP/IP, Volume I*, by Jeff Doyle and Jennifer Carroll
- *OSPF, Anatomy of an Internet Routing Protocol*, by John Moy

Go to the online course to take the quiz.

Chapter Quiz

Take the chapter quiz to test your knowledge.

Your Chapter Notes

active state

A state in which there is no Feasible Successor in the topology table and the local router goes into Active state and queries its neighbors for routing information.

AD

See administrative distance

adjacency

A relationship formed between selected neighboring routers and end nodes for the purpose of exchanging routing information. Adjacency is based upon the use of a common media segment.

administrative distance

Rating of the trustworthiness of a routing information source. Administrative distance often is expressed as a numerical value between 0 and 255. The higher the value, the lower the trustworthiness rating. If a router has multiple routing protocols in it's routing table it will select the route with the lowest administrative distance.

Algorithm

Well-defined rule or process for arriving at a solution to a problem. In networking, algorithms are commonly used to determine the best route for traffic from a particular source to a particular destination.

ALLSPFRouters

A multicast group used in the OSPF routing protocol. The ALLSPFRouters address is 224.0.0.5.

ARP

Address Resolution Protocol. Internet protocol used to map an IP address to a MAC address. Defined in RFC 826.

asymmetric routing

Asymmetric routing is when a path from network 1 to network 2 is different from the path from network 2 to network 1. The paths to network 2 are different than the returning path from Network 2 to network 1.

Asynchronous Transfer Mode (ATM)

Asynchronous Transfer Mode. The international standard for cell relay in which multiple service types (such as voice, video, or data) are conveyed in fixed-length (53-byte) cells. Fixed-length cells allow cell processing to occur in hardware, thereby reducing transit delays. ATM is designed to take advantage of high-speed transmission media, such as E3, SONET, and T3.

automatic summarization

Consolidation of networks and advertised in classful network advertisements. In RIP this causes a single summary route to be advertised to other routers.

Autonomous System (AS)

A collection of networks under a common administration sharing a common routing strategy. Autonomous systems are subdivided by areas. An autonomous system must be assigned a unique 16-bit number by the IANA. Sometimes abbreviated as AS.

Autonomous System Boundary Router (ASBR)

Autonomous system boundary router. An ASBR is located between an OSPF autonomous system and a non-OSPF network. ASBRs run both OSPF and another routing protocol, such as RIP. ASBRs must reside in a nonstub OSPF area.

Backup Designated Router (BDR)

A router that becomes the designated router if the current designated router fails. The BDR is the OSPF router with second highest priority at the time of the last DR election.

Bellman-Ford (algorithm)

Class of routing algorithms that iterate on the number of hops in a route to find a shortest-path spanning tree. Distance vector routing algorithms call for each router to send its entire routing table in each update, but only to its neighbors. Distance vector routing algorithms can be prone to routing loops, but are computationally simpler than link state routing algorithms.

best path
The fastest path to a certain destination. The fastest path being based on the routing protocol's metric.

Border Gateway Routing (BGP)
Border Gateway Protocol. Interdomain routing protocol that replaces EGP. BGP exchanges reachability information with other BGP systems. It is defined by RFC 1163.

boundary router
A router that sits on the edge two discontiguous classful networks. A boundary router can also be known as a router that sits on the edge of two different networks that have different routing protocols. Sometimes the word boundary router is loosely used when discussing OSPF and Autonomous System Boundary Routers.

bounded updates
Updates that are sent only to those routers that need the updated information instead of sending updates to all routers.

cable
Transmission medium of copper wire or optical fiber wrapped in a protective cover.

classful IP addressing
In the early days of IPv4, IP addresses are divided into 5 classes, namely, Class A, Class B, Class C, Class D, and Class E.

classful routing protocols
Routing protocols that use classful ip addressing. They do not use subnet mask information in their routing operation. They automatically assume classful masks.

Classless Inter-Domain Routing (CIDR)
Technique supported by BGP4 and based on route aggregation. CIDR allows routers to group routes together to reduce the quantity of routing information carried by the core routers. With CIDR, several IP networks appear to networks outside the group as a single, larger entity. With CIDR, IP addresses and their subnet masks are written as four octets, separated by periods, followed by a forward slash and a two-digit number that represents the subnet mask.

console port
DTE through which commands are entered into a host.

contiguous
Consistent or adjacent. In terms of contiguous networks, the word contiguous means network blocks that are hierarchical in nature.

Contiguous Address Assignment
Addressing that is not fragmented and follows a hierarchical format allowing for network summarization.

converged
The past tense of converge. When intermediate devices all have the same consistent network topology in their routing tables. This means that they have converged.

convergence
Speed and ability of a group of internetworking devices running a specific routing protocol to agree on the topology of an internetwork after a change in that topology.

cost
An arbitrary value, typically based on hop count, media bandwidth, or other measures, that is assigned by a network administrator and used to compare various paths through an internetwork environment. Routing protocols use cost values to determine the most favorable path to a particular destination: the lower the cost, the better the path.

count to infinity
Problem that can occur in routing algorithms that are slow to converge, in which routers continuously increment the hop count to particular networks. Typically, some arbitrary hop-count limit is imposed to prevent this problem.

Database Description (DBD)
A packet which contains an abbreviated list of the sending router's link-state database and is used by receiving routers to check against the local link-state database. Routers exchange DBDs during the Exchange phase of adjacency creation.

datagrams
Logical grouping of information sent as a network layer unit over a transmission medium without prior establishment of a virtual circuit. IP datagrams are the primary information units in the Internet. The terms cell, frame, message, packet, and segment also are used to describe logical information groupings at various layers

of the OSI reference model and in various technology circles.

data-link

Layer 2 of the OSI reference model. Provides reliable transit of data across a physical link. The data-link layer is concerned with physical addressing, network topology, line discipline, error notification, ordered delivery of frames, and flow control. The IEEE divided this layer into two sublayers: the MAC sublayer and the LLC sublayer. Sometimes simply called link layer. Roughly corresponds to the data-link control layer of the SNA model.

Designated Router (DR)

OSPF router that generates LSAs for a multiaccess network and has other special responsibilities in running OSPF. Each multiaccess OSPF network that has at least two attached routers has a designated router that is elected by the OSPF Hello protocol. The designated router enables a reduction in the number of adjacencies required on a multiaccess network, which in turn reduces the amount of routing protocol traffic and the size of the topological database.

Diffusing Update Algorithm (DUAL)

Diffusing Update Algorithm. Convergence algorithm used in Enhanced IGRP that provides loop-free operation at every instant throughout a route computation. Allows routers involved in a topology change to synchronize at the same time, while not involving routers that are unaffected by the change.

discontiguous

Components that are fragmented. For example a discontiguous network comprises of a major network that separates another major network.

discontiguous address assignment

A fragmented network assignment that does not follow a consistent pattern.

discontiguous network

Fragmented network addressing. Networks that do not have a hierarchical scheme. It is impossible to summarize discontiguous networks.

distance vector

see Bellman-Ford (Algorithm)

domain

A portion of the naming hierarchy tree that refers to general groupings of networks based on organization type or geography.

DROthers

DROthers are routers that are not DR or BDR. They are the other routers in the OSPF network.

DSL

Digital subscriber line. Public network technology that delivers high bandwidth over conventional copper wiring at limited distances. There are four types of DSL: ADSL, HDSL, SDSL, and VDSL. All are provisioned via modem pairs, with one modem located at a central office and the other at the customer site. Because most DSL technologies do not use the whole bandwidth of the twisted pair, there is room remaining for a voice channel.

dynamic routing

Routing that adjusts automatically to network topology or traffic changes. Also called adaptive routing.

dynamic routing protocols

Allow network devices to learn routes dynamically. RIP and EIGRP are examples of dynamic routing protocols.

Enhanced IGRP (EIGRP)

Enhanced Interior Gateway Routing Protocol. Advanced version of IGRP developed by Cisco. Provides superior convergence properties and operating efficiency, and combines the advantages of link state protocols with those of distance vector protocols.

equal cost load balancing

When a router utilizes multiple paths with the same administrative distance and cost to a destination.

equal cost metric

A metric that has the same value on multiple paths to the same destination. When multiple paths have equal cost metrics a router can execute equal cost load balancing among those paths.

Ethernet

Baseband LAN specification invented by Xerox Corporation and developed jointly by Xerox, Intel, and Digital Equipment Corporation. Ethernet networks use CSMA/CD and run over a variety of cable types at 10 Mbps. Ethernet is similar to the IEEE 802.3 series of standards.

Feasibility Condition (FC)

If the receiving router has a Feasible Distance to a particular network and it receives an update from a neighbor with a lower advertised distance (Reported Distance) to that network, then there is a Feasibility Condition. Used in EIGRP routing.

Feasible Distance (FD)

The Feasible Distance is the metric of a network advertised by the connected neighbor plus the cost of reaching that neighbor. The path with the lowest metric is added to the routing table and is called FD or feasible distance. Used in EIGRP routing.

Feasible Successor (FS)

A next hop router that leads to a certain destination network. The feasible successor can be thought of as a backup next hop if the primary next hop (successor) goes down. Used in EIGRP routing.

Fiber Distributed Data INterface (FDDI)

Fiber Distributed Data Interface. LAN standard, defined by ANSI X3T9.5, specifying a 100-Mbps token-passing network using fiber-optic cable, with transmission distances of up to 2 km. FDDI uses a dual-ring architecture to provide redundancy.

flapping link

Routing problem where an advertised route between two nodes alternates (flaps) back and forth between two paths due to a network problem that causes intermittent interface failures.

flash

Technology developed by Intel and licensed to other semiconductor companies. Flash memory is nonvolatile storage that can be electrically erased and reprogrammed. Allows software images to be stored, booted, and rewritten as necessary.

Frame Relay

A packet switched data link layer protocol that handles multiple virtual circuits using between connected devices. Frame Relay is more efficient than X.25, the protocol for which it generally is considered a replacement.

gateways

A device on a network that serves as an access point to another network. A default gateway is used by a host when an IP packet's destination address belongs to someplace outside the local subnet. A router is a good example of a default gateway.

high order bits

The 'high order bit' of a binary number is the one that carries the most weight, the one written farthest to the left. High order bits are the 1s in the network mask.

hold time

The maximum time a router waits to receive the next hello packet or routing update. Once the hold time counter expires that route will become unreachable.

hold-down timers

Timers that a route is placed in so that routers neither advertise the route nor accept advertisements about the route for a specific length of time (the holddown period). Holddown is used to flush bad information about a route from all routers in the network. A route typically is placed in holddown when a link in that route fails.

hosts

Computer system on a network. Similar to node, except that host usually implies a computer system, whereas node generally applies to any networked system, including access servers and routers.

hub-and-spoke

A wan topology whereupon various branch offices are connected via a centralized hub or headquarters.

ICMP

Internet Control Message Protocol. Network layer Internet protocol that reports errors and provides other information relevant to IP packet processing. Documented in RFC 792.

IGRP

Interior Gateway Routing Protocol. IGP developed by Cisco to address the issues associated with routing in large, heterogeneous networks.

Interior Gateway Protocols

Internet protocol used to exchange routing information within an autonomous system. Examples of common Internet IGPs include IGRP, OSPF, and RIP.

Intermediate-System-to-Intermediate-System (IS-IS)

Intermediate System-to-Intermediate System protocol (IS-IS) is based on a routing method known as DECnet Phase V routing, in which routers known as intermediate systems exchange data about routing using a single metric to determine the network topology. IS-IS was developed by the International Organization for Standardization (ISO) as part of their Open Systems Interconnection (OSI) model.

Internet Service Provider (ISP)

An ISP is a company that provides access to the Internet to individuals or companies.

IP

Internet Protocol. Network layer protocol in the TCP/IP stack offering a connectionless inter-network service. IP provides features for addressing, type-of-service specification, fragmentation and reassembly, and security. Defined in RFC 791.

IPv6

A network layer protocol for packet-switched internet works. The successor of IPv4 for general use on the Internet.

IPX

Internetwork Packet Exchange. NetWare network layer (Layer 3) protocol used for transferring data from servers to workstations. IPX is similar to IP and XNS.

ISDN

Integrated Services Digital Network. Communication protocol offered by telephone companies that permits telephone networks to carry data, voice, and other source traffic.

LED

Light emitting diode. Semiconductor device that emits light produced by converting electrical energy.

Level 1 Parent route

A first level route in the routing table that has subnets "catalogued" under it. A first level parent route does not contain any next-hop IP address or exit interface information.

Level 1 route

A route with a subnet mask equal to or less than the classful mask of the network address.

Level 2 child route

The subnets that belong to the parent route.

Level 2 route

A subnet is the level 2 route of the parent route.

Link-state

Link-state refers to the status of a link including the interface IP address/subnet mask, type of network, cost of the link, and any neighbor routers on that link.

Link-State Acknowledgement (LSAck)

Link State Acknowledgment Packets are OSPF packet type 5. LSAcks acknowledge receipt of LSA (Links State Advertisement) packets.

Link-State Advertisement (LSA)

Link-state advertisement. Broadcast packet used by link-state protocols that contains information about neighbors and path costs. LSAs are used by the receiving routers to maintain their routing tables.

link-state database

A table used in OSPF that is a representation of the topology of the autonomous system. It is the method by which routers see the state of the links in the autonomous system.

Link-State Packet (LSP)

Broadcast packet used by link-state protocols that contains information about neighbors and path costs. LSPs are used by the receiving routers to maintain their routing tables.

Link-State Request (LSR)

Link State Request packets are OSPF packet type 3. The Link State Request packet is used to request the pieces of the neighbor's database that are more up to date.

link-state router

A router that uses a link-state routing protocol.

link-state routing protocol

A routing protocol in which routers exchange information with one another about the reachability of other networks and the cost or metric to reach the other networks. Link state routers use Dijkstra's algorithm to calculate shortest paths to a destination, and normally update other routers with whom they are connected only when their own routing tables change.

Link-State Update (LSU)

Link State Update packets are OSPF packet type 4. Link State Update packet carries a collection of link state advertisements one hop further from its origin.

load balancing

In routing, the capability of a router to distribute traffic over all its network ports that are the same distance from the destination address. Good load-balancing algorithms use both line speed and reliability information. Load balancing increases the use of network segments, thus increasing effective network bandwidth.

Local Area Networks (LANs)

The term Local Area Network (LAN) refers to a local network, or a group of interconnected local networks that are under the same administrative control. In the early days of networking, LANs were defined as small networks that existed in a single physical location. While LANs can be a single local network installed in a home or small office, the definition of LAN has evolved to include interconnected local networks consisting of many hundreds of hosts, installed in multiple buildings and locations.

loopback

127.0.0.1 is an IP address available on all devices to test to see if the NIC card on that device is functioning. If you send something to 127.0.0.1, it loops back on itself, thereby sending the data to the NIC on that device. If you get a positive response to a ping 127.0.0.1, you know your NIC card is up and running.

loopback address

127.0.0.1 is an IP address available on all devices to test to see if the NIC card on that device is functioning. If you send something to 127.0.0.1, it loops back on itself, thereby sending the data to the NIC on that device. If you get a positive response to a ping 127.0.0.1, you know your NIC card is up and running.

loopback interface

A virtual interface used for management purposes. Unlike a proper loopback interface, this loopback device is not used to talk with itself.

loop-free

Free of loops.

MAC address

Standardized data link layer address that is required for every port or device that connects to a LAN. Other devices in the network use these addresses to locate specific ports in the network and to create and update routing tables and data structures. MAC addresses are 6 bytes long and are controlled by the IEEE.

media

Plural of medium. The various physical environments through which transmission signals pass. Common network media include twisted-pair, coaxial and fiber-optic cable, and the atmosphere (through which microwave, laser, and infrared transmission occurs). Sometimes called physical media.

metrics

Method by which a routing algorithm determines that one route is better than another. This information is stored in routing tables. Metrics include bandwidth, communication cost, delay, hop count, load, MTU, path cost, and reliability. Sometimes referred to simply as a metric.

multiaccess network

Network that allows multiple devices to connect and communicate simultaneously.

Network Address Translator (NAT)

Mechanism for reducing the need for globally unique IP addresses. NAT allows an organization with addresses that are not globally unique to connect to the Internet by translating those addresses into globally routable address space.

neighbor

In OSPF, two routers that have interfaces to a common network. On multiaccess networks, neighbors are discovered dynamically by the OSPF Hello protocol.

Network Interface Card (NIC)

A piece of computer hardware designed to allow computers to communicate over a computer network.

network prefix

Number of bits that are used to define the subnet mask. For example the subnet mask 255.255.0.0 is a /16 prefix.

next-hop

The next point of routing. When routers are not directly connected to the destination network, they will have a neighboring router that provides the next step in routing the data to its destination.

non-broadcast multiaccess (NBMA)

Term describing a multiaccess network that either does not support broadcasting (such as X.25) or in which broadcasting is not feasible (for example, an SMDS broadcast group or an extended Ethernet that is too large).

Non-Volatile RAM (NVRAM)

Non Volatile Random Access Memory. Random access memory that, when the computer shuts down, the contents in NVRAM remain there.

null interface

The null interface provides an alternative method of filtering traffic. You can avoid the overhead involved with using access lists by directing undesired network traffic to the null interface. This interface is always up and can never forward or receive traffic. Think of it as a black hole.

Null0 summary routes

Another mechanism to prevent routing loops. EIGRP always creates a route to the Null0 interface when it summarizes a group of routes. This is because whenever a routing protocol summarizes, the router might receive traffic for any IP address within that summary. Since not all IP addresses are always in use, there is a risk of looping packets in case default routes are used on the router which receives the traffic for the summary route.

Open Shortest Path First (OSPF)

Open Shortest Path First. Link-state, hierarchical IGP routing algorithm proposed as a successor to RIP in the Internet community. OSPF features include least-cost routing, multipath routing, and load balancing. OSPF was derived from an early version of the IS-IS protocol.

Operating System

A software that performs basic tasks such as controlling and allocating memory, prioritizing system requests, controlling input and output devices, facilitating networking, and managing file systems.

OSPF area

A logical set of network segments (CLNS-, DECnet-, or OSPF-based) and their attached devices. Areas usually are connected to other areas via routers, making up a single autonomous system.

packet

Logical grouping of information that includes a header containing control information and (usually) user data. Packets most often are used to refer to network layer units of data. The terms datagram, frame, message, and segment also are used to describe logical information groupings at various layers of the OSI reference model and in various technology circles.

partial update packet

When a router detects a change in a metric it sends a partial update about that specific change to bounded routers instead of sending periodic updates.

passive state

A passive state is a state when the router has identified the successor(s) for a certain destination and it becomes stable. A term used in conjunction with EIGRP.

path vector protocol

A path vector protocol is a routing protocol that marks and shows the path that update information takes as it diffuses through the network. BGP is a user of the kind of protocol because it verifies what autonomous systems the update has passed through to verify loops.

poison reverse

Routing updates that explicitly indicate that a network or a subnet is unreachable, rather than implying that a network is unreachable by not including it in updates. Poison reverse updates are sent to defeat large routing loops.

Power-On Self Test (POST)

Set of hardware diagnostics that runs on a hardware device when that device is powered up.

PPP

Point-to-Point Protocol. Successor to SLIP that provides router-to-router and host-to-network connections over synchronous and asynchronous circuits. Whereas SLIP was designed to work with IP, PPP was designed to work with several network layer protocols, such as IP, IPX, and ARA. PPP also has built-in security mechanisms, such as CHAP and PAP. PPP relies on two protocols: LCP and NCP.

prefix aggregation

Also known as network summarization. A number of IP addresses and IP prefixes can be summarized into a single IP prefix and be announced to other routers only the resulting less specific prefix (aggregated prefix) instead of the more specific IP addresses and prefixes that it covers.

private addressing

An address that is used for internal networks. This address follows RFC 1918 addressing. Not routable on the internet.

privileged EXEC mode

Privileged Exec Mode is the administration mode for the router or switch. This mode by allows you to view router settings that are considered only accessible to the administrator. This mode also allows you to enter global configuration mode. To get into the privileged exec mode you must use the enable command.

protocol-dependent module

A component that is dependent on a certain routed protocol. For example, protocol dependent modules in EIGRP allow it to work with various routed protocols. PDMs allow for EIGRP to keep a topology table for each routed protocol such as IP, IPX RIP, AppleTalk Routing Table Maintenance Protocol (RTMP), and IGRP.

Quality of Service (QoS)

quality of service. Measure of performance for a transmission system that reflects its transmission quality and service availability.

Random Access Memory (RAM)

Volatile memory that can be read and written by a microprocessor.

Read-Only Memory (ROM)

Nonvolatile memory that can be read, but not written, by the microprocessor.

redistribution

Allowing routing information discovered through one routing protocol to be distributed in the update messages of another routing protocol. Sometimes called route redistribution.

redundant paths

Multiple paths to a destination that are usable upon failure of a primary path.

reference bandwidth

The bandwidth referenced by the SPF algorithm when calculating shortest path. In OSPF the reference bandwidth is 10 to the power of 8 divided by the actual interface bandwidth.

reported distance (RD)

Reported distance is the total metric along a path to a destination network as advertised by an upstream neighbor in EIGRP.

Route poisoning

Routing updates that explicitly indicate that a network or subnet is unreachable, rather than implying that a network is unreachable by not including it in updates. Poison reverse updates are sent to defeat large routing loops. The Cisco IGRP implementation uses poison reverse updates.

route summarization

Consolidation of advertised addresses in OSPF and IS-IS. In OSPF, this causes a single summary route to be advertised to other areas by an area border router.

Router

Network layer device that uses one or more metrics to determine the optimal path along which network traffic should be forwarded. Routers forward packets from one network to another based on network layer information.

Occasionally called a gateway (although this definition of gateway is becoming increasingly outdated).

Routing Information Protocol (RIP)

Routing Information Protocol. IGP supplied with UNIX BSD systems. The most common IGP in the Internet. RIP uses hop count as a routing metric.

routing table

A table stored in the memory of a router or some other internetworking device that keeps track of routes to particular network destinations. A router uses this list of networks to determine where to send data.

Routing Table Maintenance Protocol (RTMP)

Routing Table Maintenance Protocol. Apple Computer proprietary routing protocol. RTMP was derived from RIP.

scale

To alter to a certain size according to need. For example a routing protocol is scalable when the router's routing table grows according to the addition of new networks.

serial

Method of data transmission in which the bits of a data character are transmitted sequentially over a single channel.

Setup mode

When a Cisco router boots up and does not find a configuration file in NVRAM it enters setup mode. Setup mode is a dialogue of questions that the administrator must answer in order to configure a basic configuration for router functionality.

shortest path first (SPF)

Routing algorithm that iterates on length of path to determine a shortest-path spanning tree. Commonly used in link-state routing algorithms. Sometimes called Dijkstra's algorithm.

Smart Serial

Cisco Smart Serial interfaces have 26-pin connectors and can automatically detect RS-232, RS-449, RS-530, X.21, or V.35 connectors.

SPF schedule delay

After inputting the command show ip ospf you will see the parameter SPF schedule delay X secs (The X meaning number of seconds). This is the delay time of SPF calculations.

split horizon

Routing technique in which information about routes is prevented from exiting the router interface through which that information was received. Split-horizon updates are useful in preventing routing loops.

static routing

Routing that depends on manually entered routes in the routing table.

successor

The path to a destination. The successor is chosen using DUAL from all of the known paths or feasible successors to the end destination. Used in EIGRP.

Summary Route

Route summarization reduces the number of routes that a router must maintain. It is a method of representing a series of network numbers in a single summary address.

supernet

Aggregation of IP network addresses advertised as a single classless network address. For example, given four Class C IP networks-192.0.8.0, 192.0.9.0, 192.0.10.0, and 192.0.11.0 - each having the intrinsic network mask of 255.255.255.0, one can advertise the address 192.0.8.0 with a subnet mask of 255.255.252.0.

Supernet route

A route that uses an arbitrary address mask, which is shorter than the default classful mask. Used to represent various subnets.

supernetting

Combining several IP network addresses into one IP address. Supernetting reduces the number of entries in a routing table and is done in CIDR addressing as well as internal networks.

Telnet

Standard terminal emulation protocol in the TCP/IP protocol stack. Telnet is used for remote terminal connection, enabling users to log in to remote systems and use resources as if they were connected to a local system. Telnet is defined in RFC 854.

TFTP Server

a server that hosts the TFTP protocol that allows files to be transferred from one computer to another over a network, usually without the use of client authentication (for example, username and password).

Token Ring

Token-passing LAN developed and supported by IBM. Token Ring runs at 4 or 16 Mbps over a ring topology. Similar to IEEE 802.5.

topology database

Also knows as the topology table, the topology database holds the information about the successor, feasible distance, and any feasible successors with their reported distances. Used in EIGRP routing.

topology table

Contains information regarding EIGRP routes received in updates and routes that are locally originated. EIGRP sends and receives routing updates from adjacent routers to which peering relationships (adjacencies) have been formed. The objects in this table are populated on a per-topology table entry (route) basis.

triggered update

A routing update that is triggered by an event in the network.

TTL

Time To Live. Field in an IP header that indicates how long a packet is considered valid.

Type/Length/Value (TLV)

The data portion of the EIGRP packet. All TLVs begin with 16 bit Type field and a 16 bit Length field. There exist different TLV values according to routed protocol. There is, however, a general TLV that describes generic EIGRP parameters such as Sequence (used by Cisco's Reliable Multicast) and EIGRP software version.

Ultimate Route

Also known as a level 1 route, an ultimate route is a route in the routing table that includes a next hop address and an outgoing interface.

unequal cost load balancing

Load balancing that uses multiple paths to the same destination that have different costs or metrics. EIGRP uses unequal load balancing with the "variance" command.

unified communications

A communications system for voice, video and data. The system integrates wired, wireless and mobile devices to create a secure solution for enterprise networks.

Variable Length Subnet Masking (VLSM)

variable-length subnet mask. Capability to specify a different subnet mask for the same network number on different subnets. VLSM can help optimize available address space.

vector

A vector is a quantity characterized by a magnitude (for instance hops in a path) and a direction.

Wide Area Networks (WANs)

Data communications network that serves users across a broad geographic area and often uses transmission devices provided by common carriers. Frame Relay, SMDS, and X.25 are examples ofWANs.

wildcard mask

A 32-bit quantity used in conjunction with an IP address to determine which bits in an IP address should be ignored when comparing that address with another IP address. A wildcard mask is specified when setting up access lists.

XNS

Xerox Network Systems. A protocol stack developed by Xerox that contains network protocols that closely resemble IP and TCP. XNS was one of the first protocol stacks used in the first local area network implementations.

CCNA Exploration
learning resources

Cisco Press, the authorized publisher for the Cisco® Networking Academy®, has a variety of learning and preparation tools to help you master the knowledge and prepare successfully for the CCENT™ and CCNA® exams.

From foundational learning to late-stage review, practice, and preparation, the varied print, software, and video products from Cisco Press can help you with learning, mastering, and succeeding!

Companion Guides

Companion Guides provide textbook-style support with additional content from leading Academy instructors.

Network Fundamentals, CCNA Exploration Companion Guide	1-58713-208-7 / 978-1-58713-208-7
Routing Protocols and Concepts, CCNA Exploration Companion Guide	1-58713-206-0 / 978-1-58713-206-3
LAN Switching and Wireless, CCNA Exploration Companion Guide	1-58713-207-9 / 978-1-58713-207-0
Accessing the WAN, CCNA Exploration Companion Guide	1-58713-205-2 / 978-1-58713-205-6

Labs and Study Guides

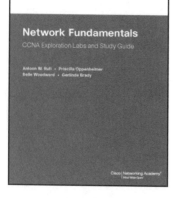

Labs and Study Guides provide study tools and labs, both from the online curriculum and from leading Academy instructors.

Network Fundamentals, CCNA Exploration Labs and Study Guide	1-58713-203-6 / 978-1-58713-203-2
Routing Protocols and Concepts, CCNA Exploration Labs and Study Guide	1-58713-204-4 / 978-1-58713-204-9
LAN Switching and Wireless, CCNA Exploration Labs and Study	1-58713-202-8 / 978-1-58713-202-5
Accessing the WAN, CCNA Exploration Labs and Study Guide	1-58713-201-X / 978-1-58713-201-8

Other CCNA resources

1-58713-197-8 / 978-1-58713-197-4	31 Days Before your CCNA Exam, Second Edition
1-58720-183-6 / 978-1-58720-183-7	CCNA Official Exam Certification Library, Third Edition
1-58720-193-3 / 978-1-58720-193-6	CCNA Portable Command Guide, Second Edition
1-58720-216-6 / 978-1-58720-216-2	CCNA 640-802 Network Simulator (from Pearson Certification)
1-58720-221-2 / 978-1-58720-221-6	CCNA 640-802 Cert Flash Cards Online

For more information on this and other Cisco Press products, visit www.ciscopress.com /academy

Cisco Press

Learning is Serious Business. **Invest Wisely.**